WALKING THE BEACH TO BELLINGHAM

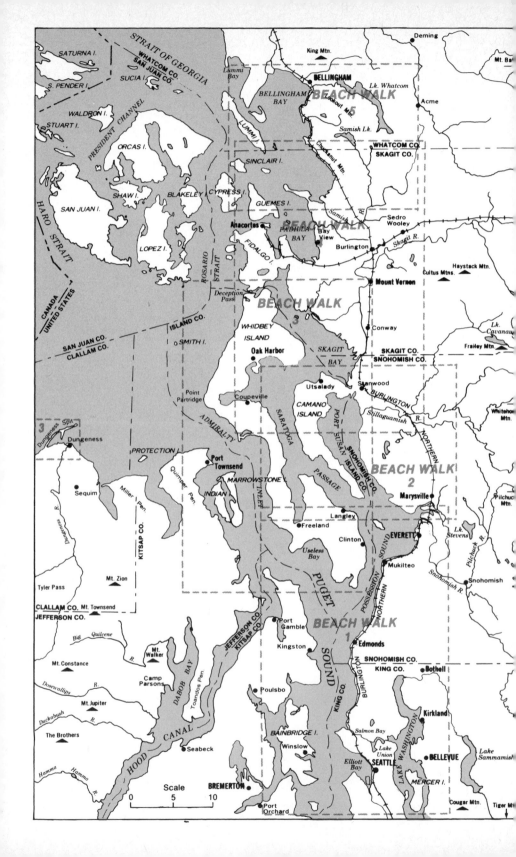

WALKING THE

BEACH TO

BELLINGHAM

Harvey Manning

MADRONA PUBLISHERS   *SEATTLE*

Published by
Madrona Publishers, Inc.
P.O. Box 22667
Seattle, Washington 98122

10 9 8 7 6 5 4 3 2 1

Library of Congress Cataloging-in-Publication Data

Manning, Harvey.
  Walking the beach to Bellingham

  1. Washington (State)—Description and travel—
1951–1980. 2. Beaches—Washington (State) 3. Walking—
Washington (State) 4. Manning, Harvey—Journeys—
Washington (State) 5. Manning, Harvey—Diaries.
I. Title.
F895.M36 1986   917.97'0443   86–21516
ISBN 0–88089–015–0

Contents

WALKING THE BEACH TO BELLINGHAM

Traveling with Spiders

By 1976 I was a quarter-century too late to make the first ascent of Mount Everest. Neither was I likely, having developed a dread of water too deep to see bottom, to sail a small boat around the world. All in all, my lust for high adventure had simmered down to quite a low level. This is not to say the juices had dried up. What they'd done was stew around in an odd corner of the pot and ferment up a quirky appetite for *low* adventure.

While onetime climbing pals were hopping into aircraft to hobnob with grizzly bears in the Brooks Range, to trek in Nepal, to ski in New Zealand, to float the Grand Canyon, to kayak around Cape Horn, I was working up a plan to go down to the Seattle waterfront carrying a sleeping bag and a rucksackful of kipper snacks, apples, Snickers, and Pepsi Cola and take deck passage on the Alaska ferry. Not to "do" Alaska—I wouldn't so much as get off the boat—would turn right around and come straight home.

While one of my daughters was Keltying through Latin America, another was bicycling across Canada, the third was doing stand-up comedy in Chicago, my son was looking to be blown up by terrorists in Ireland or North Africa, and my wife was jetting over the Greenland Icecap to Wales, I was pondering an intriguing new means of travel. A friend by the name (solely) of Orpheus told me to watch university bulletin boards for cryptic notices giving a destination, dates of departure and arrival, and a phone number. Those who on the appointed day boarded the old bus with "Greyhound" or "Trailways" or "Sequim School District" barely painted out would be assured (machinery permitting) of reaching their destination on or about the stated date. However, by majority vote the group might elect side trips—to a national park, county fair, arts and crafts festival, concert, or rodeo. A show of hands would be enough to bring a halt for a swim in a handy river or lake, or to buy ice cream cones. When a site attracted, the group would camp overnight. When not, it would drive on, perhaps stopping briefly on the prairies to howl at the moon with the coyotes. In the Gypsy Bus System (which is not a system, no more than an anarchy has a bureaucracy) a journey has a destination, but *getting* there is the trip.

I've not yet taken the Alaska ferry or caught a Gypsy Bus. I will, though, one of these days. I'm sure of that because I *did* walk the beach from Seattle to Bellingham. Low adventure gets in your blood.

It may be alleged that I took the beach hike because I was too poor and too chicken about airplanes to trek in Nepal. However, hoping not to offend my legion of friends who have taken enough color slides there to keep the carousels on their projectors spinning until they *have* no more friends, I deplore the very desire to visit Everest base camp. To be sure, long lines of sahibs and coolies plodding up and down the passes, climbers rest-stepping by the hundreds up the "orange peel route" on Mount Rainier fascinate me. So do ant colonies. If ants evolved a leisure culture, they would do these things. Spiders, by contrast, would also travel extensively; however, they would go not by jet, but by Gypsy Bus, because they would not be seeking to capture the world in color slides but to web its pieces together in unity. I know these things from watching ants and traveling with spiders.

A warning to the reader of this book: It is *not* a hiker's guide. From 1976 to 1978 I hitched together the mountain fronts of the Olympics and Cascades, the rivers flowing from mountains to saltwater, and the beaches north from the "sea in the forest" to the Sea of San Juan. The 3,000 foot miles of that web (not to omit the 35,000 supporting miles in the 1969 Volkswagen beetle) are described in the four volumes of *Footsore: Walks and Hikes Around Puget Sound.*

No attempt should be made to use the present book—a personal narrative—as a route guide. The risks are too great of being arrested and thrown in a rural jail, shot in the britches by an enraged duck-buster, irreversibly damaged while straddling a barbed-wire fence, or drowned in a soup of fertilizers, pesticides and cow shit.

A further frustration to those trying to use this book as a guide is that while the story is told largely from south to north, sometimes it travels north to south, occasionally west or east, and some of the narratives combine walks taken over a number of years.

If this isn't a guidebook, what is it? A book of sermons, perhaps.

I preach that air travel be scaled back, as a start, to the level of twenty years ago, further reductions to be considered after all the Boeing engineers have been retrained as turkey ranchers.

The state Game Department should establish a season on helicopters—fifty-two weeks a year, twenty-four hours a day, no bag limit.

Passenger trains must be restored, as a start, to the service of forty years ago and then improved from there.

The Gypsy Bus System must not be regularized (the government would regulate it to death) but publicized cautiously through the underground.

I would discourage, if not ban, trekking to Everest base camp and flying over the Greenland Icecap. Generally, people should stay home. Forget gaining a little knowledge about a lot and strive to learn a lot about a little.

Among my homes while attending the University of Washington was a room in an old millworkers' lodging house on the north shore of Lake Union. My next-door neighbor and I met frequently on the railroad tracks, scavenging spilled coal. "Little Johnny," as he was known in the Northlake community because he was an inch or two below five feet, had grown to young manhood in Cornwall, in a village very near the coast, and I supposed he had spent many a spare hour on the beach. Well, no. He'd been there once, on a Sunday school picnic. There was so much to keep him busy in the village. At the turn of the century he'd journeyed to Seattle to stay with his cousins here and perhaps to seek his fortune. He'd been at Northlake ever since and I supposed he'd spent many a spare hour watching the University grow from a frontier academy to an institution of national repute. Well, no. He'd been up to the campus once, in 1909, for the Alaska-Yukon-Pacific Exposition. There was so much going on along the lake. In 1946 a relative died and left him three houses and the village grocery. Back home in Cornwall, I'm sure he never went to the beach. A grocery always has so much that needs doing.

Still intent in those days on Denali, if no longer Everest, I was baffled by Little Johnny. I understand now. In his place, I do think I'd spend a lot of time at the beach—an hour from his village by bicycle. Why not train up to Wales for a weekend? On the other hand, I recall driving to the High Sierra after not having been in California for a dozen years, and approaching the state line verging on panic from the atavistic fear of falling off the edge of the world.

Ants are singlemindedly intent on gathering the leis of Hawaii, the jackpots of Las Vegas, the glaciers of Alaska. Spiders, when they go aroving, cast their airships loose and take potluck with the winds.

In 1976 I was not so intent on arriving in Bellingham as the narrative may make it seem. While casting loose from Cougar Mountain as I did five or six days a week for two years, as often as not the winds blew me to climb Cultus or Sparpole Hill or Porcupine Ridge, to follow the Skagit River or the Puyallup from the saltwater to the mountain front—to pursue the "alley" ambitions that had been gestating in the back of my mind. Nevertheless, the trip had been growing on me.

The more immediate cause of my setting out in 1976 was a visitation by the Great Pestilence which in a few months took old friends, beloved cousins, aunts and uncles, my hundred-year-old grandmother, and Mother. I wasn't feeling so hot myself.

During youthful recreations at the Eastlake Gardens (not far from the north end of Lake Union in Seattle) I knew a fellow who had been a male vocalist with the Phil Harris band, whose signature song was:

> Smoke, smoke, smoke that cigarette,
> Smoke, smoke, smoke.
> And when you smoke yourself to death,
> Tell St. Peter at the Golden Gate,
> "You're gonna have to wait,
> I just gotta have another cigarette."

In 1976 I smoked my last one forever. In hours I felt my death upon me. I was resigned, I was ready, I was practically willing. However, the doctor wouldn't let me go. She told me to take a long walk. So, I walked to Zion, I walked to Bangor, I walked to Busy Wild Mountain, I walked to the Devil's Garden, I walked to the Olympia Brewery, I walked to four books full of places.

Accepting my mortality permitted me, at last, to walk Bainbridge Island in search of my childhood sandbox, where I used to bury our dog, Tramp, and for the site of the beachfire where, in a summer twilight, the alto soloist in the choir of Asbury Methodist Church met the yeoman off the U.S.S. *New Mexico.* After my prowls I discussed them with the onetime yeoman. Mother had been gone long enough for Dad to enjoy reminiscing about her, about their fifty-three years together. He reviewed the rough draft of this book before his death from cigarette poisoning.

On the walk from Seattle to Bellingham, I became unable to say the word, "Indian," because there aren't any such. The waters I was walking beside became *Whulj* ("the saltwater we know"). I didn't see many of the people whose ancestors had arrived hereabouts 12,000 years ago. Not many of them are to be seen nowadays on the "Indian reservations." One reason is that beach property is too valuable not to be stolen. Another is that during the nineteenth century the people of the Whulj suffered such a visitation of the Great Pestilence as would bear comparison with that of the Black Death on Europe, and then such a Holocaust at the hands of the European invaders as would bear comparison with that committed by the Nazis.

The walk from Seattle to Bellingham was done for its own sake— which is to say, my sake. The *Footsore* guidebooks were written partly to pay trip expenses, and partly to divert people from their antlike swarmings to the North Cascades National Park, to make them good spiders webbing about in wildlands in and near their cities.

Something more seemed to me to need saying. This book is a try, written for my childhood, for Dad and Mother and the aunts and uncles and cousins by the dozens, wife and daughters and son and granddaughter, and for that branch of the human family which got here 12,000 years before mine.

Seattle to Everett

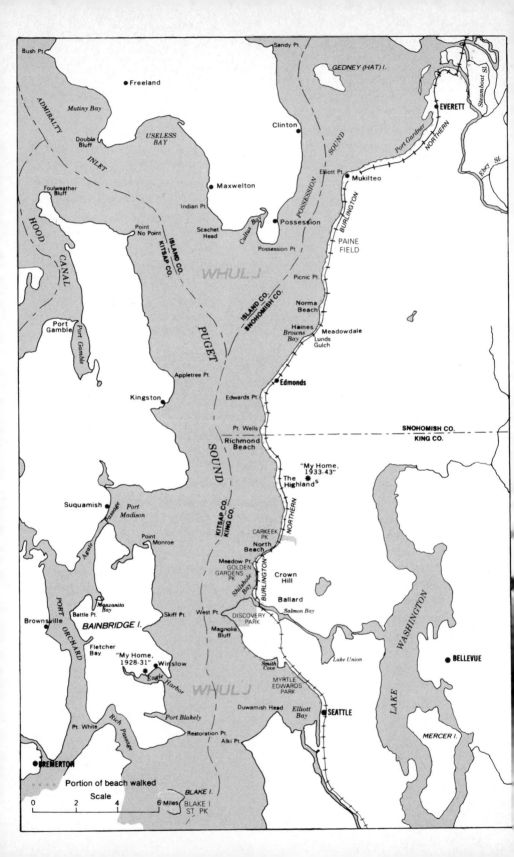

1. Bainbridge Island Mile 0–³/₄

1925-1930

Fish in the bay, fish in the boats, fish on the docks, fish in the markets, fish in the restaurants. Fish on the winds, fish in my nose, fish on
my dish. Anadromous fish and schooling fish and leaping fish and bottom fish and shellfish and starfish and jellyfish, alive and dead, stewed
up with seaweed and kelp and algae, sewage and garbage and bilge, sea-
soned with chlorides and iodides of sodium and potassium and iron and
gold.

One sniff and I'm four years old, riding along Seattle's Railroad
Avenue in the back seat of our brand new 1929 Model A Ford Tudor
sedan, just off the ferry from Bainbridge Island.

Before the Island, I remember being tied to a tree to keep me from
toddling out of the yard where we lived on Seattle's Phinney Ridge, and
I remember Grandfather Hawthorn, who died two months before I was
born. That is, I remember Dad's and Mother's memories.

After the Island, memories that are truly mine come in a crowd, a
turmoil of seven homes and three schools and two journeys the width of
America, all in three years.

The Island was the time between myth and history, it was the safe
home.

On the Island I owned my first dog, Tramp, who'd lie asleep in the
sandbox while I buried her tail to snout. There lived my first hero, Ed
Loverich, later a University of Washington basketball star, so tall even
in grade school that group pictures cut him off at the neck.

Cousins came visiting. Dad would borrow a gas launch and we'd
chug out the mouth of Eagle Harbor and around the shore to Rolling
Bay or Port Madison, nose up on a beach, and we'd wade and splash,

duck and dogpaddle until our goosebumps turned blue, and then build castles and dam creeks and skip stones and gather agates and shells until our skins were cooked pink. We'd retreat to the alders and maples over-hanging the sand, and Mother and an aunt or two would unpack the picnic basket on a blanket, and Dad and an uncle or two would fetch the crate of pop cooling in the waves.

Tuna fish sandwiches with sand. Strawberry pop the temperature of Puget Sound, shaken up in the bottles to erupt a geyser of pink bubbles in a cousin's face. Cousins—as much fun as brothers and sisters without the bother.

In our Island times we had two ways to get to Seattle. At Winslow we boarded a passenger-freight steamer christened the *Bainbridge* when built in 1914 for the Eagle Harbor Transportation Company and renamed the *Winslow* after that firm merged in 1927 with the Kitsap County Transportation Company, the White Collar Line. At Port Blakely we caught the brand new (1928) *Bainbridge*, a diesel auto ferry of the Puget Sound Navigation Company run by Alexander Peabody, whose father brought the Black Ball ensign from the family's clipper ships on the Atlantic to the North Pacific in the 1890s.

In 1935, after our Island times, the White Collar Line was swal-lowed up by the Black Ball Line. In 1938 our *Winslow* was scrapped. By World War II the Black Ball had digested every other competitor and ruled the Inland Sea as imperiously as Brittania. The relationship steadily deteriorated between the people of the state and "Captain Black Ball," and in 1948 Peabody let it be known he was willing to sell his fleet of twenty-one vessels: steam and diesel-electric, steel and wood, built between 1900 and 1930; six of them around Puget Sound (including one at Winslow) and others in California, including a dozen that served on San Francisco Bay until it was bridged. Celebrating the purchase of the fleet by the state in 1951, Governor Arthur B. Langlie hailed "a new era of Puget Sound transportation now we are rid of Captain Peabody."

To ride the ferries was to hate the Captain. Only after exiling him to Canada did we realize he was the last mariner—pirate though he may have been—to command our ships. Under Governor Langlie we were subjected to the uncivil engineers who had already sunk the mosquito fleet and now hankered to scuttle the ferries. They schemed: an underwater tube from Alki Point to Bainbridge; a floating bridge from Fauntleroy to Vashon Island, or from Fort Lawton to Bainbridge, or Richmond Beach to Kingston.

Economics frustrated their dream of a freeway under or over the Sound so the surly engineers lopped off segments of freeway and sent them hurtling across the waves. The first new postwar ferries, 1954-1959, were of a size and speed comparable to the old; the *Evergreen State, Klahowya,* and *Tillikum* carried 100 cars at 13 knots. But in 1967 the "superferries" were launched, *Hyak, Kaleetan, Yakima,* and *Elwha,* 160 cars, 17 knots; and in 1972 the "jumbos," *Spokane* and *Walla Walla,* 206 cars, 18 knots. Seattle's Colman Dock and the adjoining Grand Trunk Pacific were demolished in 1965 for a new Seattle Ferry Terminal. A bridge over Agate Pass connected Bainbridge to the Kitsap Peninsula, and a floating bridge spanned Hood Canal. With one brief slowdown to 18 knots afloat, a car could speed a mile a minute from Seattle to Port Angeles, and the world was smaller and life was shorter, nastier, and more brutish.

Many a time over the years, on the way to mountains or ocean, I have joined the sad, swift parade across the Island and never seen a thing I recognized.

Wednesday, March 15, 1978

10:30 a.m., I drove the beetle off the *Walla Walla* at Winslow, carrying a set of U.S. Geological Survey maps—the Duwamish Head, Shilshole Bay, Suquamish, and Bremerton East quadrangles. The margins were scribbled up with Dad's answers to my questions—his store of memories, and Mother's. My plan was to circle the entire Bainbridge shore to see if any of their memories were mine too.

I stopped to walk along Manitou Beach, one of the places the gas launch used to carry me and the cousins. Strawberry bubbles tingled in my nose and sandwich sand gritted in my teeth—but so they do on every sunny day on every Puget Sound beach I have walked. Rolling Bay, Port Madison, Manzanita…I walked, I looked, I sniffed—only the unchanged primordial stink brought with it genuine memories.

In the afternoon shadows a woodland lane dead ended on the beach at the sign, "Fletcher Landing." Cormorants perched on derelict pilings, relics of the dock of the ferry that used to cross to Brownsville and the road to Bremerton, where the Navy Yard periodically tended Dad's "New Momma."

I walked the beach south. Some of the forest homes had the look of very old cabins remodeled for year-round living. One may have been where Grandmother Hawthorn summered with her two youngest daughters. One may have been the cabin loaned to Dad by a retired veteran of the Great White Fleet.

I walked north onto the spit that all but closes off Fletcher's Bay, an estuary barely a stone's throw wide. Farm boys and girls from up and down the Sound, and fishermen, loggers, and millhands, and a few enterprising sailors from Bremerton, came here by steamer, launch, sailboat and rowboat to trip the light fantastic at Ma and Pa Foster's dancehall.

Nowadays, strangers who stand on private beaches studying maps are suspected of being tax assessors, developers, or worse. In the twilight a woman came down from a house to ask if she could help find what I was looking for. She smiled to hear I'd already found it—at least part of it. Here, on a summer evening by a beachfire, Dad and Mother met.

Friday, March 17, 1978

10:30, Winslow again, to complete the circuit. Crystal Springs, White Point, Pleasant Beach—names in my folks' conversations, nothing more. I did know Fort Ward, though not from childhood. In World War II the Seattle-Bremerton trip was a half-hour longer than usual because the ferry had to pause here, in Rich Passage, while antisubmarine nets were opened. (After the war, Japanese Navy records disclosed that one of their subs had followed a ferry through the nets and taken periscope photographs of capital ships in the Navy Yard. Or so I have heard.)

Bainbridge Island Country Club....According to Dad I sometimes was in the Kenworth when he delivered hay-grain-feed-seed-or-whatnot to the mansions on the knoll. Today I trespassed along the beach to Restoration Point and stood on the tip, "supers" hurtling by on my right, to and from Bremerton, "jumbos" on my left, to and from Winslow. Only the water gave me any sense of home.

On the beach at Port Blakely a woman came out of a house (the maps again). She confirmed that the pilings across the bay were remains of the ferry dock. She showed me a photo taken two decades before my Island time; the shore was a solid row of buildings—the largest lumber mill in the world—and the harbor was a forest of masts.

I drove over the hill, around the head of Eagle Harbor, and up the slope above the bay. Far across the Sound, dim in the daylight smog, rose the towers of Seattle. The towers were not in my memory, but in that place, I knew, was the source of the electric brilliance in the night sky of old. I'd not been here since 1930, but guided by the remembered bright lights I drove unerringly to our house, remodeled but unmistakable.

I descended the slope to a new marina, its offices in an old building, a building I felt certain I knew. I walked on by to a jumble of rickety pilings and rotten planks, and I knew them, too. The marina owner proved to be a student of local history. These were, indeed, the ruins of the Winslow Dock. I did truly recognize the old building. He showed me faded lettering on the wall: "Anderson," the name of the fellow who bought the warehouse in 1930, thereby causing our departure from the Island. Beneath, still legible, "Galbraith."

Earlier poke-abouts of Winslow had been fruitless because I'd been in New Winslow, built around the ferry dock, moved there from Port Blakely in 1936. Here was my Winslow—the dock, the warehouse, the street where Tom Loverich had his store and restaurant.

My marina-owner friend had consulted archives, interviewed residents, and learned everything about the past of the place worth knowing except one thing—what had made the clusters of small holes scattered at random in the galvanized-iron walls of the warehouse. None of the old-timers still around—Anderson's daughter, Ed Loverich (my hero), and the woman who was our next-door neighbor up the hill by the sandbox—had an explanation. I did.

When the rats grew too bold, Dad would invite the Gun Club in for a night of sport. They'd sit in a ring on bales of hay in the middle of the warehouse. Whiskered noses would poke from sacks of chicken scratch, shotguns would go BLAM BLAM, and the iron walls would rattle with birdshot. As the hours passed and the jugs emptied, a hunter would now and then leap from the bales in hot pursuit and a .12-gauge fired too close to the walls would leave its mark.

The Winslow Dock soon would be gone, demolished for marina expansion, leaving as the central relic of Old Winslow the warehouse, shot full of holes in Duke Manning's great and famous rat hunts.

2. Seattle Waterfront

Mile 0–3¹/₂

Tuesday, February 1, 1977

From home at night on Bainbridge Island we looked far across the darkness of the waters to Seattle's constellation of bright lights. On Saturday afternoon, Dad would close the Galbraith warehouse he managed and walk up the hill to our house, and we'd wash up and doll up and walk down the hill past the warehouse to the Winslow Dock where we'd board the *Winslow*. The deckhands would pull in the gangplank and Cap Franks would toot the whistle and take the steamer out past the sailing ships moored in the harbor, past the plant on the point at Creosote where pilings were treated, and over the Sound to Elliott Bay.

At Seattle we'd get off on Galbraith Dock, Pier 3, and climb the bluff on a sidewalk so steep it had concrete cleats to keep us from sliding back to the waterfront. A big black cat crouched above the doorway of the Alley Kat Cafe, a place cozy as a pirate's cave, the air so rich in hot grease that our clothes and hair carried the aroma of steaming-hot fish encased in crackling brown batter home to the Island.

The bright lights led to an Oriental palace—the Orpheum or Fifth Avenue or Paramount—where we waded ankle-deep carpets, escorted by ushers as dazzling as Marines in dress blues. Gilt columns and red-black-yellow-green tapestries drew every eye up to the glitterings and sparklings of glass and electricity suspended from the vaulted ceiling. Tapestries quivered and chandeliers tinkled as a pipe organ emerged by some sorcery from the deep. Spotlights transfigured singers and tap dancers, banjo players and acrobats and comedians, jugglers and magicians; and then the curtains flurried open and closed and open again, revealing the magic movie screen. The lights went dark and Harold Lloyd teetered on a window ledge high above the street and all the washed-up, dolled-up kids and folks from Seattle and the steamer towns screamed.

We used the other route from the Island when going to visit the aunts and uncles and cousins scattered through the city. We drove the Model A around the head of the bay and over the hill to Port Blakely where we'd catch the *Bainbridge.* Cap Wyatt would pilot the ferry out past the country club on Restoration Point and over the Sound to Colman Dock.

Our first stop was Washington Fish & Oyster for a sack of shrimp, hours from the depths of Puget Sound, minutes from the kettle where they were boiled alive. As the Model A carried us away from the water-front, we'd pinch off the big heads with their beady eyes and cat-whiskers, unwrap the buglegs on their curled stomachs, slip off the tails, pop the pink-white flesh in our mouths, and reach into the paper sack for the next.

While Dad was busy dodging Railroad Avenue's trains and trucks, Mother would peel for two. Sometimes he'd steer with his knees, a trick he also performed on the Island with the Kenworth truck, me on his lap convinced I was steering—as were our neighbors, appalled to see the Island's mightiest machine, loaded with hay, grain, feed, seed, coal, or building materials (with Tramp standing on the hood by the radiator cap) thundering along country lanes commanded by a child.

You can't peel a sack of shrimp without the juices squirting loose. For days the Model A would recall Washington Fish & Oyster, Railroad Avenue, aunts and uncles and cousins by the dozens.

Along the waterfront we'd pass raggedy masses of blankets hud-dled about fishpackers' waste bins, Indians filling gunnysacks with heads and tails and guts.

These eaters of unspeakable chowders were not the noble savages of the Oriental palaces who whooped and hollered around wagon trains. The Fourth of July night of 1929, as Mother was driving me home from the Bainbridge Island picnic, they attacked the Kenworth with cherry bombs. Mother slammed the truck in reverse and backed up all the way to the picnic. Dad jumped in and drove to the ambush, jumped out and knocked the leader down. Late that night the tribe gathered in the field below my sandbox. Mother stood at the kitchen window with a pistol as Dad went out, alone, unarmed, to parley.

(Or so I was telling my enraptured children many years later when Dad hooted, "Like hell I was unarmed—and my father didn't raise any sons stupid enough to go down in that field." According to him, it was Tom Loverich who parleyed with the chief and convinced him that the drunken cherry-bombers were at fault and that Manning was standing on his porch cradling a .12-gauge shotgun expecting to die this night but not before he put five rounds of birdshot in five Indian bellies. The cruelest correction of my half-century-old memory was that during the entire Battle of Winslow I was sound asleep.)

In Island times the Mile 0 of my dreams of adventure was located in Seattle where Cap Franks and Cap Wyatt brought us to shore on their respective docks. Later, when my Eastern aunts and uncles began to visit from Massachusetts by train, Mile 0 moved several blocks up from the waterfront to King Street Station and Union Station, side by side on King Street.

Later yet, as a University of Washington student but still a country boy, I thrilled to the rush of the nation's arterial blood, the bustle of significant human beings in portentous comings and goings. One night when Mary, the barmaid at The Rainbow, screeched, "You don't have to go home but you can't stay here!" I took it as a signal to set forth: to San Francisco and the earthquakes, Chicago and the gangsters, Florida and the oranges; Grand Central Station and fame, fortune, pretty girls. I rode the trolley to King Street, emptied my wallet on the counter, and asked the ticketseller how far I could go, the plan being to wake on a foreign scene hungover and hungry and destitute and live a Smollett novel homeward. My money was refused and I was handed a blur of asterisks and double-daggers, railroad typography designed to intimidate as railroad architecture was designed to awe. College boys on picaresque were supposed to go by bus.

King Street hits the water at the site of the coal bunkers that were the terminus of the city's first railroad, the Seattle & Walla Walla, which never got to Walla Walla, or even across the Cascade Mountains but did reach the Newcastle mines burrowed into Cougar Mountain, just across Lake Washington from Seattle.

South of King Street lay the Pacific Steamship Terminal, base of the coastal liners *Emma Alexander*, *Ruth Alexander*, and *Dorothy Alexander*. It was on the *H.F. Alexander*, named for himself by the father of those sisters, that Mother voyaged to and from San Pedro, California in the fall of 1924 to visit her bluejacket bridegroom. The next summer I was born.

Farther south I spent my only shipboard night ever (except in Mother's womb) on the M.V. *Standard Service*, berthed in Todd's Shipyard for maintenance between runs to Alaska. I bunked in Dad's cabin and messed with the crew, expecting in years ahead to bunk and mess like this around the world.

North of King Street, at the Municipal Float, motor sailers debarked liberty parties from the Pacific Fleet for Fleet Week, the gala of the Seattle year. Dad's ship was the "New Momma," the U.S.S. *New Mexico,* 32,000 tons, main battery of twelve 14-inch guns, commissioned in 1918 and for some time flying the four-star flag of ComPac. When that honor was transferred to the new "Prune Barge," the *California,* "Momma" was demoted to three-star ComBatDiv, and as other new battlewagons entered service, on down to ComBatDiv 5.

North of the Municipal Float is Yesler Way, the original Skid Road along which oxen dragged logs to Yesler's Mill on Yesler's Wharf, the original home of the mosquito fleet that served as the Sound's earliest ferry system.

During the Island time the mosquito fleet headquarters were further north still, on our Galbraith Dock, Pier 3, and Colman Dock, a succession of structures bearing the same name. The Colman Dock we knew dated from 1908 and was partly rebuilt in 1912 after the ocean liner *Alameda* steamed into the middle of it at full speed. The dock in the late twenties was in a period of transition caused by the shift from the dominance of water transport to wheeled transport. Earlier, the cargo decks of passenger steamers had accommodated automobiles along with other freight, all side-loaded through the cargo doors. As the vehicles proliferated, some vessels were converted to car ferries, and in 1916 a ramp was installed on Colman Dock to expedite loading. In 1923, by which time twenty-three auto ferries were operating on the Sound, a slip was added to the dock to permit bow-loading.

When my friend Suibhna the Sailor Man comes to port, I pick him up at his ship, berthed on the Duwamish Waterway, and we lunch at Ivar's Acres of Clams. The appeal for Suibhna is that always while he sails the wide world o'er, he longs for a bucket (or two or three) of steamers freshly picked from his home beaches. The appeal for me is that the restaurant occupies the remnant of the Galbraith Dock. I order seafood, of course, but prawns or scallops or halibut cheeks, not clams, because the single bucket I can afford at restaurant prices is as insulting as a mere dozen oysters.

Every second or third summer I satisfy my clam hunger. Done right, that's often enough. During a period of morning minus tides, joined by a fellow gourmet, I haul packs down the beach, over headlands, miles from civilization, to a wilderness camp. Each day before breakfast we walk far out on a rock shelf toward a sea stack where a pair of bald eagles are defending their nest against gulls and crows. Amid pools where seals are teaching their pups to fish, we kneel in green seaweedery and mine clams from the gravel beneath, filling a couple of buckets apiece. At the end of a day of beachwalking and surfwading we build a driftwood fire and put on the first bucket. A cup of Wyler's limeade fortified with backpacker's rum passes the time until the clam hinges relax. Then it's take off the first bucket, put on the second. Ladle littlenecks into the Sierra Club cup, pry the shells open, and cut the attachment muscles with the Swiss Army knife, dip the morsels in hot lemon butter, and alacazam. A cup of clams, a cup of steaming nectar, more clams, more limeade, and the next bucket is ready. Two of us once consumed in three nights clams that had a street value of $500.

Seattle's working waterfront moved long ago to the Duwamish Waterway. The "Gold Rush waterfront" of Alaskan Way, as Railroad Avenue was renamed in the 1930s, is now mainly for play. But there are still ferries to Winslow and Bremerton, the *Princess* boats to Victoria, and the mosquitolike *Good Times* to Blake Island. There is also the Alaska ferry, and I plan someday to walk aboard with my sleeping bag and a rucksackful of apples and kipper snacks and spend a week voyaging up and back on the sea lanes Dad knew in the *Standard Service*.

A plaque at Waterfront Park commemorates the August 31, 1896, docking of the *Miike Maru* with a cargo of tea, inaugurating regular service to the Orient, marking "the birth of Seattle as an international port." On July 17, 1897, the S.S. *Portland* arrived from Alaska with the "ton of gold" that was immediately deposited in the pockets of Seattle merchants, who thereupon announced that it was the Queen City's manifest destiny to annex the North.

A plaque at the site of old Piers 9 and 10 notes that here, May 23–27, 1908, crews disembarked from thirteen battleships of the Great White Fleet that had carried the Stars and Stripes 46,000 miles around the world. Without this voyage and the veteran of the trip who retired to Fletcher's Bay and the cabin he loaned Dad near the one Mother summered in, I wouldn't be on my way to Bellingham, or anywhere.

At 4:15, I left the row of restaurants and curio shops and entered the waterfront parks established when the Downtown Movers & Shakers learned what the successors of Skid Road's Madam Damnable had always known —that there is as much money to be made from play as work. In the chill twilight murk I walked alone between the railroad tracks and the seawall.

I passed the site of my first man's job in the summer of 1942, at Washington Egg & Poultry Coop. I ran the freight elevator connecting the upstairs cannery to the ground-floor warehouse, hauling down tons of glass jars of chicken ravioli and Twistee Noodle Dinner to feed the home front, and tons of one-pound tins of boned turkey and chicken to provide Thanksgiving dinner on Guadalcanal.

Myrtle Edwards Park (City of Seattle) led to Elliott Bay Park (Port of Seattle) to Smith Cove, where a few docks still work unloading Toyotas and Datsuns. Here, before the invention of nylon, the swift silk liners of Nippon Ysen Kaisha met the crack silk trains that highballed east flying the white flag that sidetracked all other traffic, even Pullmans and fast mail.

At the grain terminal in the Port's park, a Greek ship was loading wheat from the Palouse Hills. Next day it would be gone, out in the Pacific, on the way to the Indian Ocean or the Atlantic. It was my intention when I was twelve to sail a small boat, alone, out there among the dragons. After my hike that summer to Marmot Pass I decided instead to make the first ascent of Mount Everest, solo. I also didn't do that.

3. Magnolia Bluff

Mile 8–3½

Friday, March 19, 1976

Spring was on the face of the bluff, new-greening leaves spangled by red and rose blossoms of currant and salmonberry, puddles and mucks warmed to the temperature that sets off the frogs. I clambered across driftwood and turned south on the beach beneath a cliff of naked clay. Killdeer ran off squealing, only their prints and mine tracking the fresh-washed sand of morning.

A raindrop hit me square in the eye and I looked up blinking, expecting to see a storm arriving. But there was only the merest vapor overhead and the one lone drop had exhausted it. Stronger squalls bustled around the horizons, enveloping the Olympic peaks in snow clouds, slanting rainlines down on the lowlands. Nobody, nowhere, would be safe today from the cannonading and battering, looting and raping. Yet there were Blue Holes, and I'd seen them from Cougar Mountain.

A person wired tenuously together by a symbiosis of vices abandons one vice at his peril. On this, my twenty-third day without a cigarette, I needed the metronome beat of legs in motion and the music of frogs, gulls, crows, and waves to drown out the interior clamor of squeaks, groans, and the clatter of my rusted machinery falling apart. I'd gladly have taken on all the black furies in hand-to-hand combat to hold back for an hour the coming of night, when the walking would have to stop but the sleep wouldn't begin.

A sign announced "End of Public Beach." Bulkheads of pilings, boulders, and concrete were set in sand and shingle. Houses clung to narrow ledges. Lanes carved in the bluff crept this way and that down from the plateau 275 vertical feet above.

A series of time-lapse photographs compressing a century to an hour would show a ceaseless avalanche of clay, sand, and gravel, of trees that continue growing even as they slide down to the waves that chew them up and float them away, and of humans beaverishly erecting houses that are ripped apart even as they are nailed together. People build atop the plateau whose brink breaks into chunks that ride the mud downward like ice floes on a river in spring. They build at the base of the bluff where the chunks and the houses they carry overwhelm them.

They divert the rains into drains that grease the skids. They challenge gravity with retaining walls that become battering rams. They defy the sea with bulkheads that are pounded by waves and undermined by currents. The beach is strewn with twisted iron, half-dissolved slabs of concrete, splintered pilings, fragments of floors and roofs and kitchens and patios. The lost wagers of a century of gamblers.

Or won? There are folks who have lived briefly on the bluff and in reviewing the long years since are consoled to think, "At least I spent a summer on Perkins Lane, and part of a winter, too."

Stretches of bluff too vertical to support man or alder rise naked to the fringe of madronas which, mistaken for magnolias, gave the bluff its name. In the four miles from West Point to Smith Cove, only one street manages to reach all the way to the beach. From its dead end, a row of shanties perched on pilings hugs the foot of the bluff, a path hacked in the cliff providing the only access at high tide. When "the ocean waves roll and the stormy winds do blow," pilings creak, shanties shudder, and spray flies over the roofs. Friends come to the party, slipping and laughing along the treacherous path in the howling night, jugs of wine in hand and pockets full of pears and cheese.

At Smith Cove, I sat on a log for a lunch of kipper snacks and an apple and a last look at Seattle, my home city.

Cities of the Inland Sea have distinctive markers that let hikers on distant mountains identify them. Tacoma has a smelter stack, the tallest mass of masonry in the West. Tacoma, Shelton, Everett, Port Townsend, Port Angeles, and Bellingham have steam plumes from lumber mills or pulp mills or both. Bellingham and Anacortes have oil-refinery plumes, and Chehalis a plume from a coal-fired electricity plant. "Big Valley City" (Renton, Tukwila, Kent, Auburn, Sumner, Puyallup) lies close below the flow of jets in and out of Seattle-Tacoma Airport, and "Overlake City" (Mercer Island, Bellevue, Kirkland, Redmond, Bothell) spreads along the east shore of Lake Washington. Cultus Mountain hulks above "Skagit Delta City" (Mount Vernon, Sedro Woolley, Burlington), the Black Hills above Olympia, and the Blue Mountains above Bremerton. The Issaquah Alps, where I live on Cougar Mountain, are a remnant of a range older than the Cascades. They ring Issaquah and serve as a "pointer" westward to Seattle.

Seattle, however, scarcely needs a pointer; it has Towers. First was the Smith Tower, so far in advance of its time that for half a century after its completion in 1914 civil engineers traveled from around the nation to admire what was described in their professional literature as "the greatest erection west of Chicago." One night in 1945 when Cousin Al was home on furlough we slipped the watchman a buck to take us to the top. People who grow up where the loudest sounds at night are hooting owls and barking dogs, where the woods are so dark nobody can make a trip to the privy without a lantern, live with a continual, nagging hunger. Every now and then a country boy reaches the breaking point and runs about in the night banging on friends' doors, giving the cry that in ancient Greece was "Evoe!" and in our time is "Let's go see the bright lights!"

Al and I had begun the evening with pitchers of beer at the Eastlake Gardens, progressed to burlesque comedians and stripteasers at the Rivoli Theater, and now on the summit of 1945 Seattle looking down to city lights and out to country darkness, we were sure we'd gone as high as we could ever go.

But in 1962 the Space Needle was erected to symbolize the World's Fair which was produced by the same Downtown Movers & Shakers whose other enterprises generated the smog that swallowed up our innocent old Smith and its 1929 companion, the Northern Life. From this seething chemical cauldron, Towers began erupting, so many and so high they often seem, seen by hikers on far peaks, a glass-aluminum Avalon adrift on a brown sea. Or Babel?

Clarence Day, in *This Simian World*, reflected on the quite different cities that would be built by a race of intelligent felines. At night, save for operas on every corner, they would be absolutely silent, the streets carpeted to muffle pawfalls, and totally dark save for sparks from the swords of clashing cavaliers. No student of zoos, said Day, can be surprised that educated apes are delighted by neon, fireworks, and motorcycles. The human city is simply the monkey house writ large. The Towers blaze through the night, the simian "up yours" to entropy.

After departing Smith Cove, I rounded a bend in the shore that put the city out of sight and blocked off the industrial clatter of the Duwamish Waterway; wavelets now could be heard rippling. I followed the ebbing water far out from the bluff on a glistening gray plain. Wet sand mirrored the sky. I walked through clouds.

At West Point the good reek of salt was overpowered by the suffocating stench of a sewage-treatment plant, the Worthy Cause built here in the 1960s. A few steps took me back in time to clean air and to the West Point Lighthouse of 1881. Then this too was behind me, and I stood on the tip of the spit in the pristine wilderness of 1850. Wind from the north chilled my right cheek, wind from the south my left. My wind gauge hovered around 15 knots, jumped briefly to 25. My thermometer registered 44 degrees. My nose dripped.

Loud, bold waves from the northwest met bold, loud waves from the southwest. Mysteriously (to a person who was inattentive to high school physics), both sets of waves continued intact through the chop of the riptide; magically (to a person uninterested in what physics hath taught), driftwood rode the north-flowing tidal current across both wave systems.

The frenzy of the rip was backlighted by sunrays slanting from south of the Olympics. A blackness north of the Olympics huffed and puffed itself up into a cauliflower palace. The lowering sun ignited the white cliffs of Whidbey Island twenty miles north. West, over three miles of water, lay the Bainbridge shore between Port Madison and Eagle Harbor and Port Blakely. Due south six miles, jutting from bluffs of West Seattle, was the spit of Alki Point, where in the gray drizzle of November 13, 1851, the brig *Exact* landed a roving band of real estate speculators, and the women began to weep and the men to plat.

I stood here now and looked out upon Main Street: Sailboats dancing over whitecaps and stinkpots slicing through them. Fishing boats, tugs towing barges, tugs towing log rafts. Green-and-white ferries shuttling from West Seattle to Vashon Island, Elliott Bay to Bremerton and Winslow, and Edmonds to Kingston. Ships from all over the world emerging from Admiralty Inlet, the water slot up north between Whidbey Island and the Kitsap Peninsula. Most turned left into Elliott Bay and Seattle; a few continued south toward Tacoma, Olympia, and Shelton. White NOAA vessels turned right for Manchester, and gray U.S. Navy ships for Bremerton.

In a half-hour on the point I counted five ships, a dozen work boats, scores of play boats, and ferries beyond counting. A goodly enough total for today. There used to be more vessels, many more. Starting in 1837, long before there was a Seattle, the *Beaver* of the Hudson's Bay Company voyaged the Inland Sea. In 1853 the *Fairy* began the first regular connection between Elliott Bay and Olympia, the next year the *Major Tompkins* linked the bay to Victoria, and in 1865 the sloop *Alexander* provided scheduled service between Seattle and Port

Blakely. Though sailing vessels continued as important cargo carriers here longer than anywhere else in the nation, the steamer was the future, and by the mid-1870s Seattle was home for more of them than any other port in the area. Not mills or coal mines or railroads or speculators or even saloons and Madam Damnable's bordello did so much to build Seattle as the mosquito fleet. Over the years some 2,500 vessels traveled the water roads. And then there was one, the *Virginia V,* in 1973 placed on the National Register of Historic Places.

4. Fort Lawton to Golden Gardens   Mile 8–12¹/₂

Tuesday, February 1, 1977

One February I kept daily weather notes. Only twice during the entire month did a glow in the clouds so much as imply the possibility of a sun. Every other day, every other one of those twenty-eight brief twilights, a low ceiling slid north in a ceaseless cyclonic swirl. Between storms the motion slowed and exhalations of forest and sea, man and machine coagulated in a gray filth of rotting air. In Seattle's February limbos are the beginnings of Seattle's April suicides.

This morning the miasma lowered to Cougar Mountain's tree tops and seeped through windows and pores into the space behind my eyes. Not to go walking was to risk slipping into the abyss.

The military recognized early on that the strategic spot for the defense of Seattle was Magnolia Bluff, where they situated Fort Lawton. It was never provided with guns, though, because nobody could imagine who might attack Seattle. (Tacoma?) So toothless was this stronghold that soon after the turn of the century its ramparts were overrun by Seattle's engineers, who piped raw sewage through the fort to West Point. After seven more decades of dispiritedly mowing the lawns of parade grounds that never saw a proper parade, in 1972 the Army abandoned 535 acres of the fort. Attacks were instantly mounted by a legion of Worthy Causes—a golf course, a museum, a college, a penitentiary, an artist colony, a North American Bayreuth, an Indian sports arena. The Friends of Discovery Park, as it was christened, repulsed them all and preserved most of the fields and forests for walking. Buffered by the park from civilization (except its epitome, the sewage plant), the beach, too, was saved for public feet.

I intended to follow the beach from West Point north around the bluff, but the tide was too high. By sidewalk I descended from the park through residential neighborhoods to Hiram Chittenden Locks.

Chittenden Locks. Named for the Army engineer who directed the digging (1911-1917) of the Lake Washington Ship Canal from Salmon Bay through the Fremont Cut to Lake Union, and on through the Montlake Cut to Lake Washington, which was lowered to the level of Lake Union.

Ballard Locks (the common name). A postcard standard, one of the Seven Wonders of Seattle, for decades second in size in the world only to the Gatun Locks of the Panama Canal. It is the connection between saltwater at sea level and freshwater at 21 feet above mean high tide. It was expected to make Lake Washington a world port. It didn't. Except for play boats, most of the traffic has been fishing vessels based at Salmon Bay Terminal.

Ballard. Until 1907 an independent city, seventh largest in the state, with seventeen shingle mills and three sawmills. Where in 1909 Frank Hawthorn, a Pennsylvania farm boy become schoolteacher turned North Dakota homesteader, brought his family after Australian wool put him out of the sheep business and hailstorms out of the wheat business. It is the location of Ballard General Hospital, my birthplace. Until 1940 or so, it was the location of Ballard Ferry Dock, the terminal of a ferry to Suquamish—and of the ferry to Port Ludlow that in 1938 was the first leg of my route as a Boy Scout to Camp Parsons and Marmot Pass.

Miasma condensed to a drizzle. The fog horn on West Point, unseen, warned of the edge of the world.

One Sunday in the early 1920s, Mother, aged fifteen, paddled a canoe through the locks, the five miles to Bainbridge Island and the five miles back; in winds from the north and winds from the south; through Main Street tugs and barges, fishing boats, mosquito fleet, Pacific Fleet, ocean freighters, coastal liners, lumber schooners, rumrunners, Prohibition agents, killer whales, and dragons.

I passed the statue of Leif Ericson, who in his own time on his own seas sailed beyond the edge of the world; not in a *drakar,* a dragon ship designed for piracy, but in a *knarr* built for the open ocean.

I walked by the site of the ferry dock to a row of restaurants offering crab from Alaska, lobster from Maine, shark from Florida, prawns from Australia, and even salmon from Puget Sound or nearby. Noon was coming on and the exhaust fan of a sidewalk eatery exhaled memories of the Alley Kat. I hungered for fish and chips, but among the rotten things of the day was a toothache that kept me from opening my jaw enough to chew. However, the wall menu listed peanut butter milkshakes, a delicacy I'd found, until now, only in a restaurant in Puyallup where we used to stop, sunburned and dehydrated, returning from climbs of Mount Rainier. Walking on, I looked in restaurant windows at folks sipping Manhattans and crunching shrimp. Dolled up, warm and cozy, they looked smugly out on a cold drizzle, a bronze Viking, and a tramp spooning a peanut butter milkshake through his whiskers.

The restaurants ended at the sands of Golden Gardens Park, where I first walked, having earlier crawled, on the trail that leads to Bellingham.

5. Carkeek Park to Meadow Point

Mile $14^1/_2$–$12^1/_2$

Wednesday, February 18, 1976

Muscles gone flabby at a desk need to be stretched. Sour juices need to be sweated out of the pores and vile vapors out the ears. It was a morning for a getaway. Since 1952, when we moved from Seattle to Cougar Mountain, the direction of escape had been east, farther from the city. But today the east was altogether a darkness that said millions of tons of snow were being dumped on the high Cascades and billions of gallons of icewater on the low. To the west a Blue Hole shone.

A scant hour from my desk I stood in Carkeek Park, two miles north of Golden Gardens, on a skybridge arched above railroad tracks, breathing cold wind. Tatters of cloud rushed north across the Hole, darkening waves to steely gray, letting through touch-and-go sunbursts that torched off the whitecaps. My wizened fungus of a woodland soul expanded hugely.

Carkeek Park. From 1942 to 1945 this was my getaway from the University of Washington campus. Before that, in the spring of 1942, during our final weeks of high school, my friend Arild and I came here by Model A to gather beer bottles from the driftwood, toss them far out in waters colored by the setting sun, and bombard them with rocks until stars flickered in the waves. In the spring of 1938, Boy Scout Troop 324 hiked down the trail through the woods and dropped their packs in the meadow beside Piper's Creek. Other troops of the North Shore District erected tidy tent villages. We unrolled our blankets in the grass and slept open to the sky, a slum, ranked dead last in the Camporall.

In 1920 or so, Mother walked from here (a brickyard then) north four miles to Richmond Beach, and then ran all the way back to Ballard to be on time for her solo in the church choir.

The tide was high, the beach drowned, but the rail avenue was open. I walked the tracks south. Pigeons waddled, crows sliced the wind, gulls rode it. Waves slammed against the granite seawall and sloshed over the rails. An alder-maple jungle climbed the 200-foot bluff of glacial drift. By the grace of God's waters and God's glacier and James J. Hill's railroad, I walked in wildness.

The bluff lowered to a bank—North Beach, once upon a time the scene of many a Sunday school picnic and, as the piling stubs told, a port of call for the mosquito fleet. During the summer of 1941 Cousin Al and I, at the end of hot days mowing lawns of Blue Ridge manors, descended by trail, pulled off our sweat-soaked clothes, and plunged in. Since then the trail has been blocked by houses, the public excluded unless it walks the tracks.

The bluff reared up in billows of alder catkins reddening toward spring. I passed a work train and cleanup gang, the mudbucket scooping gray slime from the tracks, the crew repairing the sensor wire that warns a control room in the city that the tracks have been overwhelmed again. In my childhood the sensing was done by a speeder sent in advance of the locomotive or, in lack of a speeder, by the cowcatcher, in which case the newspaper headlines would announce that a train had been stuck in the mud again.

The bluff and tracks curved left around a corner. By one odd chance and another, I'd never before rounded that corner, hadn't even examined the map, never in my mental geography had connected Carkeek Park to Seattle. My pace picked up, in anticipation. This day of 1976 I would see what I had not seen in 1945, or 1942, or 1938, or ever.

When Seattle's Downtown Movers & Shakers (DMS) yearned for a fish tank to entertain the tourists who stayed in their hotels, ate in their restaurants, and shopped in their stores, they chose for their Worthy Cause a chunk of empty, useless, free land—that is, a public park. However, this time the crime of attempted rape couldn't be laid at the feet of the DMS, because the site, Meadow Point, was also selected by the custodian of the Pacific Science Center, a moldering but sanctified relic (the Center, that is) of the World's Fair. Previously the custodian, a marine biology professor at the University, had gained great fame and adoration for her championship of marine ecosystems. Though at that time the pet after-dinner speaker of the DMS, Professor Dixy Lee Ray was then still a heroine of environmentalists.

To the consternation of the professor and the DMS, a group of wretches agreed a fish tank would be dandy for tourists and school kids—but not on Meadow Point. The case was powerfully and repeatedly presented in a slide-illustrated lecture by Wolf Bauer, who afoot and in kayak had minutely studied the shores of Puget Sound.

Wolf explained the parts of a mature—a "complete"—beach: first, the wave-washed zone which extends up to the highest normal tide; second, above that, the semi-permanent driftwood line which is shuffled only by storm tides; third, inland of that, the dune line which is accumulated by winds blowing grains of sun-dried sand, gradually building a ridge above reach of most tides; fourth, inland of that, dammed by the dune, a lagoon; and finally fifth, the uplands of the bluff. In the narrow band between deep water and forest is a series of distinct systems of plants and creatures, "infinite riches in little room."

Wolf described Seattle's saltwater shore. South of Elliott Bay are bulkheads-houses-seawall-boulevard, not one natural inch. In primeval times, there were complete beaches on three spits, but Three Tree Point and Alki Point were domesticated early on. Point Williams survived until after World War II, "protected" within Lincoln Park, but then honored by another Worthy Cause—a swimming pool. Elliott Bay is now totally industrial-commercial from Alki Point around to Smith Cove. Magnolia Bluff's beach remains largely natural, but "young" and thus incomplete. Waves are still in the process of attacking the cliff. There's no driftwood except temporary litter, no dune line, and no lagoon. West Point once had all these parts, magnificently, and they had survived the Coast Guard, Army, and even Seattle's raw-sewage pipe, but they succumbed in the 1960s to an exceedingly Worthy Cause, the METRO sewage-treatment plant. North of Shilshole Bay were harbor and railroad, nothing natural, no beach complete. *Except at Meadow Point,* where the DMS wanted their fish tank.

The aquarium was ultimately installed downtown at Waterfront Park, much handier anyhow to the hotels and restaurants. Meadow Point was preserved. But Hell hath no fury like a professor scorned. Elected governor of the state of Washington by the DMS, she came down on the environment like a wolf on the fold.

From Carkeek Park to North Beach the way had been familiar. I approached the corner in growing excitement, wondering what marvels awaited beyond. I rounded the corner and saw a few yards ahead a spit! A palpable spit! A driftwood line much eaten by beachfires but with some logs intact, silver-bleached, grass-nurturing, and bird-and-critter sheltering. There was a dune line, much trampled but perceptibly elevated. Even a patch of reeds and cattails, remnant of the lagoon.

How could Wolf Bauer, most systematic and thorough of observers, have missed seeing it?

In rounding the corner I'd been smacked in the face by a thirty-knot wind. I looked to the south to see a Blackness gobbling up the Blue Hole and convulsing the Sound from shore to shore. At the tip of the spit, where piling stubs marched out into breakers, I watched the squall veer inland, missing me. Another, following hard behind, swerved west, destroying Bainbridge Island. It was like having a grandstand view of a war without the risk.

But I was sad to have learned that Wolf was fallible, his inventory of the spits of the Seattle shore so obviously incomplete.

A few steps more and I stopped dead. Just ahead was a bathhouse. I knew that building! Many a summer day, long ago, the cousins and I went inside to change into our swimming suits. This was Golden

Gardens. Wolf was infallible after all—the spit I'd just "discovered" was the one the fish-tank controversy had been all about. I'd known it well since childhood. Yet today's thrill remained. In childhood I'd known the civilized side of Meadow Point. After all these years I'd discovered the wild side.

Now that I'd connected Carkeek Park to Golden Gardens—to Seattle—a thought arose. North of Carkeek Park were other bulges in the shore I'd never rounded, other scenes of childhood and youth never hitched together. A great notion began forming—a spidery notion of spinning a web from here to there to there.

Friday, April 18, 1980

The U.S. Geological Survey's Snohomish Quadrangle, surveyed 1893–1895, published 1897, has "FT LAWTON" on Magnolia Bluff, though construction had not yet begun at survey time. In 1897, the tidal marshes of Smith Cove almost meet those of Salmon Bay, an estuary arm of Shilshole Bay, virtually making an island of the bluff. Lake Union empties through a creek to Salmon Bay. The only sizable settlement in the vicinity is Ballard, on the north shore of Salmon Bay. Through it runs the Great Northern Railroad, only just completed to Seattle (1893). Seattle is confined to the far side of Lake Union, on the slopes dropping to Elliott Bay.

Seattle had a population of 42,837 in 1890. In 1908, when the city was nearing its 1910 figure of 237,174, the U.S. Geological Survey published the Seattle Quadrangle. Urbanization is now complete from Elliott Bay to Salmon Bay. Ballard sprawls west along the Salmon Bay shore to Shilshole but stops a mile south of Meadow Point. On the heights north of Ballard and east of Meadow Point are several country roads and two dozen scattered houses. There is also a tract marked with a cross, the map symbol for a cemetery.

I'd been to Crown Hill Cemetery once before, with Mother, to put flowers on the graves. Today was my second visit.

Dominating the family plot was a solitary monument erected by and for the man who bought the plot: Harrison W. Clark (1841-1910), "A MEMBER OF CO I NY VOL INF." In the 1890s he came out from Chautauqua, New York, with Gramma Clark (my great-grandmother), Julia (1847-1915). During 1899, the year after the Klondike Gold Rush,

1,200 houses were built in Seattle. Grampa Clark was building his share in Ballard, including the house on Phinney Ridge that Mother grew up in and where, in 1925, I was brought home from Ballard General Hospital. The Clarks' daughter, Carrie (1867-1929), my grandmother, was so tall that to walk hand in hand with her I had to reach high in the air. As a boy, her husband, Frank Hawthorn (1859-1925), had heard a horse galloping by the farm in Pennsylvania and the rider shouting "They've shot Lincoln!" The five-year-old ran in the house and hid under the bed, knowing they'd be coming after him next.

The daughters lay in a row: Aunt Eva (1887-1951), Aunt Mary (1894-1963), and Aunt Grace (1899-1971) with her husband, Uncle Bill (1897-1976). There was one aunt I never knew, Jessie (1898-1912). The next-to-youngest daughter, Aunt Ruth, was buried elsewhere, as were three sons, Uncle George, Uncle Jim, and an uncle I never knew, Harry, killed by an Indian in North Dakota (a hunting accident). Mother, youngest of the nine, was here, Kathryn D. Manning (1906-1976). A single space in the plot remained vacant, reserved for Dad.

I drove to Golden Gardens and walked north to Carkeek Park.

The 1897 map shows the Seattle seen by Grampa Clark, the veteran of the Grand Army of the Republic, arriving to build a metropolis.

The 1908 map shows the city my mother came to in 1909—on these railroad tracks. Empty country then, this stretch of shore. A building of some sort on Meadow Point. A single house at North Beach, above the piling stubs. In the three miles north from there to the map edge, just seven houses—all atop the bluff. Below the bluff, only the water, the tracks.

Across the Sound lay Eagle Harbor of Bainbridge. North of the Island, on the Kitsap Peninsula shore of Port Madison, was Indianola, where Grandmother Hawthorn rented a summer cottage, before the one at Fletcher's Bay. Between land masses on the northern horizon opened the water gap of Admiralty Inlet, where Dad arrived on the "New Momma." His mother's father, Thomas Simpson, was partly a farmer, partly a fisherman who had sailed a schooner from his home port in Nova Scotia to the fishing banks in the North Atlantic. Dad's mother was Louise (1876-1976). When she was a child in Nova Scotia the population of Seattle (1880) was 3,553.

Steamers sidewheeled then and sternwheeled and propeller-churned along the Sound, pluming white wood smoke, and black coal smoke. Tall ships spread their wings. A few cedar-dugout canoes still paddled by. At night, there was darkness on the waters and shores, and the only bright lights were the moon and the Milky Way.

6. Carkeek Park to Richmond Beach

Mile 14$\frac{1}{2}$–18$\frac{1}{2}$

Friday, March 12, 1976

A cold front was rolling in from the North Pacific, and the surf was oceanic. Spindrift flew by my eyes, wind roared in the forest. Low clouds raced north pierced by spotlights of cold sun. Yet pussies were hung along the willow boughs and coltsfoot bloomed white in blue clay. In the cattails the frogs racketed—quieting as I neared, resuming behind my back. Wrens and bushtits scrambled. Robins chirped. Sparrows warbled. A hawk circled.

Lightly I stepped along the ties. After the Meadow Point walk a few weeks ago, I'd cut my food intake to the starvation level. Crazed with sanctity, on February 24 I threw away, half-smoked, my last cigarette forever. Having already lost its beer, my body decided I wasn't worth fooling with anymore. Yesterday I'd gone to the doctor, purely as a perfunctory preliminary to the funeral. Her diagnosis was less final than mine. Exercise would fix me up, she said, and she further advised me to get my mind out of its internal derangements by taking a long walk. It so happened I was on my way to Bellingham anyhow.

A hundred feet offshore "grew" an islet of maple trees. I could see in the bluff the gray cavity from which it had slid. The cleanup gang had left plenty of ooze on the track for the rains to wash away, as the rains had been doing hereabouts for 13,000 years.

Before the Recent Epoch of geologic time came the Pleistocene

Epoch, commonly referred to as the "Ice Age." The epoch was composed of at least four *glaciations,* defined as periods when the ice advances from centers of accumulation. They are separated by *interglacial periods* when the ice retreats. The glaciations are broken into *stades* (major advances) separated by *interstades* (major retreats). A stade itself is made up of lesser advances and retreats, lasting years or decades or centuries. One of these lesser advances, the "Little Ice Age," began in medieval times, and compelled the Norse settlers of Greenland to unite with the Eskimos for survival. It also gradually forced Norwegian farmers to switch from grain crops which no longer could ripen to hay they could feed to cows, and in the late eighteenth century caused ice advances that overwhelmed villages in the Alps. In the next century retreat began and continued until the mid-twentieth century, when glaciers in the Cascades and Olympics resumed their advance. A few hot summers and they quit. Several hard winters and they revived. Back and forth.

Future geologists may add our Recent Epoch to the Pleistocene. It cannot now be said whether the world is in an interglacial period, or perhaps merely an interstade. Certainly, there presently is far more glacier ice than in all but a very few previous moments in the history of the earth.

In any event, the Fraser Glaciation, last (if it indeed is) in the Pleistocene series pushed the Puget Lobe of the Cordilleran Ice Sheet south from Canada. In its Vashon Stade the ice crossed the border about 16,000 years ago and at an average rate of a tenth of a mile a year reached its limit south of Olympia about 14,000 years ago. The ice thickness then sloped from 7,000 feet at Bellingham to maybe 3,000 at Seattle, 1,200 at Olympia, and zero a few miles south. During the Everson Inter-stade that followed, the ice retreated to Canada. The Sumas Stade was an advance occurring around 11,000 years ago, but this time the Canadian ice barely slid over the border.

On most of the Inland Sea, outcrops of bedrock are uncommon. The ground surface is mainly *glacial drift*—materials transported by the Pleistocene ice. An *erratic* is a boulder that rode the glacier—or sometimes an iceberg—until dumped. *Till i*s an unsorted mixture of particles of every size from clay to boulders, compacted to a concretelike *hardpan.* Most drift is sorted by meltwater: *sand* and *gravel* are deposited in river beds and deltas by water of greater or lesser velocity; *clay* settles out in lakes and ponds from ice-milled rock flour.

The area north of Seattle last melted free about 13,000 years ago. Since then the drift has been under attack by the Inland Sea—or rather, a series of Inland Seas.

When the glacier stretched unbroken from the Olympics to the Cascades, walling off the ocean, the Inland Sea was freshwater Lake Russell, which received the rivers of the two mountain ranges and drained through its outlet south around the corner of the Olympics to the ocean. At different times its surface was at different heights above modern sea level and thus there are fossil shore bluffs (that is, bluffs carved in a preceding era) high above and some distance inland.

When the ice melted, two things happened concurrently. First, the earth's plastic-like crust, which had been pressed down by the huge glacial weight, elastically rebounded upward, gradually regaining its preglacial level. This happened about 6,000 years ago in the Seattle vicinity—earlier farther south, later farther north. The amount of the downbowing and rebounding varied with the thickness of the ice. There was none of either beyond the ice margin, south of Olympia, some 450 feet of down and up in southern Whidbey Island, and as much as 1,000 feet in Alaska.

Second, at the time the ice dam created by the glacier vanished and the salt flowed in, the oceans were lower than they are now, because much of the world's water was still locked up in continental glaciers. As the glaciers shrank, sea level rose some 400 feet from the Pleistocene low, attaining approximately today's level and virtually stabilizing (a very slow rise continues) about 4,000 to 5,000 years ago.

Until about 6,600 years ago the land rose at around twice the rate of the sea. Shore bluffs were carved and beaches planed flat, then lifted beyond reach of the waves, one more cause of the fossil beaches found frequently around the Inland Sea, although they are in many places covered over by the slumping bluffs. The land's uplift and the sea's uprise were both substantially completed about 5,000 years ago, and the shore has since then remained at essentially the same elevation.

The bluff composed of glacial drift has determined the character of the Inland Sea more than anything else. Its imported sands and gravels provide abundant beach material, far more than waves could have milled from hard rock in the available time, and so the beaches tend to be wide (at low tide), except where the waves, blocked by seawalls and bulkheads, can't get at the bluff. Due to the same lack of time, the beaches are mostly so young that whenever the tides are very high, waves attack the bluff, helping gravity and rain bring the walls tumbling-slipping-oozing down.

Carkeek to Hidden Creek

North from Carkeek Park stretches the largest wilderness in the City of Seattle, one and a half miles long to the city limits (it continues many more miles beyond) and up to 250 feet high, laced with ravines fingering inland. Too treacherous even for fancy engineers with their costly drainage pipes, anchor cables, and sleek testimony at public hearings, the Pleistocene bluff is forested by alders and maples, jungled by stickery salmonberry canes, poison-spiked devil's club, and the dagger-thorned vines of "hellberry"—this a mixture of two Eurasian exotics, Himalayan and evergreen blackberry, that have run amok in Puget Sound country, to the horror of farmers and hikers and the joy of the birds and critters who find refuge in the tangles from other Eurasian exotics, the neighborhood cats and dogs.

For this wilderness the Pleistocene must be thanked. But nature itself couldn't have done the job. The Seattle shore south of Elliott Bay is also glacial drift, but there the beachwalker is under the steady, glassy scowl of picture windows. Nature's partner was James J. Hill.

When Hill brought his railroad over the Cascades and down the Sound shore from Everett to Seattle he was hailed for rescuing the Queen City from the ignominy of being connected to civilization solely by a branch line from Tacoma. But in the era of the Environmental Impact Statement one reflects that an EIS for Hill's Great Northern would compare to those for the Sack of Rome, the Burning of the Alexandria Library, and the Sinking of Atlantis. As Grandfather Hawthorn and other North Dakota homesteaders used to say, "First we had the drought, then we had the hail, then we had the locusts, and then we had James J. Hill."

Between Port Gardner in Everett and Shilshole Bay in Seattle the seawall and the roadbed obliterated most tidelands. When the Seattle tide table shows a high of 9 or 10 feet or less, and winds are moderate, virtually all unmolested beaches of the northern Sound are walkably wide even at high water. On railroad shores, though, beachwalking is meager until the tide drops to 2 feet or so. Moreover, the seawall robs the waves of a continuing replenishment of sand and gravel, and in sweeping away what's there, the longshore currents leave "starved" beaches of boulders and cobbles, misery to the ankles and Achilles tendons.

But in any tide and any weather and on any day, always there is the trackwalking.

> Then we'll sing one song of the poor and ragged tramp,
> He carries his home on his back;
> Too old to work, he's not wanted 'round the camp,
> So he wanders without aim along the track.

So sang the wandering Wobbly, Joe Hill. The heirs of James J. Hill don't love Joe Hill's heirs. Some of us are drunk or stoned, some deaf, and some too preoccupied by mountains or birds to keep an eye and ear to the rear. The railroad is put to heavy annual expense doing the paperwork on squashed walkers. But shooing us away would cost even more. Inspection crews on speeders, maintenance crews installing new ties or fresh ballast, cleanup crews mopping up pieces of bluff, train crews on locomotives and cabooses, all ignore the tramp or wave a friendly greeting.

A slot canyon sliced in sand and clay isolated a thin ridge from the bluff, obviously a favorite place now, as it was thirty-odd years ago, for kids to risk their necks. Straddling the skinny crest, I gazed over whitecaps, big ships and little boats, Olympic snows and clouds. Northward, silver tanks on Point Wells briefly blazed in a flash of sun. Beyond, in another sudden flare, a white dot flamed on leaden waters—the ferry crossing from Edmonds to Kingston.

All was as it had been.

I rounded a bulge to a valley where a creek flowed far out on a delta point. Piling stubs. Relics of a dock upon which I sat thirty-four years ago and watched a winter sunset.

Hidden Creek to Richmond Beach

Fathers earned the living, mothers kept the house, and kids had the diseases. That was how the work of the world was allotted, and I tried to do my share with as good grace as my folks did theirs. But having run the gauntlet of children's diseases, I broke loose with a caper, leap, and yell, shouldered the Trapper Nelson, and climbed up up up from wilderness forests to the tundra crests of mountain ridges.

> They go so high,
> Almost touch the sky,
> I'll always climb them 'til I die.

So we sang in the twilight at Campfire Point, on the Hood Canal beach of Camp Parsons, capital of the Boy Scout universe.

Whenever my new freedom was threatened by symptoms I suppressed them, on the theory that going to the doctor didn't cure but caused illness. The strategy worked until one morning in April, 1941 when I was going on sixteen and companions had to take my pack and fashion me a crutch to hobble nine miles from Lake Dorothy to the road. I'd done with measles and mumps and chicken pox and other plagues of little kids, but now, in common with half my generation, had graduated to "growing pains." The disease was tolerable. It was the doctor who nearly killed me: he said, stay out of the mountains a year.

1938: the sunset at Marmot Pass and the above-the-cloudsea sunrise on Delmonte Ridge.

1939: on one hike, the pellmell glissade from Flypaper Pass to the Anderson Glacier; on a second, the hushed entry into alpine fairyland, Deception Basin and Mystery Glacier.

1940: the epic retreat along Lost Ridge in a screaming-hollering Three Day Blow.

1941: why bother having the year at all?

Returning west in 1933, after a year living with Dad's folks in Lowell, Massachusetts, we settled on the rolling plateau of glacial drift north of Seattle, mostly wooded by second-growth Douglas fir dating from the clearcutting of a third of a century before. Now in the summer of 1941, banned from the mountains, I roamed the near countryside, exploring trails and ancient wagon roads. Compared to old-growth forests and cascading rivers, precipices, and glaciers, it was dull stuff.

One day Arild was at our house, located in a gone-wild orchard circled by second-growth fir, and I was telling him my latest discoveries—collapsed chicken houses, junked Model Ts, lovers' lanes—nothing to compare with Shangri La. He asked if I'd found Hidden Lake.

"Where's that?"

"There."

He pointed beyond the foreground trees to a ridge in the "Boeing Tract," also forested, I'd always supposed, by more of the same second-growth. Very wrongly, I now learned. Eight years I'd lived with that ridge as my western horizon, seeing the trees sway in high winds, turn white in snowstorms, dissolve in low clouds, etch black lines in sunset, and not realized it was virgin forest, a square mile preserved by William Boeing (the elder), the logger-become-airplane-builder, as his personal pleasuring gound, enhanced by damming a swampy bottomland on the main creek to create Hidden Lake.

The rich man's pleasuring had ceased when he went broke in the Crash. For a decade the wilderness had been deserted by humans, save for stealthy poachers, like Arild, come to steal the trout. The time had come for a peasant boy's pleasuring.

Arild led me on an introductory tour, and thereafter I was on my own. A scant half-mile on country roads took me from our house to the edge of the tract. The poachers' path ascended the ridge, entered the cathedral gloom beneath green arches that hid all the sky except a scattering of blue stars. On the ridge crest the path intersected a trail connecting the estates of The Highlands to their water supply in Hidden Creek. Rich little ladies rode horses here, reporting peasant boys to the waterworks caretaker, who prowled about carrying a shotgun for grouse and peasants, so that one walked very quietly. Beyond the danger zone the creek trail followed the flow to the lake, a pool of silence rippled by ducks, rounded the shore from an inlet delta of golden sand to an outlet waterfall, continued on to concrete tanks of long-abandoned fish-rearing ponds, and on down the forest gorge to railroad tracks, beach, dock.

I explored these and other trails and animal traces, left paths altogether to bull through head-high salal, crawl over and under logs, slide into black-mucky devil's-club bottoms. I fantasized breaking abruptly out of twilight into a meadow—by a freak of microclimate, an *alpine* meadow. With a naked moraine. And through the power of prayer, a tiny glacier.

An afternoon in early December of 1941. A brilliance of winter sunlight flooded the classroom, the teacher opened the window to let in breathings of new life, and I couldn't wait for the school bus that carried us country kids back to where we came from. I skipped out early, hitch-hiked home on Highway 99, and while school friends were still wondering where I'd gotten to, was sitting on the dock looking towards Marmot Pass, watching the sunset, marveling that there could be such fury with no sound. The fires died, the band of green dissolved in cream, pinks and yellows faded to milky blue, time resumed, and I stood up and turned east to the forest—and impassable night.

My way home therefore lay northward along the tracks. Phosphorescence in the waves danced with the glint of stars. Goblins chuckled in the woods. Cities and homes were blacked out, and ships and boats too; automobile headlights and traffic signals were taped to slits and beach fires forbidden; air raid wardens were watching for stray beams that might guide the enemy in. It may have been the darkest night on Puget Sound since the Europeans came and lit whale-oil and kerosene lamps, perhaps darker than since the Asians arrived and built campfires.

The goblins attacked! The quick wink of a hooded flashlight revealed khaki and rifles. Acquitted of being Japanese, I proceeded past the gravel pit being guarded against sabotage, into Richmond Beach, and so home by highway. It was the only occasion the U.S. Army ever expressed interest in me, and for that reason was the most dangerous night of my war.

In 1945 the rotogravure section of the *Seattle Times* showed the Boeing Tract being skidded down the bluff to the beach and rafted to a mill—"just like the good old days of tidewater logging," brayed the reporter, dancing on the grave of what could have been Seattle's greatest wildland park. I had never been back, until today.

The creek rattled delta gravels as before; the new map called it "Boeing" Creek. Seawall and tracks were unchanged, though the parade of trains had dwindled to a sorry few.

Only gulls and cormorants now found sitting room on the dock, reduced to six pilings above the water and other stubs barely breaking the surface, a lot of wood, actually, to survive thirty-four years of marine jaws that bite and waves that pound—plus how many years before Arild had shown it to me?

The Highlands. In 1908 Seattle's old money sought refuge from the elbows of new money, bought 380 acres of virgin forest, built Cyclone fences, roads, waterworks, mansions—and a dock. Considering that the auto road to the city was tortuous at best and impossible in flood or snow or thaw, and that the Great Northern milk train ran at hours better suited to cows than magnates, the dozen miles by water road to the

Seattle waterfront must have been much the most comfortable, whether by a mosquito on a scheduled run or by a magnate's yacht, based at Salmon Bay and summoned by telephone.

I trespassed in The Highlands once, ascending the woods road from the dock, emerging astonished into manicured trees, shrubs, lawns, and gardens. As enchanted as I was bewildered, I wandered from mansion to palace to castle. Too late I heard a rumbling "Fee fie foe fum!" A car rounded a corner and braked to a stop. I turned to confront—not a magnate but the *Seattle Times* paperman, who saw my peril at a glance and gave me a ride past the dungeons and the men-at-arms guarding the gate to a safe return home by country road.

The north wall of the Hidden Creek valley was now beyond recognizing with its rows of picture windows. Where the creek trail had been there was now a road, which I followed to a marshy basin that didn't belong there until I recalled hearing of a cloudburst that had not enough forest floor to soak it up and had therefore rushed off roofs and patios and streets, washed out the dam and drained Hidden Lake.

The south wall, surprisingly, was wild as ever, the forest spared from logging because the old firs were mostly snagtops and wolves not worth hauling to the mill. Just as I remembered, the beach road switchbacked up the bluff and, just as I remembered, opened out in a park that would have gratified a grandee in the reign of Good Queen Anne.

I didn't push my luck. In fairy tales the peasant boys are rescued, but not the dirty old men. I returned to the tracks and continued north, to the scene of my encounter with the khaki goblins.

7. Richmond Beach

Wednesday, February 2, 1977

Dad, rather at loose ends since last October 30, when Mother died, joined me for the day, and we drove to Richmond Beach where the gravel pit was now a King County park. It used to be a two-mile walk on country roads and woodland paths from our orchard. This was the spot for Scouts to assume the traditional costume and swim fifty yards for the First Class test. Winter was the bravest season, when the surf smashed loud and the wind blew cold and in minutes a naked Scout turned blue all over.

We used to tear apart barrels, nail leather toe straps to the staves and push off from the top of the pit, skiing a few feet and tumbling the rest of the way to the tracks. Less painful sport was on the high sand hill outside the tracks. We'd run to the brink of the 50-foot cliff, fly like Superman, drop like a shot duck, splash in the sand, and roll laughing to the beach.

Dad and I crossed over the tracks on the skybridge, new since our day, to the sand hill, eroded to less than half its old height, and the cliff now gently sloping to beach level. A bathhouse was on top, where scotchbroom once grew concealing burrows where one could see that people had been lying—one wondered for what purpose.

During the Depression, entertainment was provided regularly on the beach south of the sand hill. A column of black smoke towering thousands of feet, visible throughout Seattle's North End, announced the show. In the evening the audience assembled to watch a wooden ship burn. Afterward the strippers would salvage the brass and copper. Here in 1923 the *Glory of the Seas,* laid down in a Massachusetts shipyard in 1869, the last American clipper ship ever launched, was burned. Among the pyres we attended in the 1930s may have been those of the tall ships which rode at anchor in Eagle Harbor in the 1920s. Perhaps we saw the *Conqueror* burn, a five-masted barkentine originally out of Yarmouth, Nova Scotia, which appeared in the movie *Tugboat Annie,* filmed on the Sound; possibly too the *Eleanor H,* which had carried Walla Walla wheat to Australia and Newcastle coal to South Africa. It was commanded by Captain Anderson, and his son was once my best friend. In 1929 I went to his birthday party in the captain's cave-snug cabin, the paneled wood, glowing brass, and thick-glassed portholes speaking of a planet of waters.

On a hot summer day Dad would get home from the shop at 5:30, we'd all three change to swimming suits, and by 6 o'clock be neckdeep in the tangy green water whose temperature in July is at least two or three degrees warmer than in January. We'd change to dry clothes standing in a blanket, two holding the curtain while the third squirmed.

We'd eat potato salad, hamburger-noodles-tomato sauce casserole, and watch the sun go down.

We'd look west to the Olympics—Marmot Pass, where in 1938 I first saw wilderness and knew it was wilderness. We'd look across the Sound to the Kitsap Peninsula and, south a ways, Bainbridge Island.

Puget Sound. Where Indians paddled canoes for thousands of years. Where Captain Vancouver sailed the *Discovery* in 1792, followed for a century and a third by more and more, then fewer and fewer, tall ships. Where in 1837 came the Hudson's Bay Company's cranky little wood-burning *Beaver*, the first steamship on the Northwest Coast, first of the mosquito fleet that would cleave the Inland Sea until 1939, on the eve of World War II, when the *Virginia V* quit its Seattle-Vashon Island-Tacoma run.

World War II. On this beach we learned of events in the Pacific not reported by the American press, and not believed when announced by the Japanese. Picnicking families stopped swimming, eating, and laughing to watch ocean-going tugs shepherd capital ships that had been ripped by explosions and blackened by fires. It was my closest contact with the war aside from being almost arrested on suspicion of being Japanese.

8. Richmond Beach to Edmonds   Mile 18½–22½

Thursday, February 17, 1977

The Cascades and Olympics were a black void, but beneath a Blue Hole a winter wind drove waves to explosions of spring-bright surf. I walked the tracks north from the park to the site of the station, where in our time the residents still caught the train to work or shop in Seattle. The 1897 map, surveyed just after completion of the Great Northern Railroad, shows several dozen structures in and around "Richmond," named in 1889 for the seat of the earl who killed Richard III. Most were near the station, as was the dock, the only one shown on the map between Ballard and Edmonds. The wagon roads connecting Richmond to these towns surely were secondary to the railroad and water road, both of which served commuters, summerers, and workers at the Richmond Beach Shipbuilding Company, which in 1909 launched Seattle's famous fireboat, the *Duwamish*.

In 1897 the settlement ended at Point Wells, a spit several times the size of Meadow Point, larger even than West Point, and then with but a single house. The town of Richmond Beach still ends at "The Point," where a Cyclone fence encloses a tank farm of fifty-odd huge silver cylinders, the intricate piping of an asphalt refinery, and a tanker dock. This "silver city" of Standard Oil was already old in the 1930s.

Once when the *Standard Service* was in its home port here, I spent a night inside the fence with Dad and ate a day's meals in the mess hall. Outside the fence the Depression raged and we lived on potatoes, farina, and hamburger. Within, steaks and chops and roasts all were served at the same supper, bacon and eggs, ham, sausage, hotcakes, waffles, and French toast at the same breakfast. Every meal was topped off by an array of cakes, pastries, and pies—fruit pies and cream pies: banana cream, coconut custard, lemon meringue, and chocolate chiffon. Urged on by table mates, I nearly pied myself to death.

At the far end of the fence the tank farm ended, but not the spit, not quite. I followed a creek through a grove of willows to the cattails of a lagoon, crossed the undisturbed dune line and the jumble of driftwood to the waves. Beyond the fence was a complete beach, a remnant of a pristine spit fit to delight Wolf Bauer—and me. Wolf had been a good teacher and had sent me back to my geology textbooks to refresh what I learned from other good teachers at the University of Washington. As the journey went along I was getting to be something of a professor myself, able to deliver at least an elementary lecture, to wit:

The *coast* is an indefinitely wide strip landward from shore. The *shore* is the narrow zone between low-tide shoreline and high-tide shoreline. The *shoreline* is where land and water meet.

The chief agents that erode the shore are wind-generated *waves* that carve *wave-cut cliffs* whose debris forms *beaches* of cobbles, gravel, and sand. Waves that strike the shore obliquely move along the shore creating *longshore currents* which transport materials, depositing some on beaches and using some to build *spits* and *bars*. In any locality the orientation of spits and bars is determined by the direction of the dominant longshore current, which is determined by the dominant winds and the orientation of the shore. (*Tidal currents* go back and forth and accomplish little.)

As waves erode the land, the beach widens. The retreating cliff leaves a *wave-cut bench*, a platform of rock (or, in most of the Inland Sea, the glacial drift dumped by the ice) usually covered with sand and gravel that gradually are moved seaward by the *undertow* and dumped in deep water, accumulating a *wave-built terrace*. At the outer edge of the terrace is the dropoff all Puget Sound children are warned against, because here it is that waders drown.

The width of bench and terrace, which together constitute the beach, depends partly on how long the waves have been at it. The Inland Sea isn't old enough for much erosion of its comparatively few hard-rock shores, but the drift is readily attacked, and thus beaches of good width are virtually universal wherever there has been substantial wave action— and where no obstacle starves the waves.

A longshore current picks up a load when it hits the shore and drops it when it runs out in deep water and loses momentum. When a current fills an offshore area, creating a shallows, surf churns up material to form an *offshore bar* that may be raised above the normal high-tide line by storm tides and ultimately be connected to the shore, enclosing a lagoon—another route to a "complete" beach.

Longshore currents straighten shores by the following process: When the shore bulges abruptly out or curves abruptly in, the currents tend to keep going straight, soon losing energy in deep water and dropping loads. Thus *spits* are built. When one of these terminates in open water, it forms a *point* (a different species from the point built by a creek *delta*). When it connects the mainland to an island, the latter becomes a *tombolo*. When a spit crosses an indentation and intersects the shore on the far side, it encloses a lagoon—another route to a complete beach. When a spit pushes across the mouth of a bay and nearly or completely closes it off, it's called a *baymouth bar*.

The shore north of Seattle, generally a north-south line, gives free run both to storm southerlies and sunshine northerlies. The former, commoner and stronger, do the bulk of the transport and would, if working alone, form the sediments into points jutting northward. But northerlies do enough to modify the points to cause them to jut westward, resulting in triangular *cuspate forelands*.

On a shore walled by a bluff of unstable drift, the spits and bars are man's favored habitat. Here he either fills the lagoon to make dry ground for refineries, sewage plants, and picnic tables, or dredges basins for stinkpots hitched to picture-window ramblers. Here he heaps up breakwaters and seawalls and bulkheads to fend off storm waves that in a state of nature carry driftwood over the dune line into the lagoon. The most complex and intricate parts of the shore are precisely those most readily reduced to sterile simplicity.

Thus the miracle of this small scrap of perfect beach.

Bluff wilderness began, a green mile with a half-mile extension up Deer Creek Canyon, from whose mouth emerged a path, doubtless the route of local Scouts coming to assume the costume.

Offshore were ancient pilings. From when? Nothing was shown here on the 1897 map, and I'd walked off the edge of the 1908 map. The 1973 map placed Woodway Park atop the bluff and I did remember Highlands-like mansions in the forests behind fences along the road from Richmond Beach to Edmonds. The pilings said there must have been a Woodway Dock. If so, did folks ascend the bluff, which rises 240 feet—and falls so steadily that the naked muck was now greened only by a few toppled alders? Did Woodway Park residents of early days dig a new wagon road up the bluff every spring, and all winter make their way somehow to Edmonds or Richmond Beach to catch a mosquito or the train? Walking by, I saw nothing to answer the questions.

A comparison of the 1897 and 1973 maps showed that decades of slumps and derailments at the notorious "Woodway Slide" at last had impelled the Great Northern to move out from the bluff to a causeway through offshore shallows—shallows built by thousands of years of slumps.

A kemptness on the brink lured me up through lumps of clay, clumps of willows grayed by pussies, and copses of scotchbroom freckled by yellow blossoms. The wall culminated in a 30-foot band of vertical till. I started up a slanting ledge obviously gouged by peasant boys. Two hell-black hounds appeared at the brink, flashing fangs and howling for blood. A rude path led up a clay gully to a ladderway of roots, to an alder leaning against the till cliff. I clambered up the branches and danced along a bouncing limb onto the brink.

My first paying job, at the age of nine—50¢ for half a Saturday—was mowing the lawn of the local squire, Doctor Brown (a veteran of the Philippine Insurrection, with a U.S. Army cavalry saber to show for it). Lurking in the bushes now, my peasant-boy eyes goggled at what by those old rates would have been a $20 lawn. The castle was a brick hall of three stories plus garret and two gables, with attached donjon keep and glass walls fronting on the Olympics and the Inland Sea. Surely this was the seat of a marquis or earl, certainly it was fit to house a king, whenever we decided we wanted one.

To the south the shore jutted to Point Wells and Highlands Point and dimmed in haze to Meadow Point and West Point, all soon to be lost behind me. North was my new view, between Point No Point (Kitsap Peninsula) and Double Bluff (Whidbey Island) to Admiralty Inlet. Out that narrow slot the nearest land, San Juan Island, was fifty miles away, too far for the eye, so there was a thin sliver of water horizon, a glimpse of the edge of the world.

I clambered down the beanstalk before the hounds could smell the blood of an Irishman. Walking north around Edwards Point, I passed another silver city—the tank farm, tanker pier, and asphalt refinery of Union Oil.

A half-mile up the hill, I remembered, lay Edmonds City Park, where in 1940, as Senior Patrol Leader of Troop 324, I led our three patrols to be ranked in the top three places in the Camporall, redeeming the shame of 1938 at Piper's Creek.

At the point the bluff swung far inland and for a mile the shore was a baymouth bar. A remnant of the ancient bay-become-lagoon was preserved in marsh, but most had been filled in in the late 1960s by the spoils from the dredging of Edmonds Yacht Basin, a half-mile-long harbor behind a boulder jetty that sheltered an armada the equal of Seattle's Shilshole Bay.

Not an inch of bar was intact. Land not put to work by Union Oil and the Port of Edmonds was solidly houses and apartments, business and industry, and parking lots. I paused at the Amtrak Station, the sole stop between Seattle and Everett, to read the schedule. No problem was posed by asterisks and double-daggers: trains ran north daily at 6:32 and 9:50 p.m., south at 6:10 and 10:44 a.m.., and that was all of that. The total traffic I saw the entire day was one short freight, one speeder, and one puny Amtrak with not a single face in the window that might be on picaresque.

An Edmonds restaurant's ventilator fan loosed on the wind and into my nose the aroma of the Alley Kat....

A New York newspaper columnist, Don Marquis, arrived in his office one morning in 1916 to find a statement in his typewriter:

> expression is the need of my soul
> i was once a vers libre bard
> but i died and my soul went into the body of a cockroach
> it has given me a new outlook upon life

Though handicapped by his training in free verse, a prejudice against punctuation, and an inability to work the shift key for capital letters, the cockroach, archy by name, contributed frequently to Marquis' column. Most notable of his friends was

> mehitabel the cat...
> mehitabel s soul formerly inhabited a
> human also at least that
> is what mehitabel is claiming...
> who were you
> mehitabel i asked her i was
> cleopatra once she said well i said i
> suppose you lived in a palace you bet
> she said and what lovely fish dinners
> we used to have and licked her chops
> mehitabel would sell her soul for
> a plate of fish any day

In the 1950s Broadway got to know mehitabel, as played by Carol Channing. I met mehitabel a decade earlier, in the reprint of a book illustrated by George Herriman, the fellow who did the comic strip that starred Krazy Kat, another female feline famous in my childhood, the model of the Alley Kat I knew so intimately. During my high school years I committed the entire mehitabel corpus to memory, and recited selections with such gusto as often to bring the faculty monitor to our table in the high school lunchroom. I have ever after found in her words, as often as in Shakespeare or the Bible, tags fitting life's bad times and good. The opening lines of the "song of mehitabel" are never far from my mind:

> i have had my ups and downs
> but wotthehell wotthehell

yesterday sceptres and crowns
fried oysters and velvet gowns
and today I herd with bums
but wotthehell wotthehell

I looked in on the antiseptically white restaurant where fish-stuff was homogenized and square-cut and served in a plastic dish with a plastic fork and a plastic coleslaw, all the rich grease and good reek sucked out by the ventilator fan and thrown away on the wind.

I went out to the tip of the ferry dock and sat upon the planks in the winter wind to tell sad stories of the death of kats and to eat my kipper snacks and apple. wotthehell. A ferry was unloading. Olympic peaks moulded of pure snow were emerging from clouds. The sand bluffs of Whidbey shone beneath the Blue Hole. In the slot between snow and sand opened the window on the dragons.

9. Edmonds

1933-1943

Friday was our family show night at Edmonds' Princess Theater, closer to home by half than the Oriental palaces of downtown Seattle, and much cheaper—15¢ each for Mother and Dad, 10¢ for me. At 7 p.m. the house went dark and the curtain opened on slides advertising Edmonds business firms, followed by "Prevues of Coming Attractions," then a newsreel—"The Eyes and Ears of the World"—a cartoon, and a travelogue or "Pete Smith Specialty." After all this the curtain rustled to a dramatic close, paused pregnantly, and reopened to a growling lion, searchlights illuminating giant block letters, or a spinning globe with a radio antenna atop the North Pole. Lying outside the Seattle zone in Snohomish County, the Princess didn't have to wait for major movies until months after their first runs at the downtown Seattle palaces, as did the Seattle neighborhood theaters, but got them the very next week while they were still hot:

The *Voice of Bugle Anne*, with Lionel Barrymore quavering and a beagle dying. *Smiling Through*, with a beautiful young bride getting shot right in the middle of her wedding gown. *Trail of the Lonesome Pine*, more shooting and dying and tears, now in Technicolor. *Snow White and the Seven Dwarfs*, the stepmother so scary I had to close my eyes. *Gone With the Wind* ran so long I fell asleep and never saw Atlanta burn.

In all our years at the Princess (we didn't go every Friday, only forty-nine or fifty a year) the largest crowds (the owner set up chairs in the aisle until forbidden by the Fire Department) were for the Will Rogers-Irwin S. Cobb *Steamboat Round the Bend* series. Will Rogers was probably the most loved man in America. We were thrilled to be on the beach of Vashon Island in 1935 and wave at him and Wiley Post as they flew close over the water, having taken off from Seattle's Boeing Field to circle the globe. We were stricken to learn of their fatal crash a few days later in Alaska.

Edmonds was our show town. It could have been my school town—half my Ronald Grade School class chose Edmonds High. I bused with the rest a bit farther in the other direction, south to Mother's old school, Seattle's Lincoln High.

Edmonds was our getaway town. We could take the ferry to Kingston on the Kitsap Peninsula, then another from Port Gamble over Hood Canal to Shine on the Olympic Peninsula. Far better, though, was the ferry that went north on the Sound to Admiralty Inlet, then between Point No Point and Foulweather Bluff, and across the mouth of Hood Canal to the Olympic Peninsula's Port Ludlow, a voyage of nearly two hours. Cancellation of this run was among the crimes for which Captain "Black Ball" Peabody was forced to flee to Canada.

A radio program of the period opened, "Tired of the everyday world? Ever long for a life of adventure? We offer you—*escape!*" Each and every day of the year ferryboats offered escape from the dull and the bad; evil spirits cannot cross water (except on a bridge, in automobiles).

In June 1943, having saved up my A-stamp ration of four gallons a week, I drove my 1930 Model A coupe to Edmonds and the ferry. The wake of white foam lengthened over the lime-green sea, the dock and the town shrank, the mainland shore dimmed in salt haze and disappeared behind the tip of the Kitsap Peninsula. The University of

Washington world of poetry and philosophy, professors and coeds, faded out, not to be seen until the start of Summer Quarter in a week.

That evening, the solitary camper at Sequim Bay State Park, I sat on the dock above waters smooth as oil and red as the dying sun, pulled out the pack of Dominoes bought on impulse in Edmonds, and smoked my first cigarette.

Next morning a crunching in a boot reminded me where I'd put my glasses for safekeeping. As the U.S. Army was to tell me two months later, I was legally blind. Squinting to distinguish forest from sky I drove miles up a steep, rough, single-lane road, pausing often to let the radiator stop boiling.

A snowbank blocked the way. A shovel was stuck in the snow, as if someone were anticipating my need. I shoveled for an hour, then clenched my jaw, held my breath, eased out the clutch and gentled in the gas and squeezed past, the left-front tire snubbing snow, the right-side running board hanging over air.

So it was that in 1943 I returned to the high Olympics from which I'd been banished since 1940. In Deer Park's grove of Christmas trees and fields of flowers I was greeted by the skywatcher who had lived in a cabin there through the winter, watching for Japanese bombers. He was about to go down to Sequim for his first grocery shopping since November, but the snowbank changed his mind; he'd left the shovel on the chance of someone answering his need.

To watch a ferry go out is to lose a possible chapter in a potential life. I had to deal with the ferries. But first there was the shore north from Brackett's Landing, as this place was called when settled in 1866. In 1880 a speculator named it for Senator Edmonds of Vermont, who had a bundle of senatorial loot the speculator hoped to get his hands on (but didn't). The 1897 map shows that by then the town had several business blocks, a large dock, a wagon road south to Richmond and Ballard, but no road north to Everett. There was, however, a trail, Jim Hill's rails, and it was still there.

10. Edmonds to Picnic Point

Mile 22$\frac{1}{2}$–28$\frac{1}{2}$

Friday, April 2, 1976

From a nicotine-starved night siege I awoke to a sunshine riot, the sort of spring day when Swedes wake from the long Northern winter and take off their clothes and make movies, and Puget Sounders blink the fog from their eyes and jump off the Aurora Bridge.

> I must down to the beach again,
> To the kelp and the fleas and the clams.

Warm sand exhaled a low-tide reek of salt and iodine, rotting weedery and dead jellyfish. Mild air wafted essences of trees greening, flowers whitening and reddening and yellowing. Piped through a nose no longer anesthetized by cigarette smoke, these potent gases overpowered my reason. This was a day of a hundred hours, or a thousand, or a googol, and never would there be another night, and maybe I'd walk to Samarkand for tea or Xanadu for honey-dew. There'd be no good works done this day. It was good-in-itself, not a means but an end, not a servant of the future, but a redeemer of the past. I sped along the Great Northern tracks as if driven by steam.

> Walking, lads, walking's the bit
> For fellows whom it hurts to sit.

In the static mode an observer may unify the pieces of a puzzle, but only as a blueprint—kinetics adds the third dimension of depth, and the fourth of history. The motion, however, must be on the human scale, which happens also to be that of birds, waves, and clouds. Were a bullet to be made sentient, it still would see or hear or smell or feel nothing in land or water or air except its target. So, too, with a passenger in any machine that goes faster than a Model A. As speed increases, reality thins and becomes at the pace of a jet airplane no more substantial than a computer readout.

Running suits a person who seeks to look inward, through a fugue of pain, to study the dark self. A person afraid of the dark had better walk—strenuous enough for the rhythm of the feet to pace those of heart and lungs, relaxed enough to let him look outward, through joy, to a bright creation.

> do you think that I would change
> my present freedom to range
> for a castle or moated grange
> wotthehell wotthehell
> cage me and i d go frantic
> my life is so romantic
> capricious and corybantic
> and i m toujours gai toujours gai

Edmonds to Meadowdale

Mapless, planless, thoughtless, careless, I steamed north.

Nothing was familiar. It was as if I'd never been here before. Yet I *had*, and remembered well those two days in June 1938. Where *was* everything I remembered? My final test for First Class Scout was the overnight 14-Mile Hike. Only three times had I hiked overnight, once to the Camporall at Carkeek Park and twice to the Cascade foothills, all three times in the mass security of the full troop. This trip allowed only a single companion. This was the test that had kept most of the troop Second Class.

Warren and I carried our Trapper Nelsons away from our orchard and down a lonesome road. We were passed every hour or so by a car rattling over the gravel washboard and in the five-odd miles to Edmonds we passed by a dozen chicken ranches and stumpranches. It wasn't wilderness, but it was country.

After a brief interruption by Edmonds, we returned to country, on the railroad tracks between water and woods. When we'd covered the required seven miles, or close enough, we dropped our packs on a narrow beach. Measured against the three Boy Scout *Handbook* criteria for a camp, ours had plenty of salt-soaked, sun-dried driftwood for a fire, water provided by the handpump of a nearby farm, and for shelter, above us arched God's great blue tent.

Supper, my assignment, was a triumph. On Mother's advice I'd rejected *Handbook* menus (kabob, bread-on-a-stick, potatoes-in-the-coals) and boiled noodles in a coffee can, fried hamburger and an onion in a pan, and mixed them up with a can of tomato sauce, alacazam.

Later we unrolled sleeping bags with toes barely above high tide, heads against the seawall atop which ran the rails, where the freight of the nation moved day and night.

After February 1933, when I was asphyxiated with ether for re-moval of my mastoid bone, I was regularly chased around the basement by the Devil, who came out of the furnace of the Seattle house where we lived in 1931, the year I entered Daniel Bagley Grade School. (The Devil: The Problem of Evil? Punisher of sins such as: failure to run to the school restroom in time? Speaking with a western accent the whole year we lived in Massachusetts, and with a Massachusetts accent a whole year after we returned west?)

After December 1936, when I was gassed for a tonsillectomy, the pursuer became a tornado-like Something that always got me just as I'd fallen, gasping, at the door of our house in the orchard and was hollering for my folks to open up. (A Something: a vengeful God? Fear of infinity? Of girls? Of locomotives?) The nightmare ordinarily woke me every month or two; the night of the 14-Mile Hike, due to train traf-fic, every hour or less.

Modern locomotives may squash a walker who fails to keep an ear cocked to the rear, but are hardly the stuff of nightmares, or good dreams either. Gone are the black steel violence and the white steam fury and the wheels that run by the grace of God.

After that night's ordeal came breakfast. The ingredients of War-ren's breakfast were wholesome enough, including home-cured bacon and homemade bread, but the eggs had not been kept cool, as is essen-tial when the rooster is running with the hens. Attached to each yolk was a miniature chick, complete to feet and beak, ghastly in the sizzling grease.

I fell into the irregular stride of tie-walking, maddening to a trail-hiker, autonomic to the old hobo. Where was the pump, the farm? Gone with the thirty-eight years, replaced by a row of picture windows. Be-yond the houses the bank lept up 140 feet to a tanglewood bluff and once more the way was in wild solitude. Far north a white spot shone on the water, the ferry from Mukilteo to Whidbey. Over my shoulder, ferries shuttled between Edmonds and Kingston.

The bluff swung inland around a marsh where tons of fill had re-cently been dumped and a mansion plunked down on top. Why did I feel a pang? I was beyond the far point of our 14-Mile Hike.

There used to be a place called Browns Bay. Troop 324 hiked there to the wildland shore down a woods road too mucky for cars most of the year.

After World War II bitter battles were fought on the beaches. We natives asserted ancestral rights against foreigners ignorant of the common law of the Inland Sea, against the alien invaders from the dry-land continent who built fancy houses and stout fences to wall us off from the water.

That was the pang. For the lost refuge of frogs and blackbirds—and Scouts.

Wild bluff, resuming, was sliced by a ravine deserving to be a park. It already had the Worthy Cause, signed "City of Lynnwood Sewage Plant." I recalled a field of weeds beside Highway 99, a weathered sign, "LYNNWOOD. Watch us grow." It did grow and now it excreted on the shore with the same self-satisfied scorn as Seattle.

Since rounding the bulge to where Browns Bay had once been I'd been puzzled by the view ahead to a village on the bluff, sloping down to a pier. Nearing, I read the sign, "Laebugten Fishing Wharf." There never was any Laebugten on this shore, not in my time. Yet the pilings and over-the-water building had an air of age. Someone had changed the name—this was *Haines*.

"Simply messing about in boats . . ." The fisherman who returns from a day on the salt complaining about a lack of fish doesn't understand the sport. What makes a water rat is the "simply messing about."

"Boat" means *row*boat, of course. In winter, when the marsh behind our house became a lake, Uncle Bill launched his rowboat so Cousin Bruce and I could mess about in cattail baylets winding amid grass islets. At the Cousins Consani's summer place on Martha Lake I couldn't rest easy until oars were in hand. Sailboats were the future, the voyage around the world, but rowboats were the present—and the past: Bainbridge Island was a circle of beach entirely surrounded by rowboats.

Memories of Haines Boathouse were only vicariously mine, through Dad. I went saltwater fishing with him just once, on Elliott Bay, rowing out from the docks as the bright lights dimmed in the dawn. I'd have liked to go dozens of times a year, as he did, but a fishing trip on the open Sound was not for children because a squall might ambush from a clear sky, in minutes whip up whitecaps that broke over gunwales. A situation in which one man was desperately bailing and the other struggling at the oars to keep the bow in the wind was no place for kids. By the time I was of an age to "pull my own oar," the mountains had drawn me away from the water, so my sole connection to the sport was eating almost as much salmon as hamburger. I was years getting over the notion that they both were "Depression food," for poor folks.

Dad fished from a number of launching points. Ray's Boathouse was located at Shilshole Bay. At Edmonds was Carpenter's, just south of the ferry dock. (Nearby was a fishtrap, until those devices were outlawed in 1935.) North of the dock an old water rat rented rowboats: "four-bits a day—no fish, no pay." At Browns Bay was a ramp for launching your own boat, if you had one, as Uncle Bill did. Next north was Cleveland's, which featured Briggs and Stratton inboard motors, very hoity-toity. Next door was Haines, especially popular because the launching elevator made putting-in so much easier than a ramp.

The "big hole" off Whidbey's Possession Point was four miles away, an easy row in moderate waves and winds—and favorable tides. Against a tidal current running twice as fast as any two men could row, they would have to pull up on the beach and build a fire and make coffee and wait for the turn. But sometimes while absorbed in mooching or spinning or trolling they got caught. Dad and his partner once were sluiced a dozen miles west and north, across the mouths of Cultus Bay and Useless Bay, and might've kept on to the Strait of Juan de Fuca had they not been rescued off Double Bluff by a kickerboat.

The kickers of the 1930s were small, cranky, and few. The sound of men at sea was the rattle of oarlocks, the gurgle of eddies behind blades, the slap of waves cut by a wooden hull. Those are *sounds*. As do airplanes in the sky and motorcycles on the trail, kickers make *noise*.

The marine equivalent of walking is rowing. Both have a human pace. In rowboat days the Inland Sea was of a scale for heroes. Now it has shrunk to a children's playground.

The world is smaller and noisier. The rowboats are gone, but then so are the fish.

Meadowdale to Picnic Point

The sunshine emptied homes on the bluff, the rumor of it spread inland, and everybody headed for the beach. I asked a fellow sitting on a log where I was and he said, "Meadowdale." I knew the name. Originally a summer colony with a train station and a mosquito dock, now it was a commuter community, but not of the all-American variety. Often in the rainy season the papers reported the village was on the slide again, houses staging their annual race to the railroad tracks. Among the gamblers on the bluff was Cousin Al. He ought to be walking down to the water today.

On another sunny day, soon after Al returned from the Air Corps in 1945, we went to Carkeek Park, twelve miles south. Swarms of kids were straddling logs and paddling around, ramming and turning turtle, bobbing up, blinking and gasping. We found our own logs and paddles and went to sea and were beset by fleets of ten-year-olds mobilizing to repel the two twenty-year olds. They attacked us singly, as did the German submarine that sank the *Royal Oak* at Scapa Flow, and in flotillas, as did the British cruisers and destroyers that hounded the *Bismarck*. Rammed and splashed by galleys, brigs, triremes, junks and frigates, we, the superdreadnoughts, turned on our tormentors and overturned rows of warships, drowning captains and commodores and admirals. The cry went up and down the beach, bringing task forces of twelve-year-olds, and even eight-year-olds. Torpedoes hissed, bombs splashed, ack-ack chattered, and 16-inchers roared, hours and hours, until everybody had such sunburns as would keep us moaning through the night, and the mothers called in the fleets to go home for supper.

Here today at Meadowdale, a fine large creek issued from a wild valley onto a broad delta fan. I crawled through a rusting fence to gone-wild lawns and charred timbers of what had been Meadowdale Country Club and now was an undeveloped Snohomish County Park. A path followed the creek up Lunds Gulch, largest wildland since Piper's Creek in Carkeek Park.

Returning from green twilight to the beach and bright sun, I rounded a bulge to another thrust of buildings on pilings, the roofs swaybacked, the planks sagging, awaiting a final nudge to become driftwood. "Norma Beach Boathouse," said the faded sign. On slump terraces of a small valley, a community of houses, which were as old as the trees and seemed as natural a part of the landscape, was gracefully riding green waves down the hill.

(Later, reading the 1897 map, I saw here the only name between Edmonds and Mukilteo, "Mosher," with a dock, two structures, a wagon road inland past Martha Lake to the Bothell-Everett road, a trail to Everett and Mukilteo, and a "Lumber R.R." inland three miles to a dead end. Its shore terminus was spectacular—a fall-line plummet of 300 feet, which meant it was an incline where cars were raised and lowered by steam donkey. The map showed a network of other roads and trails: up the bluff from [future] Meadowdale; from [future] Lynnwood Sewage Plant to Edmonds and the Mosher railroad. Some of these skidroads and skidways later were incorporated in the sinuous "Snake Trail" that gradually was improved into today's boulevards.)

Again the bluff reared up—very far up, to a sand wall where I could hear children laughing. No doubt they were leaping.

(Later, reading the 1953 map, I realized this was the most stupendous bluff between Seattle and Everett, 420 feet tall. Yet across the face of the precipice the map showed "Puget Sound Drive." I returned another day to walk an abandoned half-mile of boulevard, leaf-littered and mossy, where road-builders had at last conceded defeat. On either side of the sand cliff the blacktop ended in air. From within the reconstructed wildland I looked over the tops of alders and maples that hid the tracks below, out to waters whose salt haze erased works of man on the far shore. All was as it had been. A fleet of canoes would not have been a surprise—just the Haidas on the way to raid Suquamish.)

The bluff was broken by a long, narrow terrace—perhaps a beach when Lake Russell was 50 feet higher than today's sea level, or before the land rebounded 50 feet, released from the weight of the ice. Forest yielded to homes. Another summer colony of old. On the beach were rows of pilings.

Soaked in creosote (as at Creosote, on Eagle Harbor), pounded deep in the beach, pilings live longer than the men who drive them. The wood fully in the air, above the reach of high tide, and the wood fully in the water, below the drop of low tide, lasts indefinitely. The weak spot is the zone of twice-daily alternation of air and water, the zone of waves. There the creosote gradually leaches out, teredos (shipworms) bore in and eat the piling to a wasp waist, and finally the top is stormed off. Along beaches of the Inland Sea are full-height pilings, pristinely solid, others perilously wasp-waisted, others become stumps of pilings, and others abraded to stubs flush with the beach, circles of wood amid sand and shingle.

In 1976, seventy years after construction and perhaps forty-five since the last maintenance, the Highlands Dock retained a few full-height pilings. When Moran Ship Yard in Seattle was demolished in the

1960s, the underwater forest "planted" early in the century was logged by divers and made excellent lumber.

The wooden circles in the sand tell stories dating to the earliest European settlements:

Booming grounds. Starting in the 1850s, loggers worked inland two or three miles from beaches. At first they pulled logs along corduroy or skid roads with teams of oxen or horses. John Dolbeer gave the industry a mighty boost in 1881 by inventing the donkey engine.The first logging railroad in Washington was built the same year. Brought to the bluff by whatever means, logs were slowly lowered on rail trams or loosed on timber skidways to rocket down and splash in the bay. Men in caulked ("cork") boots and tin pants, jaws full of snoose, danced from log to log, pushing and pulling with pike poles to organize the big sticks inside log-boom rectangles which were moored to pilings forming log rafts for tugs to haul away.

Fishtraps. The efficient way to catch salmon is not to go out hunting but to lie in ambush on their migration routes to the rivers where they spawn. The efficient way to ambush is not in a boat but with a trap, a line of nets tied to pilings driven in a line at right angles to the routes. Except for emptying the nets into collector boats for hauling to the cannery, the only attendance needed is a resident guard, posted in a shack on the pilings to ward off pirates. The Inland Sea's first traps, other than those of the original residents, were installed in the early 1880s. In 1915 there were 600 licensed traps in Washington waters. The sole objection to traps was that they required capital and tended not to be owned by Ballard Norwegians. Thus in 1935 an initiative was passed by the voters, traps were outlawed, a blow struck for the little man against the capitalist, and Puget Sound now has a little-man fishing fleet a dozen times larger than the salmon runs justify, and each salmon costs a dozen times more to catch than it would to trap.

Mosquito fleet. Some docks of the interurban-suburban-rural transit system were built by individuals or companies, others by port districts, highly specialized units of local government. Kitsap County (in which Bainbridge Island lies) alone had twenty-two such districts, each operating at least one public dock serving the likes of the *Winslow* that carried us to the bright lights, the *Tyee Scout* to Camp Parsons, and the *Virginia V*, which in 1939 took Troop 324 to Camp Sealth, on Vashon Island, to help Campfire Girls build trails.

The pilings linger, telling of bullteams and boomers. Of night attacks by Ballard Vikings. Of dolled-up folks going to town for fish and chips and a show.

From Edmonds the shore north is a long concave arc. As I approached the north tip, an offshore islet materialized from salt haze. Gradually it resolved into a grove of poplars cut off from the bluff by the railway. A landmark visible from afar, it had seemed much too far to reach today. Now I was there. Where? A fellow came by, barefoot in the sand, and I asked.

"Picnic Point," came the answer.

The name had been in the news—2,500 acres had been bought by Standard Oil for a refinery, but the Snohomish County environmentalist militia chased the company north to Whatcom County, leaving the Chevron Land Development Co. to console its stockholders with plans to build a new city, among whose amenities would be Picnic Point Park, not given or sold, but *leased* to the county by the thrifty oilers.

The ten-year-olds were straddling logs to refight Salamis and Lepanto, littler kids were paddling innertubes, the littlest were building castles. Girls were running in bikinis, splashing and squealing, and boys were running berserk after. Dogs were chasing frisbees and gulls and barking at a young woman galloping down the creek on a white horse. High school students had skipped classes and were sitting in rows on logs drinking beer. The air was rich with the chemical of driftwood smoke, more addictive than tobacco. The fires were wanted because despite the warm sun the air temperature (said my thermometer) was only 55 degrees, and the breeze was brisk enough out on the tip of the point that kites were frolicking. There'd nevertheless be parties tonight, the first beach parties of the year, fires blossoming up and down the dark Sound.

I stepped over waves sparkling up the delta to meet the creek sparkling down. Amid poplars beside the tracks were concrete slabs, old foundations. Piling stubs thrust out toward the water. Until twenty-odd years ago Picnic Point had a wharf-boathouse. But these slabs were from an older construction. Did I hear ukeleles in the moonlight? The mosquito fleet brought families to the summer colony on the bluff—and to the cabins here in the poplars. Perhaps on a fine spring Sunday after church, it brought picnickers from Ballard.

Amid the holiday throng on the sandy delta point which had no oil refinery, no sewage plant, no lighthouse, no swimming pool or fish tank, I sat on a log and ate my picnic lunch of apple and kipper snacks.

Stinkpots blasting, sailboats bouncing. Fishing boats, tugs and barges, tugs and log rafts. Log ships for Japan, grain ships for India, container ships for the world. Busy Main Street, the North Sound. I knew the South Sound too, the "sea in the forest," and the fiord of Hood Canal, and the dragon coast, but the North Sound was where I came from.

Over the waters nine miles west, at the tip of the Kitsap Peninsula, winked the lighthouse on Point No Point. The Ludlow ferry used to make a hard turn around that corner, barely missing fishermen in row-boats working the tide rip. Southward the Kitsap Peninsula shore dimmed toward Bainbridge Island, more felt than seen.

Between the winking light on the peninsula and the white cliffs of Whidbey Island, Main Street changed its name from Puget Sound to Admiralty Inlet. In through that four-mile-wide waterway limped the crippled battlewagons from the South Pacific. Arild, later, returned from Tokyo Bay in the "Mighty Mo," and before that Dad, two decades earlier, arrived in the "New Momma." Out there the world once awaited me. Not anymore.

Return from Picnic Point

2:30. Kill off the Pepsi Cola, stomp the can, and stuff it in the ruck-sack with the kipper can. Toss apple core to the gulls. Returning from Picnic Point, I turn south toward a faraway shimmer in salt haze, the Silver City on Edwards Point.

A narrow beach was still open between seawall and incoming tide, and when all is said and done, sand and gravel and even cobbles are happier walking than tracks. The eye-stinging fumes of creosoted ties are as haunting to an old beach bum as low-tide stink, but the salt smell is primordial, the memory flows in our blood.

The beach pinched out in the rising tide and I climbed the seawall: three-point suspension, weight over feet, test holds, climb with the eyes—the four rock-climbing rules as fitting here as on the South Face of The Tooth or the Northwest Ridge of Sir Donald. I sat on my summit, feet dangling over water, and ate a Three Musketeers for the legs' sake. The miles were growing long.

At Meadowdale Beach the mellow lads in a row on a log offered the whiskered old man a beer, only half in derision. He genially declined, having many miles to go before he'd drink. I used to pity the ragged old men, lower than hobos—bums, or perhaps even tramps—shambling along the tracks as they had since the Railroad Trails were built. But it's not so bad to be a ragged old man shambling along the tracks. One might be, instead, a clean old man in suit and tie, sitting at a desk in an office in a Tower.

I looked back and saw I'd lost Picnic Point's Poplar Isle in haze. But it was not lost, nothing was lost, the past was all around and only wanted the walking to be found. I'd thought there'd be pain in the finding and had avoided the past, dreading its growing mass. Yet the mass was wealth.

As I approached Edmonds, a ferry was docking. I sat on the seawall and ate an apple. The tide was climbing toward my feet. A breeze was rising and choppy waves slapped the granite blocks.

5:06, the ferry pulled out. Boys in a sailing catamaran slid by the shore. Two black fish rose up on hind legs and strode from the deep, wetsuits glistening. A lad was sleeping on the seawall.

Edmonds and trip's end. I climbed from tracks to lawns atop the bank, sat on a park bench beside the beetle, and stretched my legs. 5:12, open a can of cold beer, drain it in a single swallow, vaporize the half-quart in the thirst of twelve miles and six sunshine hours. Nose tingled, eyes teared. Light as a bubble, the mind floated free, rising into brightness emanating from both sun and belly, illuminating the great truth suddenly revealed that this was the moment it all was for. After decades of patches and fidgets, false starts and dead ends, signifying nothing, I was free to walk about the countryside saying goodbye to all the beautiful places, asking the important question, "Where did I come from?" Let others ask themselves the trivial question, "Where am I going?"

In returning south I'd regained the window on the Seven Seas. I'd never go to explore them. I needed mountains, Olympics west and Cascades east to lean against, lest I fall down.

As once I read Masefield and Conrad, I now pored over letters from Suibhna the Sailor Man and loved his tales of mama-sans, typhoons, and saloons in steaming seaports of the nations of exotic postage stamps. Yet another friend of mine, a fellow landlubber who also had dreamed of the seas in childhood, set off on a voyage around the world—and whenever the ship left sight of land had to retreat to his cabin and keep the steward on the run bringing gin to dull the horror.

My longest sea journey occurred in 1945 on the Canadian Pacific's *Princess* boat that left Seattle in early morning, docked in Victoria at noon, and returned in the evening. We voyaged down the Sound to Admiralty Inlet, to the Strait of Juan de Fuca, and over the gulf to the city where steak-and-kidney pie was on the menu, the cigarettes were Players and Black Cats, and British majors in mustaches and tweeds bicycled around the rose gardens.

5:20, the sun was high above the blue Olympic silhouette in a yellow cirrus sky. A freight train passed, the sound of discipline, the nineteenth century, different from noise, simian chaos, the twentieth century. Man can live beside a railroad, not by a freeway nor under an airway.

5:30, a ferry coming in. Open beer #2.

5:37, a freight going south—and simultaneously, another north! The Teamsters were on strike, bless their picket lines, may they stay on the bricks until their wheels turn square.

The Inland Sea had a happy transportation system, the mosquito fleet, and killed it with Model T's and A's and Mack and Kenworth trucks, and now America was bludgeoning its rail network with subsidized freeways and airways. The "railroad" companies didn't mind, they were focusing their greed on the plundering of stolen land grants. The better to do so they were mergerizing toward the ultimate goal of One Big Non-Railroad Company. Only the polysynthetic Burlington Northern survived on the shores of Puget Sound. How poignant now it was to watch the passing trains whose boxcar walls preserved such old boasts as "Northern Pacific, Route of the Vista Dome North Coast Limited," and displayed Great Northern's mountain goat that in nights of yore shone electrically bright in the downtown Seattle sky. Other walls spoke of the rails that knit the continent: Chicago, Milwaukee, & St. Paul, the Atchison, Topeka, & Santa Fe, the Southern, Southern Pacific, Union Pacific, Cotton Belt, Frisco, Rock Island Line, Pennsy, Chessie System, New York Central, B&O, C&O, B&M.

The sport of peasant boys in the days of my youth was counting the cars of freights and waving to the engineer and fireman in the mighty black engine and the brakeman in the cozy red caboose. Passenger trains were our drama, windows flashing by with a blur of faces, the golden people of Hollywood movies, the Mysterious East, skyscrapers, taxicabs, penthouses, night clubs, and luxury liners, the bright lights of the permanent party.

When I at last was invited east to join the fun, the nation had been Boeinged, Douglassed, and Lockheeded. The airplanes that filled the sky with their noise had shrunk the planet, giving the ahistorical specious adventures, the ageographical false perspectives.

> Through the window
> Of the big tin pot,
> See the world
> As the world is not.

A plumbers' convention in Schenectady, Aunt Sally's goiter operation in Fresno, steak sandwiches with a fertilizer salesman in Houston, a swim in a heated pool in Omaha, a slot machine in Carson City, a fruit salad in Honolulu are solemnized by the passage through air. Thinking by altitude to achieve significance, by massing of miles to fill lives, the mobs herd into airports and are swindled. Train stations were exciting and docks thrilling; airports are simply saddening.

In 1959 I evaded the air by taking the Canadian National from Vancouver, through the Fraser River Canyon (which had been my route to a peak with a close view of Mount Waddington) and past Mount Robson (whose summit I at least plotted against), over Alberta parklands and Saskatchewan prairies. I walked the swaying corridor to the dining car, the place setting of a dozen pieces of silver, the linen napkin folded in a pyramid, the crystal goblet wherein water jiggled and ice cubes clinked, the slice of chill melon with a twist of lemon, the lambchops with mint jelly and panties. Before retiring to my roomette I sat in the club car and watched the Canadian night roll by and drank a McEwan's Strong.

By Canadian Pacific we traveled in 1950 to the Selkirks to climb Sir Donald and gaze over the arctic enormity of the Illecillewaet Névé. The same August, while four of us were rappelling in darkness off the North Peak of Index after the hottest day of summer, canteens dry for hours, breath coming in rasping gasps, I gazed a vertical mile down to the Great Northern train gliding beside the Skykomish River and saw the shining windows and thought of the golden people within and all the water they were drinking.

5:45, the ferry out. 5:50, open beer #3. 6:00, another ferry in. The street behind my park bench was filling with cars. The sun was about two inches above Marmot Pass, where I first saw wilderness. In a sunset. My first Camp Parsons hike.

The morning after that sunset we had traversed Dungeness headwaters to Home Lake, a droplet of snow water beneath cliffs of Mount Constance, and I raised my eyes in awe to the ramparts, wondering if they'd ever been climbed.

Due west of my bench, four and a half miles across the waters, was Appletree Point. In the spring of 1940 Troop 324 carried Trapper Nelsons onto the ferry at Edmonds, carried them off at Kingston, hiked north on the beach, and camped at the point. That summer I twice followed the crest of Lost Ridge, one day in sunshine and wind, the views west to glaciers of Mount Olympus, the next in a screaming Three Day Blow, my last Parsons hike.

Marmot Pass, Appletree Point, and I were in a straight line that, if extended west, would intersect Lost Ridge and, further west, Olympus, which fell to my boots in 1949.

South of Marmot Pass was Constance, apex of the Olympic skyline. With ice ax in hand and 7/16-inch manila rope on my waist I stood there in 1948 and looked to *here.*

Farther south, The Brothers, 1949. In sunsets like this, in 1856, the coast surveyor George Davidson sat on the porch of his sweetheart's Seattle home gazing over Puget Sound to the peaks, naming them for her family. I couldn't make out his sweetheart's mountain, Ellinor, near the south end of the range, but big sister Constance was plain, and the two boys.

6:05, beer #4. Milk-blue crags and ridges outlined against smoke-yellow sky. Wizened red ball radiating five long sunrays to the ends of the sky, a wonder portrayed on the flag of Japan but seldom seen because few people watch a sunset all the way.

6:13, the ferry out.

Let it go, let them all go today, there'll be more tomorrow and I'll be on them. The present is a night-haunted misery, the future belongs to the fools and villains who are making it. All I want is the past, a ferry-boat, and a can of beer.

6:20, #5, *Rainier* beer, of course. I never sailed the small boat around the world, never climbed Everest, but in 1948 (and '49, '50, '51, and '52) I climbed this beer's namesake and was 14,416 feet tall.

6:25, sun entering the horizon, having drifted north from Marmot Pass beyond Mount Townsend, where in 1946 we climbed from Windy Lakes on a breakfast of stewed apricots and met Whiskers Jack Conrad, who had lived alone a year in Montana wilderness, never seeing a soul. When he came out to Missoula, he felt real bashful and had a notion folks were staring at him, and thought maybe he had a hole in the seat of his britches, so began feeling around back there as he walked the streets, and got surer and surer folks were staring.

The sun was slipping in just a couple inches from the north end of the range, near Blue Mountain. From its summit on a summer night in 1946 I looked down to twinkles of Sequim and over twenty black miles of the Strait of Juan de Fuca to the constellation of Victoria.

This sun, this skyline, this Main Street, I knew of old. Though the land I'd walked today was more battered and torn (as was I), water and sky were the same (and so was I). In the mirror of the past shone the inner constant.

6:30. There goes the sun.

I am not alone. Street, park strip, and beach are crowded, silent. Sunset-watchers. Past-watchers. The hope of the world.

11. Picnic Point to Mukilteo   Mile 28½–33½

Tuesday, April 27, 1976

Picnic Point is a *cuspate hybrid*, the composite result of longshore currents trying to build a spit and a creek determined to build a delta. It's also a ruin, the dune line muddled and the lagoon obliterated by railroad and auto road.

A scant mile north I came to Shipwreck Point, a classically simple spit with all the proper parts and, contrary to rule, the prettier for *not* being pristine. Snuggled in a poplar grove, served by no road or electric wires, was a cottage as weathered as the beachcombers' treasures surrounding it in the sand—driftwood sculptures, fishing nets and floats, rotten rowboats converted to flower planters. Atop a pole waved Old Glory, as innocently patriotic as Commodore Bainbridge's squadron showing the flag in ports of the Barbary States. The rib cages of two wooden ships poked through the sands. Beached to rot on the strand between waves and lagoon was a complete wooden hull, larger than a mosquito, smaller than a lumber schooner, perhaps a Northern trader.

For a higher perspective I climbed beside the cottage's water supply, a tumbling creek, on a staircase cut in clay 260 vertical feet through forest to the blufftop. I started up slowly but found myself running, breaking a sweat, and giving lungs an airing. Then down I run, hickory dickory dock.

I'd awakened in morning unrested and jangled from nightmares of cigarettes thrusting themselves in my fingers and lips, butts overflowing ashtrays, coals burning holes in clothing and furniture, smoke blinding and strangling. Running up and down the bluff put me back on track. A railroader rolled by on a speeder. We exchanged smiles, congratulating each other on being nowhere else but here. A wind from the north cooled my brow, cleared veils from the Olympics and the sun and the blue. In cattails of the trackside ditch the redwing blackbirds rasped, frogs croaked.

To the north a ferry abruptly swung out from behind a bulge of bluff, westering to Whidbey Island. I looked south and beyond the Poplar Isle saw a ferry westering from the Silver City. I turned north again and saw a ferry eastering from Whidbey.

> Yo ho ho, the wind blows free!
> Oh for the life on the In-n-n-land Sea!

Scoundrels had been here, jackstrawing the forest to open a view for new homes atop the bluff, where the map showed "Chenault Beach Road." No road descended the 120 vertical feet to the beach, nor even a trail, and indeed there was no beach.

Past the carnage lay peace—wide, deep, and wild—Big Gulch,

shown on the map as slicing one and a half miles inland to Paine Field. Not a park, though there was the Olympus Terrace Sewage Plant. (Picnic Point also was honored, I'd learned driving down the entry valley today, finding there the Alderwood Manor Wastewater Treatment Plant).

I scowled at the Worthy Cause. The attendant came out. He smiled and won. Only incidentally a sewerman, his true vocation was ranger. He told of coots, mallards, goldeneyes and buffleheads, scaups and cormorants and widgeons, a thousand gulls offshore at the outfall, thousands of migrants swimming by in fleets. He told of sandpipers and killdeer on the beach, choirs of forest birds and creek birds, and bald eagles perched on snags. He told of seals in the waves and weasels on the sand, and deer and bear that paid him no more mind than they did each other.

This was a Cause Worthier than some. Paine Field was built when "environmental impact" was still called "progress" and nobody objected to the Army Air Corps dumping raw sewage in Big Gulch to run in the open to the delta. When later the sewer pipe was buried in the creek bed, the creek was not destroyed because there wasn't one. Now there was, clean and loud and alive in new-growing forest.

In the quarter-century since the platting of "Chenault Beach" in 1942, only a half-dozen homes had been built. Overnight the sewage plant had rocketed the building lots from $400 to $15,000. The boom was on. The ranger was worried about the bears and the eagles.

At the onset of the Depression the newly poor fled city taxes and bureaucracy for the freedom of country, which had no piped water, no sewers, no garbage trucks, no fire department, few police, and roads that were mud in winter and washboard in summer. In "The County" a family could borrow space on a friend's property, scavenge scrap lumber for a tarpaper shack, dig one hole for a well and another for a privy, cut firewood in second-growth forests "nobody owned," raise chickens and a pig and grow potatoes, corn, peas and onions to supplement Relief. When things got better the land could be bought for five or ten bucks a month, electricity brought in to replace the kerosene, and City Water the well. The local squire had a telephone neighbors could use in emergencies.

No suburbs adjoined the city, only a fringe of slum beyond reach of building and health inspectors. All the way to the next city was country, interspersed with a few compact old towns, most of them built around mosquito docks and railroad stations—Richmond Beach, Edmonds, Meadowdale.

In 1942 the Puget Sound area began to share in the cure for the Depression. Platting, dead since the Crash, resumed. Fields and forests were staked and ribboned for weekend Victory Gardens.

Lumber and carpenters came home from the war. Vegetable gardens were buried in peatmoss and seeded with lawn. Beach trails were fenced shut. My backyard wilderness was logged. Commerce oozed north and south on roadside shoulders to form Highway 99 Strip City. Seattle merged into Edmonds, and Edmonds into Mukilteo and Everett, and the gaps were filled by instant synthetics—Mountlake Terrace, Alderwood Manor, Lynnwood.

In school they taught us the population of the United States was 131,669,275 in 1940, up from 122,775,046 in 1930. It was predicted to top out in the twenty-first century at 150,000,000, after which would begin the natural decline normal, healthy, and decent for a civilized nation. But the population in 1950 was 150,697,361, and in 1960 was 179,323,175—grossly unnatural, abnormal, unhealthy, indecent, and there go the bears and the eagles, and there goes country.

On the tip of Big Gulch delta I pondered a Momentous Geographic Event. At day's start I'd looked across three miles of the waters of Main Street to Possession Point, the south tip of Whidbey Island. Now I was around the corner, off the street, up the alley, beyond Puget Sound, on Possession Sound.

According to Captain George Vancouver, who in May 1792 sent Peter Puget in a ship's boat to explore the "sea in the forest," Puget Sound was *that part of Admiralty Inlet* (take note) south of what is now Tacoma's Point Defiance.

The 1866 map of the "U.S. North West Boundary Survey, Western Section" (which names only three places on the shore north of Seattle— "West Pt," "Wells Pt," and "Pt Elliott") shows three major waterways south of the Strait of Juan de Fuca: Hood Canal; Admiralty Inlet, extending south past Seattle to Vashon Island; and Puget Sound, still where Vancouver put it.

But an 1873 "Map of Washington Territory" that shows population centers (on the mainland shore north of Seattle there is only Mukilteo, on shores west only Blakely and Port Madison) pushes Puget Sound north to Elliott Bay; Admiralty Inlet begins at Port Madison.

The U.S. Geological Survey's Snohomish Quadrangle of 1897 (which between Seattle and Mukilteo adds Spring Beach, Richmond, Edmonds, and Mosher) advances Puget Sound to Edmonds, where it meets Possession Sound and Useless Bay—altogether eliminating poor old Admiralty Inlet.

The USGS Seattle Quadrangle of 1958 reverses the original relationship, demotes Admiralty Inlet to a part of Puget Sound, which runs north of Double Bluff and off the edge of the map.

Only a little less radical, *Maritime Memories of Puget Sound*, published in 1976, pronounces the boundary of Puget Sound to be a line from Point Wilson on the Olympic Peninsula through Point Partridge on Whidbey Island and onward to the mainland, incorporating into Puget Sound all of Admiralty Inlet, Skagit and Port Susan bays, Possession Sound, and a host of other waters.

(And a 1980 Seattle newspaper article describing the San Juan Archipelago was titled "Island in the Sound"!)

This is Imperial Rome all over again, a "sea in the forest" unhinged by manifest destiny. Let it go unchecked and there'd be no Pacific Ocean or Atlantic. Everything wet in the world except rain and beer would become "Puget Sound."

Rolling back the empire to Point Defiance is impractical. Perhaps the best compromise is a line from Point No Point or Foulweather Bluff, on Kitsap Peninsula, to Double Bluff on Whidbey. North is Admiralty Inlet; south, Puget Sound.

Few of the imperialists are driven purely by chauvinism or ignorance or stupidity or perversity. Mainly they behave as they do because geography abhors a vacuum. Put Puget Sound and Admiralty Inlet and Hood Canal together, add Possession Sound, Saratoga Passage, Port Susan, Skagit Bay, Padilla Bay, Samish Bay, Deception Pass, Guemes Channel, Bellingham Bay and the Strait of Georgia—assemble all the sounds, channels, straits, bays, harbors, ports, passages, passes, coves, and inlets—recite the entire rosary, and what have you got? A splendid incantation, to be sure. But how can the sum be distilled to one word that is *thunder*?

Historian Edmond Meany says Vancouver called the whole region New Georgia and all the waters, in aggregate, Gulf of Georgia. But George III lost the war and his gulf was deported to Canada.

"Inland Sea" has had long currency. Murray Morgan, in *Puget's*

Sound, declares "Puget Sound embraces the entire inland sea." One hopes he wrote that with a sigh.

"Greater Puget Sound" is as depressing as "Greater Seattle." "Sea of Vancouver" would honor a competent British professional. But this would be as inappropriate as a Northwest pedestrian walking through England, Scotland, Ireland and Wales and, upon his return home, having his friends rename the area as, say, "Great Manning."

Well then, "Salish Sea"? It smacks of anthropology. "Saltchuck"? Worse—Chinook jargon recalls gunnysacks being filled with fish intestines on Railroad Avenue.

Meany says the local folk called it "whulge," spelled by later writers "whulj," translated as "saltwater," or "the saltwater we know."

Respectful explorers don't invent names when they can find existing ones. Respectful geographers correct earlier disrespect. As our sense of history lengthens backward beyond European solipsism, we renounce "Mount McKinley" for Denali, "Mount Baker" for Komo Kulshan, and lean away from "Mount Rainier" toward Tahoma. The name that grows on one, walking the beach, is Whulj.

The bluff nodded to let people near the water. Outside the tracks on a fill defended from waves by a bulkhead, lay a row of cottages with a driftwood look. As I had the Old Salt on Shipwrecking Spit and the Gamblers of Perkins Lane and Meadowdale, I forgave them. The road was a stiff little climb up a trail: the cottagers didn't buy many refrigerators or bales of peatmoss, and they had rucksacks for carrying in their groceries.

A deserving few should be permitted to live by the water. Money should have nothing to do with the selection, which might be done by essay examination or a group of tests that would include rowing a boat, skipping stones, finding agates, and digging clams. Each of these cottages had its rowboat and driftwood and pebble garden. A row of deserving dogs barked me by. A deserving woman hoeing a tiny pea patch smiled me on, a deserving hobo.

Wildness resumed, a forest of swelling billows that in February had been the red-brown of alder catkins and now were the salad-bright green of alder leaves and the rowdy yellow of maple flowers.

Out of the billows a ferry came a-charging! A few steps more, around a corner, I saw the lighthouse, and the narrows of Possession

Sound opening to a broad gulf, and the white volcano of Komo Kulshan.

Mukilteo. Mother used to visit her sister Grace here when brother-in-law Bill filed the saws of the gang mill at Crown Lumber. Uncle Bill became noted as the best filer on the West Coast, which as any West Coast lumberman will testify, means he was the best in the world. He also was as expert a salmon fisherman as never turned professional. He was Dad's teacher and before that, Mother's. One dawn when she was twelve the two of them caught a gunnysackful of kings in Possession Sound, tied the skiff to the boom sticks, and walked the log boom a quarter-mile to shore, Bill bent double under a hundred pounds of fish.

Point Elliott. Largest spit since Point Wells, totally manhandled so long ago that the 1897 map shows no vestige of lagoon. It shows railroad tracks and two large structures (mills?), and smaller ones on spit and bluff. (Including a salmon cannery? The first in the region was built here in 1873.) No roads. The only overland connections to Edmonds and Everett are trails.

The 1873 map has "Mukilteo," that of 1866 only "Pt Elliott," named in 1841 for the chaplain on Charles Wilkes's *Vincennes*, also remembered by Elliott Bay. It was a convenient place on January 22, 1855, for Governor Isaac Stevens to camp with representatives of the twenty-two tribes or bands living north of Seattle, an estimated 4,000 souls. A handy spot to sign the Treaty of Point Elliott by which the "Snohomish, Skokomish, Duwamish, Muckleshoots, Queelewamish, Seawamish, Snoqualmie, Sakequells, Scadgets, Squinamish, Keekallis, Scoquachamas, Swimmish, Nooksacks, and Lummy" ceded all lands and waters from Seattle to Canada in exchange for the Lummi, Tulalip, Swinomish, and Port Madison Reservations, plus the right of "taking fish at usual and accustomed grounds." With this and companion treaties Governor Stevens set off the "Indian Wars" of the 1850s—and the 1970s.

I left the tracks for the beach of Mukilteo State Park, passing throngs of infants playing in the sand and hot sun.

Mukilteo Lighthouse, 1906. Now guiding log ships and fishing boats as it (and a predecessor) did sloops, yawls, ketches, schooners, brigs, brigantines, barks, barkentines, and full-rigged ships. Round tower topped with polished glass. Brightly white, from miles away seen catching the sun. When night swallows or salt haze dissolves the tower, the revolving light winks through.

In fog the horn sounds, seeming the sorrowing voice of the spirits of local speculators who in 1872, when the Northern Pacific board of directors steamed by on the *North Pacific*, were tremulously aware that only three candidates remained under public consideration for the railroad's western terminus—Seattle, Tacoma, and Mukilteo.

Mukilteo Dock. Built for ferries that are small because Whidbey Island is mostly empty, that are slow because speed is less relevant on the three-mile crossing than the humility and agility to dodge log ships and garbage barges. Two vessels were in service today: *Kulshan*, an inelegant scow (built in Oakland, 1954, 65 autos, 12 knots) with an open car deck around a center tower containing the pilot house and a cramped cabin for such passengers as might wish to leave their cars to buy a packet of salted peanuts from the vending machine; and the *Klickitat* (San Francisco, 1927, rebuilt 1958, 75 autos, 12 knots), a proper high box of a double-ender with car deck roofed by cabin deck, open promenade all around, and two pilot houses on top.

Eating apple and kipper snacks, drinking Pepsi Cola, I watched the *Klickitat* load and leave at 1:21.

Turn for home.

Wind died, sun exploded, skin burst into flame, lungs burned with creosote. Frogs were into their game of shutting down their racket as I passed them on the tracks, staring at me with their little fishy eyes, the bastards. A shirtless boy, apparently doped out of his skull, stumbled barefoot north. A train went south, a train went north, and neither struck him down. I sat on a granite seawall that scorched my behind, licked a melted Peanut Butter Mountain Bar from the paper wrapper, and drank my last Pepsi Cola, hot. A helicopter clackety-clacked overhead close enough for me to see the pilot's idiot grin. From beyond the bluff came the roar of jet engines being ground-tested, Boeings lined up at Paine Field for delivery to emirs, potentates and military juntas, the row of tin pots painted in postage-stamp colors like so many waterfront whores.

At Picnic Point I sat on a log and opened a beer. A German shepherdess nagged me to throw sticks, but when I did she didn't retrieve, just flung them away and nagged for more. Nazi bitch. I opened another beer. It didn't help. It doesn't always work. You can't win 'em all.

12. Mukilteo to Everett

Mile 33$\frac{1}{2}$–38

Wednesday, February 16, 1977

North from the ferry dock the shore was edged for a mile by aviation fuel tanks. In World War II, they and the craft they served at Paine Field, located nearby atop the drift plateau, were the sober silver of the Army Air Corps. Now they fed bordello-hued Boeing jets and had been painted California mauve and apricot and blush-pink. Amid the morning's hunter-killer squalls pursuing Blue Holes, they seemed an Oz on the banks of the Styx.

Then the rail trail resumed its pre-Technicolor isolation between gray waves and gray glacial drift.

I grew up on drift, supposing the entire world was composed of gravel pits for filling mudholes in roads and shoveling into concrete mixers, sand banks to jump on and dig caves in, clay banks for making mudballs, glacially deposited erratics to clamber around on, and till that couldn't be dented with a pick and for which it took dynamite to excavate a privy hole.

Later, in the mountains, I saw drift being manufactured by glaciers—dumping loads in moraines, flushing rockmilk from snouts, rumbling boulders along rivers.

Yet never as now had I felt so close to the ice and its meltwater: Strata of fine sand deposited by slow-flowing water in frozen winter and of coarse sand, pebbles, or cobbles dropped by swifter water in the melting time of summer. Horizontal beds that had been spread out over the floor of a valley (*bottomset*), and *foreset* beds, dipping steeply forward where materials were dumped off a delta front. Foreset gravels atop horizontal clays, where the delta advanced over a lake floor. Till atop gravel, where the ice advanced over a river bed. *Unconformities*, sharp breaks marking the end of the depositing of sediments when the ice lobe retreated, the resumption when the ice returned. All these and many more stories the beachwalker "reads" in the cross-sections sliced by waves in the bluff, annals of the eons portraying to the mind's eye the ice front, the raw moraine, the tumbling river, the gray-milky lake that were here then as they are now in the mountains.

At the north end of the Mukilteo spit, I passed a vertical wall striped in shades of gray, light to dark, the best display of *varved* clay I'd ever seen. The lighter-gray clay was deposited (so geologists tell us) in summer, the darker in winter, and thus each pair of bands (a *varve*) is presumed to represent a year. With patience, one can count the life span of a lake or pond. How many varves here? I lacked the patience. Centuries. For that long the ice front was stable at this spot, feeding milled rock into the lake to settle slowly to the bottom. About 13,000 years ago? Had the first pioneers arrived by then, via the land bridge from Asia and an icefree lane down the coast of Alaska and British Columbia? More likely they came 1,000 to 2,000 years later when the ice front had retreated nearly to Canada and the drift plateau, humped with moraines and dotted with kettle lakes, was a tundra of grass, willow, and alder resembling today's subarctic.

The pioneers were not canoe-paddlers or salmon-catchers. The easternmost reach of the Whulj, which was hundreds of feet lower than now, was near Port Angeles. Between the Olympics and Cascades lay a broad green valley roamed by bison and woolly mammoth. The pioneers were big-game hunters. Bones of a mastodon found near Sequim on the Olympic Peninsula have been dated as 12,000 years old. They were cast aside by human butchers after they smashed the skull to extract the brains.

During the summer of 1934, we went camping on the Olympic Peninsula, and while my folks and Uncle Bill fished the Clearwater and Bogachiel Rivers and Aunt Grace fried the trout (which Cousin Bruce and I ate by the dozen), I worked clay from the riverbanks, kneading it smooth, shaping ashtrays and candlesticks, baking them hard (though crumbly) in the campfire. Years later, camped with my wife Betty and our kids at my folks' property on the North Fork Stillaguamish River, again I kneaded, shaped, and baked clay, this time in non-utilitarian forms. I showed them to Aunt Grace, who'd taken up potting, and she baked them in her kiln where my crumbly gray cubes and pyramids turned brick-hard, brick-red. Whulj country provided Europeans other wealth than timber and fish: in the Concrete Age, sand and gravel for freeways and towers; before, in the Brick Age, clay for homes and factories and hotels, for the city streets of the 1890s, and the highways of the 1910s.

During the day, nine delta fans—an exceptional number—thrust out into waves from deep ravines that penetrate far inland. Powder Mill Gulch.(Site of an explosives factory? Lots of powder was needed in the privy-building era of the drift country.) Merrill and Ring Creek. (Named for a pioneer timber company. Was the mill here? Not according to the 1897 map.) Beyond a third ravine, the bluff was broken by a large amphitheater with an unnatural look (old gravel pit?). The 1897 map shows a structure here; the 1953 map shows rail sidings, a large building, an oil tank, and a long pier. Nothing remained. I ascended the gentle slope past concrete foundations and rusting junk, through copses of scotchbroom in yellow bloom and over carpets of English lawn daisies in yellow and white, these last being disoriented foreigners that blossom the year around, unable to tell a Northwest winter from a British spring. A black squall slanted rainlines to the gray bay. An Amtrak Domeliner passed, headed south, a pitiable two passenger cars, sadly adequate under a sky noisy with tin pots.

Atop the amphitheater were lawns and benches and a sign, "Harborview Park," which incidentally informed me I'd entered the City of Everett.

The tale told by a park exhibit:

> Though willingly signed, it was with some reservation that the Indian tribes of this area ceded to the United States their lands from the Duwamish to the Canadian border in the Mukilteo Treaty of 1855. The land was their life and religion.
> "Every hillside, every valley and grove is hallowed by cherished memories of incidents in happier times. Dust under our feet responds more lovingly to the tread of Indians than to strangers, because it is ashes of our ancestors and our bare feet are conscious of the sympathetic touch. At night when the streets of cities the white man will build are quiet, they will be thronged with returning hosts that have lived in and still love this good land."—Chief Seattle
> Living in this immediate bay area, the Snohomish Indians numbered near 850 during the mid-1850s. The tribes were centered around four villages. The sites of two can be seen from here. Looking beyond Everett's calm industrial harbor, you can see the site of their largest village, now part of the Tulalip Indian Reservation. The other site is to the northwest on the end of Camano Island.

There seemed a considerable understatement in the words, "it was with some reservation." Four days after the treaty was "willingly signed," the Battle of Seattle was fought. Subsequently "Chief" (a title bestowed by the Europeans) Leschi was hanged, not for being at the battle or the treaty signing—he was at neither—but because he was thought a surly wretch, the antithesis of the eloquent and amiable "Chief" Sealth (Seattle). It has been commented that the latter's preserved eloquence has the sound of other published statements by Noble Savages, a body of American literature with which Sealth's translator may be presumed to have been familiar. In fact, this savant, Dr. Henry A. Smith, didn't reconstruct the speech from notes until thirty-two years after the fact. At the time he took the notes, he had been on Puget Sound only two or three years and hadn't learned the language Sealth spoke. Nevertheless, other pioneer testimony depicts Sealth as a genuinely wise and noble man. To be sure, his amiability has been called that of Uncle Hiawatha.

Defiant to the end, Leschi was, of course, a hero in modern eyes. Is it possible revisionists might also consider Sealth a hero of another sort, the spokesman of a deep grief?

My own life covers two-fifths of the history of the city named for him. Some of the "coarse, filthy, debased natives" (as the Reverend Blaine described them in the 1850s) who gathered fish guts on the waterfront in the 1920s very likely remembered Chief Sealth. Some of the elders at the Battle of Winslow might have been, as children, with him at Suquamish on January 26, 1855, and heard cannon of the U.S.S. *Decatur* shelling the forest during the Battle of Seattle.

"850 Snohomish Indians." How many were there when Sealth was born in 1786, a decade after Captain Cook landed on the Pacific coast, four years before the exhalations of European ships blew eastward into the Whulj? In his childhood the Duwamish—neighbors of his own people, the Suquamish—had a winter village of eight long houses near what became Seattle's Pioneer Square. As many as 200 people may have lived there. When the platters arrived in 1852, there were ruins of one deserted long house.

For us European children, a part of growing up (or not) used to be running the gauntlet of the domesticated plagues—the measles, mumps, whooping cough, diphtheria, and all the others that in earlier centuries had attacked the entire population, and then in more recent times had settled down to pick on kids. Childhood was a dangerous time, one damn disease after another, yet at least we had the nursing and sustenance of our elders, who were immune. Sealth's people took the shock—

all the shocks of all the diseases—as one, children and adults alike, nobody safe.

Europe suffered a similar shock—the Great Pestilence, also known as the Bubonic Plague or the Black Death. Europe recovered because it didn't receive the second blow that Sealth's people did—the culture shock brought with the new ways of the invading whites. To understand Sealth, we must imagine how we will react when the saucer fleets descend from the sky and the conquerors sneer at our Ivy League and Oxbridge and Vatican libraries as the scribblings of "Siwashes."

Pigeon Creek No. 2 (named for what?) and a smaller companion enclosed between them a quarter-mile of shore bluff, Howarth Park. From a ravine trail I looked out from forest windows and smugly watched gray rain batter gray waves.

An acre of sand outside the tracks, a constructed beach, was protected from longshore and tidal current erosion by a bulkhead. A skybridge crossed from the bluff to a wooden octagon that provided a staircase and restrooms but had the appearance of a watchtower where sentinels might scan the horizons for alien navies.

Atop the tower, I was the alien, cut off from sight of Puget Sound by the jut of Point Elliott. Mainland and Whidbey shores diverged here and Possession Sound widened to seven miles—the "Gulf of the Northern Isles." Two waterways, Saratoga Passage and Port Susan, exited north from the gulf on either side of Camano Island. In the middle sat Little Gedney Island, better known as Hat Island because that's what it looks like.

At Everett Junction, where the through line curved along the bluff and the industrial line went out on fill, the rumble and clatter of the factories seemed to wake the drowsy railroad. A freight came herky-jerky from the yards. A switch engine scooted by. A work train rolled slowly south doing routine maintenance, a procedure I'd often watched: a big-toothed machine clamps jaws on the centers of old ties that need replacing, lifts them until they snap in two, and flings the broken halves aside. Another brute jacks up rails so the work gang can slip new ties under. A crane hoists away worn-out rails and lowers the replacements. Carloads of crushed rock are dumped on the bed and thumped by a mechanical tamper. A rolling calibrator measures heights and widths so the gang can crowbar the rails to perfect alignment. Were the number of such work trains doubled, the speed on American rails could go up by half, and half the flying tin pots could be sliced up for kipper snack cans.

At the junction, where the bluff was gulched by Pigeon Creek No. 1—an industrial ditch—began the row of old barns that had dominated the view all the way from Mukilteo. On the first were fading letters, "Weyerhaeuser Timber Co. Pulp Div." This pioneer stood quiet, in fact was in the process of being dismantled. Still alive was the adjacent "Mill Number 1." Through paint-flaking walls and sawdust-frosted windows came a contraption symphony, roarings and whirrings and whinings and snarlings of saws, planers, sanders, and shapers. From stacks and pipes and from cracks in the wall squirted jets of white steam.

For a half-mile, the Katzenjammer factory, built without blueprints by illiterate Swedes with jaws full of snoose, walled off the water. The bluff lowered to a green bank, last gasp of the Jim Hill Wilderness I'd walked since Golden Gardens. The bluff eased off to a gentle slope rising to downtown Everett atop the drift plateau. My way lay on a sidewalk over filled-in bay.

At the site of the 1903 sawmill, I passed "Everett Thermo-Mechanical Pulp Mill," Weyerhaeuser's slick new 1975 model built by university-educated engineers with briefcases full of blueprints. Esthetically the mill was a failure, boring as white shirts and 747s, not even a steam plume to mark the city for mariners on far waters and hikers on distant hills. (It proved to be an economic failure as well, doomed to be demolished in December 1980, because its principal product was disposable diapers and the mill's process could turn out only brown paper, esthetically offensive to the doting parents of America, and so much for smart engineers.)

Port of Everett Pier 1, and Amtrak Rail Passenger Station, ended the thirty-eight foot miles from King Street Station.

PART TWO

Snohomish River to Stillaguamish River

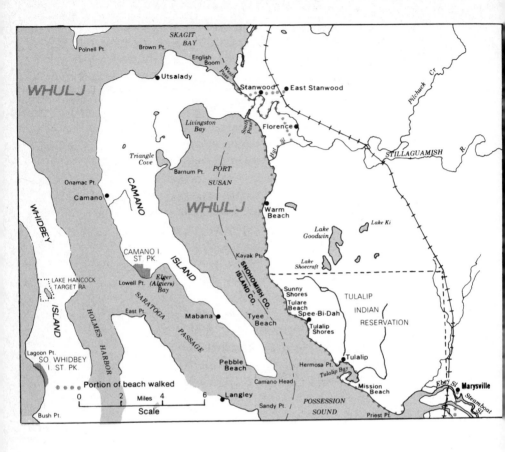

WHULJ

SKAGIT
BAY

Polnell Pt.   Brown Pt.

English
Boom

Utsalady

Stanwood   East Stanwood

Livingston
Bay

Florence

Pilchuck Cr.

Triangle
Cove

STILLAGUAMISH R.

Barnum Pt.   PORT
SUSAN

Onamac Pt.

CAMANO

Camano

WHULJ

Warm
Beach

Lake
Goodwin

Lake Ki

CAMANO I.
ST. PK.

ISLAND

Kayak Pt.

Lake
Shoecraft

WHIDBEY

LAKE HANCOCK
TARGET RA

Elger
(Algiers)
Bay

Lowell Pt.

SNOHOMISH CO.
ISLAND CO.

Sunny
Shores
Tulare
Beach

TULALIP

INDIAN

ISLAND

SARATOGA

East Pt.

HOLMES HARBOR

Mabana

Tyee
Beach

Spee-Bi-Dah

RESERVATION

Tulalip
Shores

PASSAGE

Lagoon Pt.
SO. WHIDBEY
I. ST. PK.

Pebble
Beach

Hermosa Pt.

Tulalip

Tulalip Bay

●●●● Portion of beach walked

Camano Head

Mission
Beach

Ebey Sl.   Marysville

0   2   Miles   4   6

Langley

Sandy Pt.

POSSESSION
SOUND

Steamboat Sl.

Scale

Bush Pt.

Priest Pt.

13. Everett

A book by Norman H. Clark, *Mill Town: A Social History of Everett, Washington, from Its Earliest Beginnings on the Shores of Puget Sound* (oh, sic!) *to the Tragic and Infamous Event Known as the Everett Massacre* (University of Washington Press, 1970), memorably portrays the hustle-bustle of the town-boomers on the shores of Port Gardner in 1892. Platted barely two years earlier, Everett had 800 houses and what seemed as many saloons and more of both abuilding, as were a paper mill, nail factory, shipyard, and a smelter to process Cascade ores. The ores were said to be "as rich as Monte Cristo"—a fact not to be doubted because John D. Rockefeller himself was heavily invested. Rails were being laid along the shore toward Seattle, there to connect with the branch line from the Northern Pacific's transcontinental terminus at Tacoma. This did not mean that Everett was doomed to be a mere satellite city. James J. Hill, "The Empire Builder," was pushing his Great Northern Railroad through the Cascades, the first train from Lake Superior scheduled to arrive in June 1893. Port Gardner boomers were confident Hill would choose as his terminus Everett, which as a consequence was sure to "be to the Pacific Coast what Boston and Lowell are to the East."

The scene of Clark's story was surveyed in 1893 to 1895 for the USGS Snohomish Quadrangle, published in 1897. In the map's 875 square miles, the only settlements ranking as more than hamlets are Seattle, Everett, and Snohomish. The boomers' young Everett already has stolen the Snohomish County seat from old Snohomish and is larger than Seattle's mill town, Ballard. Several major docks jut out into the bay, including City Dock.

Hill soon proved to have been cozying up to Port Gardner boomers purely to so frighten Elliott Bay speculators, who'd previously lost the Northern Pacific to Tacoma, that they'd give him their waterfront—as they did, under the name of Railroad Avenue. Seattle, all along, had been his desired terminus. However, he by no means neglected the city where his rails came down from the mountains to tidewater. He gave it to a Minnesota crony.

In 1893, Frederick Weyerhaeuser, his scalping of the East nearly complete, bought a house in St. Paul next door to Jim Hill's, handy for sitting on the veranda, smoking big cigars, talking about rails and trees. On January 3, 1900, the two neighbors struck a deal for a portion of the forty-million-acre Northern Pacific Land Grant that Hill had acquired in the course of his empire-building. For $6 an acre Weyerhaeuser bought 900,000 acres, foundation of a timber empire that by 1914 would grow to 1,514,000 acres in the state of Washington alone, obtained for an average of $8.80 an acre. In Everett in 1915 he built what was then the largest lumber mill in the world (a title held at one time or another by many a mill on the Whulj).

In the first decade of Weyerhaeuser's presence in the Northwest, under his leadership as the acknowledged chief of the timber barons, Everett flourished, the population growing from 8,000 to more than 35,000. Clark tells that in 1910 it had eleven lumber mills, sixteen shingle mills (including the largest in the world), seventeen combination lumber-shingle mills, a paper mill, shipyards, breweries, and enough miscellany to make a grand total of ninety-five manufacturing plants, each with a tall stack. A hiker on the mountain front would not then, as in more recent times, have located Everett by its steam plumes. He'd have seen only a mountain of smoke.

When times were good the baronial rule seemed benevolent, or close enough. When times were bad the workers felt the mailed fist, and it began to seem times almost always were bad. In the second decade of Weyerhaeuser in the Northwest it came to be said more and more often that the Northern Pacific Land Grant was the grandest larceny in the history of the nation; that the barons all were thieves and thugs and receivers of stolen goods, and the bigger the baron the bigger the crook; and that the lot of the working man had not improved since medieval times, when the rule was:

The law locks up the man or woman
That steals the goose from off the common,
But leaves the greater villain loose
Who steals the common from the goose.

Weyerhaeuser headquartered himself in Tacoma, well distant from the smoke and sweat and smoldering discontent of Everett—discontent that steadily heated through the summer and fall of 1916 toward the explosion of "Bloody Sunday."

That day was later memorialized for the radical ages in a poem by Charles Ashley, published in a booklet entitled "IWW Songs of the Workers."

Everett, November Fifth

...And then the Fellow Worker died, singing "Hold the Fort"—From the report of a witness in the trial involving 74 members of the I.W.W. arising from the massacre of free speech fighters on the ship Verona by a drunken sheriff's posse at Everett, Wash., November 5, 1916.

And then the decks went red; and the grey sea
Was written crimsonly with ebbing life.
The barricade spewed shots and mockery
And curses, and the drunken lust of strife.

Yet, the mad chorus from that devil's host—
Yea, all the tumult of that butcher throng,—
Compound of bullets, booze and coward boast,—
Could not out-shriek one dying worker's song!

Objective historians give as bare facts that shortly before 2 p.m. on November 5, 1916, the *Verona,* having left Colman Dock in Seattle at noon on its regular Sunday run carrying freight and passengers, steamed into Port Gardner carrying an estimated 200 or 250 Wobblies come to protest the beating of comrades who had attempted to demonstrate for free speech in Everett. Awaiting the *Verona* on City Dock were the sheriff, who had supervised the beating, and some 250 special deputies, mainly baronry subchiefs and their merchant allies.

From the dock came a shout: "Turn around and go back."
From the boat came the answer: "We won't."
From boat or dock (witnesses at the trial disagreed) came a gunshot.
From boat and dock came many gunshots.

The *Verona* backed out in the bay with thirty-one wounded and five dead aboard and perhaps a dozen dead overboard.

On the dock two men lay dying and sixteen lay wounded. To this day a person does well in any gathering of the city's elders not to ask about Everett's most historic hour. Chances are some of their fathers and uncles were on City Dock, and some on the *Verona*.

14. Everett Massacre to Marysville

Mile 38–44 ½

Saturday, January 7, 1978

In a dark noon sixty-one years and two months after Bloody Sunday, I set out north from where City Dock used to be. If there was a monument, I couldn't find it.

The landmark of the vicinity was the sulfite (white-paper-producing) pulp mill of Scott Paper, exhaling one of the columns that distinguished Everett as the last surviving three-plumer of the Whulj. (In 1979 Scott installed a vacuum cleaner in the stack to suck out particulate matter, leaving only steam. A sad loss. With a mill town, as with a dirty old man, too many baths are ruinous.)

Docks, mills, and factories lined the shore for two miles. At the first gap I walked out on a dock to view the plastics and pastels in the Everett Yacht Basin and reflected that were this fleet of stinkpots to be armed as heavily as the *Verona* and sent forth to combat the armadas of Edmonds and Shilshole Bay, there would be a spectacle to gladden the hearts of rowboaters and seals.

The Norton Avenue Boat Launch, on a fill that thrust a half-mile out through mud flats, served outboard cowboys who trailered craft from home. The 1897 map shows a lone pier, isolated from the main assemblage of docks, jutting out here to water of ship-floating depth. That was my last glimpse of 1897 because at this point I walked off the Snohomish Quadrangle onto the Mount Vernon Quadrangle, surveyed in 1909, published in 1911.

The fourteen years from 1897 to 1911, unrecorded on any of my maps, were a major time gap. North of the gap I was cut off from seeing back to 1897 and the accomplishments of Jim Hill's first half-decade in the Northwest. South of the gap I was cut off from 1911 and the results of Weyerhaeuser's first decade. On both sides of the gap, though, I could see the half-century skip to the USGS map of 1956, which shows among other constructions a breakwater two-thirds of a mile offshore—wide enough to be an island—two miles long from the site of City Dock to the mouth of the Snohomish River.

On Bloody Sunday the sun was shining. Today cold rain rode a steady wind. Umbrella cocked southwest, I walked north by pilings of old docks, memories of old mills. Beyond the rotting past lay the living present, seen dimly through the rain, a vastness of logs.

Often in my years of speeding along highways toward mountain wilderness I'd flashed past tantalizing alleys. Become at last an old settler, "no longer a slave of (high) ambition," I was free now to pursue the low, the alley ambitions. One such ambition was walking the Whulj. Another was connecting the salt to the snow by following rivers from beaches to mountains. A third was circling the mountain front, ascending those undistinguished foothills of the Cascades and Olympics ignored by climbers, hikers, and wilderness pamphleteers hurrying to the mountain interior.

In tracing the mountain front of the northerly Cascades, I'd walked hundreds of miles in Weyerhaeuser clearcuts, Scott Paper clearcuts, Georgia-Pacific clearcuts, and Washington Department of Natural Resources clearcuts. I'd ascended through the Western Hemlock Zone, best known for its most prized species, the Douglas fir (the one zone industrial foresters know enough about to rudely ape nature and practice "tree farming"). I'd climbed into the Pacific Silver Fir Zone, where knowledge thins and pretenses of tree farming end. I'd climbed higher into the Mountain Hemlock Zone where Christmas trees and subalpine flowers intermingle, and heirs of the Northern Pacific Land Theft are mining forests they haven't a notion how to regrow. These are forests nature won't be able to replace for half a millennium—assuming it can do so at all, because the tree-miners have flushed much of the soil down the rivers, not to be replaced for a dozen millennia.

Wherever any vegetable larger than grass grows I'd watched trucks creep down spur roads and highball down main line roads hauling big sticks and little sticks, old growth and second growth. I'd watched freshets of fir and hemlock and cedar merge into torrents of logs, and I'd gazed far out to the three-plumer where they flowed into the Whulj.

The plumes had become irrelevant. Mill Town is the past. The present is Log Town. Walking the shore of Port Gardner I saw hills of logs on every dock and bays of logs between. There was a sea of logs extending nearly to the two-mile-long breakwater-island, itself a range of log mountains. Trucks dumped logs. Tugs towed rafts of logs. Helicopters flew bundles of logs. And cranes lifted logs aboard ships—rows of ships—a whole fleet of Japanese *marus,* because we clearcut the wilderness to pay for trail-razzing Hondas, Kawasakis, Yamahas, and Suzukis.

Mills and docks resumed, and across the tracks so did the Jim Hill Wilderness. I climbed a viaduct street to the top of the tanglewood bluff and from under my umbrella looked out to rain-dim Possession Sound, the rain-bleary Northern Isles, and the gray void where the Olympics ought to have been. South were the ferries and pastel jet-fuel tanks of Mukilteo, the land of Oz. North, Cultus Mountain loomed vaguely, marking the Cascade front at the edge of the Skagit delta. It was 185 years and seven months since the June 4 birthday of George III when George Vancouver landed here (or nearby) and took possession of New Georgia.

Norman Clark writes that "On an afternoon in the spring of his thirty-fifth year, 1792, Vancouver walked the beach below the bluffs that rim the high ground. Standing there in an infinite wilderness, he looked west to the dark islands, west to the fabled Strait of Juan de Fuca, west to the mystic Orient.... It pleased the captain then to record that the serenity of the climate, the innumerable pleasing landscapes, and the abundant fertility that unassisted nature puts forth, require only to be enriched by the industry of man...to render it the most lovely country that can be imagined. In a mood of warm satisfaction, he ordered the issue of a generous round of grog and raised his country's flag while his men shouted and fired cannons."

Likely the sun was shining then, too.

The railroad curved around Preston Point to a Momentous Geographical Event. Though the broad waters ahead appeared to be simply more of Port Gardner, in fact they were the estuary of the Snohomish, first river of my way northward, first hitching together of saltwater waves and mountain clouds.

It was hard to get excited about the Event. A river winning the battle against the sea pushes out a delta. A sea defeating a river floods inland, widening the mouth to an estuary. The Snohomish is a loser. Moreover, while the Nisqually and Puyallup issue proudly from glaciers of Tahoma, and the Nooksack from the Nooksack Cirque of Shuksan, and the Skagit from hundreds of great peaks, and even the Stillaguamish has Big Four, Three Fingers, and Whitehorse to brag about, the Snohomish is born just twenty-five miles upstream from Preston Point, where two other rivers join and yield up their identities. I couldn't believe that the corrupt waters of this lowly alluvial merger contained the Snoqualmie—which drains from Mount Si, the South Face of The Tooth, Dutch Miller Gap—and the Skykomish—which drains from Slippery Slab Tower, La Bohn Gap, Lake Dorothy, and the North Peak of Index, on whose cliffs in one August night of 1950 I longed for a mouth large enough to suck up the entire starlight-sparkling river.

The tracks came to a sign: "Delta Junction." Around me in the rain and gloom assembled the spirits of Jay Cooke, Henry Villard, James J. Hill, J. Pierpont Morgan, John D. Rockefeller, and Edward H. Harriman. For those who can interpret the language of the rails, these names were on the maps along with those of the group's Mephistopheles, Jay Gould, and the Dutch bully, Commodore Vanderbilt, whose son Billy provided the motto of America's railroaders, "the public be damned."

I wanted a movie in which time is speeded up to compress a century to an hour or two, the camera positioned high enough in the sky to encompass the whole of Western Washington to let me watch lines of steel push north from the Columbia River and west from the Cascades, paralleling and crisscrossing and colliding head on. I wanted the camera to descend for closeups of gangs blasting tunnels and fabricating bridges, of towns turning out with brass bands and dignitaries to greet the first locomotives. The camera also would penetrate smoke-filled rooms to reveal Congress being bribed to give away the Northern Pacific Land Grab, and the Washington Legislature paid to set permissive regulations. It should show boomers being threatened with ruin if they failed to sign over the fattest slices of their towns, and stock being watered to bilk investors as far away as Germany and the Russia of the tsars.

Lacking such a movie (*The Birth of a Province*), I had to make do with still photographs—maps—supplemented by other documents:

Before the Maps

1873: Northern Pacific completes a rail line from the Columbia River to a dead end in Tacoma.

1874: Left in outer darkness, Seattle boomers begin construction of the Seattle & Walla Walla Railroad, which never gets to the wheat but does bring coal from Newcastle.

1884: Puget Sound Shore Line, a Northern Pacific subsidiary, enters Seattle from Tacoma. Trains are so scheduled that a Seattle passenger must stay overnight in Tacoma to catch a transcontinental. Train service frequently is suspended, causing much innocent merriment in Tacoma.

1885: Seattle boomers begin construction of the Seattle, Lake Shore, and Eastern, intended to reach the East via Canada; it never gets to the border but does link Seattle to Arlington, for whatever that might be worth.

July 4, 1893: A Great Northern train steams into Seattle, which lives happily ever after.

1897 Map

From Preston Point the GN main line proceeds up the Snohomish toward Stevens Pass (and North Dakota and St. Paul).

South along the river, near Lowell, the GN main line meets the Everett & Monte Cristo R.R., which runs to Snohomish and a junction there with the Seattle & International R.R., successor to the Seattle, Lake Shore, and Eastern.

The S & I runs south to Woodinville. From there its main line enters Seattle via Lake Washington; its Snoqualmie Branch runs down

Lake Sammamish to Issaquah and off the map east.

Seattle is now perfectly content, served from the south by:

Northern Pacific R.R. Seattle Line.

Columbia & Puget Sound R.R., part of which previously was the Seattle and Walla Walla, renamed in 1880 when acquired by the NP.

Though not shown on the map, the Union Pacific since 1895.

1911 Map

From Delta Junction (just off the edge of the 1897 map) the GN's Seattle and Vancouver Line crosses the river and heads north.

The line that in 1897 was the Seattle & International is now the Seattle and Vancouver Line of the NP.

From the NP at Hartford, the Monte Cristo R.R. branches east, off the map.

Though not shown on the map, in 1909 the Chicago, Milwaukee, St. Paul & Pacific—usually known as the Milwaukee Line—arrived from the East via Snoqualmie Pass and began patching together a helter-skelter system all over the landscape.

1973 Map

No trace remains of the Monte Cristo R.R. though excursion cars (not trains) ran along it, under the new name of Hartford & Eastern until the early 1930s, carrying tourists to Verlot, Silverton, Big Four Inn, and the ghost town of Monte Cristo, where Rockefeller didn't make a fortune but never missed the one he lost.

The map also has forgotten the line that originally was the Seattle & International, NP having abandoned the route in 1963.

The only names left on the map are the ramshackle Chicago, Milwaukee, etc. and the merger of everything else that has survived, the Burlington Northern.

After the Maps

1980: The Chicago etc., having spent its whole corporate life in or near bankruptcy, goes belly-up. Reminiscent of those evenings on the St. Paul veranda when Jim and Fred smoked big cigars and disposed of empires, BN and Weyerhaeuser rip off tasty chunks and leave the rest to rot.

1981: BN swallows the Frisco Line to cap a conglomeration that has 29,226 miles of track, 114,000 cars, and 3,000 locomotives, few of which ever appear in public.

Tracks ran north from Delta Junction to empty air above the river. I stood transfixed as a metal mass impelled by unseen forces swung 90 degrees sideways to close the gap. A rumble of engine and bustle of wheels dragged a freight train over the water. The bridge swung itself back, reopening the gap. It was a Momentous Historical Event: the railroad had left me trackless and on my own.

I scrambled up a gravel bank to the old Highway 99 bridge and another Event. Thus far on my journey the view east, no further than the bluff, had been short and blank. Now the valleys of the Snohomish and its parent rivers let me look through the dimness of rain to vague loomings. Closely east rose the grand bulk of "Nanga" Pilchuck, standing between the valley of the Skykomish and the South Fork of the Stillaguamish. Far north was Cultus, at the Skagit River's exit from the mountain front, and far south Mount Si, at the exit of the Snoqualmie.

In clear and windless weather the Whulj is barely visible from those peaks because early in the morning the haze-smog exhaled by nature and man is cooked opaque. However, often in the short days of winter, I was still on the heights when the setting sun slanted in under the pall, and water and land became abruptly and sharply distinguishable, the one molten gold, the other smoke-blue.

The first time this happened, in the beginning of my explorations of the mountain front, I was bewildered by the maze of winding waterways and curving shores, and I marveled that any mariner ever could find his way. Now, though, I was learning the shorelines so well that from any distance I could sort out and identify bays and straits and sounds, islands and peninsulas. My feet knew them.

Almost always, even though not visible itself, Everett could be found by the plumes rising above it: Scott's on the waterfront and the two here on either side of the Highway 99 bridge. Upriver was the thin plume of the Weyerhaeuser sawmill. Downriver was the little old red mill, silent and still, and beside it, fed by sawmill waste on a conveyor belt, the modern Weyerhaeuser kraft (brown-bag) pulp mill.

Pedestrian sidewalks identified the Highway 99 bridge over the main channel of the Snohomish as dating from the childhood of the automobile, when the machine was tolerant, having so recently been itself the interloper. A few steps took me to Smith Island, where sawdust hills and log mountains towered above a scattering of dispirited cows.

A low highway bridge took me across Union Slough, wide as the main river, which it once was, to a nameless island where plastic stink-pots were being glued together to harass the seals. Next I crossed river-size Steamboat Slough, named for the steamboats that once worked their way to a junction with Military Road in Snohomish City. Here was an exuberance of bridges, a museum display of a century of civil engineering. As close in time to Robert Fulton's *Clermont* as to me was the antique iron drawbridge of the railroad. Highway 99, designed in the 1920s when 40 m.p.h. was a spanking speed, had two drawbridges. Its fretworks of iron trusses based on massive concrete piers reminded a dirty old man of Mae West. On either side of each draw span was a lift tower containing intricate marvels of magical machinery. These were the past. The present span was Interstate 5, built for 90 m.p.h. and trucks as big as freight trains, a concrete sky supported by a forest of spindly, mass-produced pillars as sexy to an ancient pedestrian as the drug-shriveled superstars of rock music.

I crossed Steamboat Slough on the Highway 99 bridge to a nameless marsh-island owned by the Tulalip Tribes. In the 1970s Seattle struck a deal with Marine Garbage Disposal Company, which struck a deal with the Tulalips, and Seattle commenced to dump garbage here, on Everett's doorstep. My airways being no longer irritated by cigarette smoke, I was greedy for grossness. I craved tide flats in the hot sun and pulp mills belching privy-like odors, and today I gourmandized along the half-mile of garbage mountains, recalling when Seattle garbage was burned in Lake Washington marshes and the occasional east wind suffused the University of Washington campus with sickly-sweet smoke.

Highway 99 and I slunk under the double span of thundering I-5, crossed narrow Ebey Slough on a drawbridge, passed a boat yard, a log hillock, a little sawmill, and entered Marysville. Here in 1883 the first logging locomotive in Washington Territory, if not the world, set off huffing and puffing along maple rails, and here in the 1940s, returning from climbs in the North Cascades, I stopped many a time at Herb's Kerb for the best hamburgers in the world, then moved down the road to the Cottage Inn for the best pies in the world.

15. Priest Point to Tulalip Bay
Mile 47–54

Wednesday, January 11, 1978

I knew more about the oceans sailed by Captain Cook, the Antarctic plateau sledged by Scott, and the ridge of Everest where Mallory disappeared in a cloud than about the shore beyond the end of Jim Hill's steel trail. Nobody could tell me if the beaches of this white space on my mental map were walkable. Most asked why on earth I'd want to do such a thing. Mallory said of Everest, "Because it is there," but that didn't apply to me because he was an amateur, while I, in the throes of cigarette withdrawal, had been forced to find work as a pedestrian. Marshall Will Kane, asked in *High Noon* by his craven ex-deputy (named, irrelevantly enough, Harvey) why he was going out in the street to face the outlaw guns, spoke for us professionals: "If you don't know it, no use me tellin' you."

My way from Marysville to the beach of Possession Sound, the route north, was the bank of Ebey Slough. I stared in dismay.

A railroad organizes a shore, gives form, meaning, and direction. Follow the tracks forward and they'll take you to the future—to fame and fortune. Follow them back and they'll connect to your childhood, a wagon train, a Viking longship. A trackless shore is uncreated chaos, a void, an Ebey Slough.

Here where tides flow but no beach-building waves roll, river and bay seep into a reedy, thorny midworld too thick to swim and too thin to walk. At low water there is open ground—the intertidal belt of boot-sucking mud that shelves steep and slimy to the brown soup of silt and cowshit and vile leakings from Seattle's swill. Had I somehow, lizardlike, wiggled or swum along the slough bank, it would have been to a bad end in the salt marsh of Quilceda Creek, final tributary of the Snohomish. Beyond that obstacle the shore rose up in a bluff and Ebey and Steamboat sloughs joined in the estuary. Here the wind had enough of a broad sweep to make beaches. But they were not beaches fit to be walked. For nine decades the southerlies had been beaching Mill Town's castoffs on this windward shore—rotten logs, rotten boats, rotten mills. I conceded the first two and a half miles from Marysville and beetled inland on Marine Drive.

Mission Beach to Priest Point

Clean beach began on Priest Point, but the water was walled off by cheek-to-jowl houses, so I drove on north to Mission Beach, where I found a place to scramble down from the road to the beach through a jumble of planks and a forest of pilings. These were the remains of the large dock shown on the 1968 USGS Tulalip Quadrangle, the Mission Beach Boathouse. Here, on September 24, 1933 were held the finals of the Ben Paris Fishing Derby, the major league of sport fishing, with forty-two boathouses around the Whulj qualifying fishermen for the Derby finals, the World Series. Uncle Bill always made the finals and surely was on the scene that day. Was this where he tied for first place and lost the grand prize, a new Plymouth, on a flip of the coin?

Along the blufftop ran a row of green-lawn ramblers synthetically weathered by driftwood stain. At the bluff base nestled a dozen cottages on pilings, weathered by the Whulj to match the driftwood and drift-rope that decorated the doorways and windows. Sand cliff at their back doors, waves at their front, these below-bluffers came and went by plank walk, beach, or rowboat, stared southwesterly gales straight in the eye, probably didn't own bathtubs or worry about it. One could guess their hair and clothing smelled of salt and kelp; one suspected they were young with nothing to fear or old with nothing to lose.

Here began the most magnificent mile on the route thus far. The cliff rose a noble 200 feet in elegantly naked strata of sand and clay. At the base were no seawall and rails, at the brink no houses intruding on the fringe of fir and madrona. For the entire mile the bluff was pristine atop and below.

The beach was a smooth plain of moist sand, glistening gray. I took off my boots to walk barefoot, feeling the crystals between my toes. I held a pinch to my eye and it wasn't gray at all, was a mass of gems, black as coal, white as snow, and blue as sky.

Overhead hung a darkness that extended dense and solid northward. Southward, gray waters swept past green forests of Hat Island and white plumes of Mill Town to a brilliance. Was Oz beginning to glow?

The mile of wildness ended. First there were old pilings and wrecked wooden staircases. Then, 140 feet above the beach, a landscaped brink. The bluff lowered to 100 feet, then 50, and ladders, staircases, and trails descended to boathouses on pilings and bulkheads. I walked out on Priest Point, where the fair-weather longshore current strives to push a spit southeasterly and the storm current crooks the finger northwest. Behind the driftwood, where the dune line used to be, ran a solid half-mile of houses. At the end of houses and sand, where the slough mud starts, lay the mouth of what in eons past was the lagoon.

Here in 1858 at the village of Tc'iL!a'qs (as the anthropologists spell it), largest settlement of the Snohomish, one Father Chirouse founded a mission. The lagoon remnant now was a working port, a cluster of sagging docks, shops, and patched-up tugboats.

I sat on a log and opened my can of kippers. The umbrella hadn't been needed. The mildness of the air refuted the calendar. Definitely nearer, now, were the South Seas. I looked across a mile of estuary back to the breakwater-island of Port Gardner enclosing Everett's harbor. Tugs shuttled log rafts, helicopters delivered log bundles, log-loaded *marus* got underway. The mill plumes billowed fat and tall, no wind bending and dissipating the steam. Enough essence wafted here to fill my nose with the "smell of money." From industry and freeway the buzzes, whirs, bangs, squeaks, and thuds blended in a regional hum-rumble. A train horn pierced through, lonesome as the call of a loon.

Clouds sliced off the tops of Three Fingers which I first climbed in 1949, Pilchuck (1940), and Index (1950). The summits of Ebey, Wheeler, Blue, Olo, and Green—the humble mountains of the Cascade front I climb nowadays—stood clear.

To the south a black bug was creeping across yellow clouds, the last ferry I'd see on this journey. I'd lose it soon. And Everett, too, where ended the tracks of childhood.

As I headed north into darkness, back toward Mission Beach, the sun caught up and flooded over my shoulder. Gray hands turned pink. Gray beach sparkled with googols of jewels. Monochrome Kansas exploded in Technicolor. A Munchkin tugboat materialized out of the lowering sun, and a hit man for the Wicked Witch jumped into the bay and waded toward me, dragging a cable. He hooked it not around my neck but on a log and waded back to Little Tug, which turned its nose to sea, said "poopa-poopa-poopa," and made a run for it. When the cable went taut, Little Tug slowed to "*Poo*-paw-paw, *Poo*-paw-paw (*Think* I can, *Think* I can)" and shuddered and shook until the log slid off the sand, a raft escapee recovered for a shipment to Japan.

At Mission Beach I was startled to find barely three feet of boot-room between the pilings and the incoming tide. Another half-hour and I'd have been up to my ankles.

Before starting south from Mission Beach I'd checked the tide chart and noted a high of 10.8 feet at 5:50 p.m. What did *that* mean? To *me*? It now was 2:45, with three more hours of rising water. In the wild mile no long-settled logs lay against the naked base of vertical drift, only a fresh litter of chips and twigs. At a tide level of 10.8 feet—or maybe 9 feet—the beach would be gone and a walker would have to climb a ravine, or try. Or wade. Simple enough on so calm a day as this; what about in a storm?

In all my years on the Whulj I'd been an amateur blundering about. Now lacking a railroad to guide me, I as a professional was going to have to organize the shore.

Mission Beach

North of the boathouse ruins the bluff leaped from 20 feet to 50. A capping of till protected the lower drift from erosion, forming an overhanging cliff. The sandy portions of the wall, where no bloody-minded cat could crawl, were riddled with holes, a swallows' apartment house. The solidity of the till had encouraged other residences on top.

Walking the beach had made me a close student of blufftoppers—or rather, of their potential for intruding on my privacy. I'd discovered a basic law of the Whulj: *The attraction of the beach for blufftoppers varies inversely with the height, steepness, and stability of the bluff.*

When the bluff is 200 feet high and composed of too-steep sand-gravel-till, or too-ooky clay, nobody comes down to the water except children.

When the bluff is 100 feet and of a reasonable angle, adults join the kids in building trails, perhaps easing tricky passages with railings, stairs, or short ladders. The blufftopper then may visit the waves every weekend, at least in summer.

When the bluff lowers to 50 feet and is easy the whole way, some members of the family may descend on almost every nice day.

However: Even the shortest bluff, if extremely steep, requires extreme measures. Today I'd passed every manner of device from electric elevators on steel cables to rope ladders dangling from overhangs. Here, fancy new houses above the swallows' condominium sported fancy new cliffside stairways. Teams of architects, engineers, carpenters, and masons must have come by land and sea to erect the timber-and-plank towers, 50 feet tall, that were defended at the base by pilings or seawalls. But interspersed with these new grand stairways were old grand stairways that had lost their supports and now ended in midair. All in all, blufftoppers don't bother us below-bluffers very often, very long.

A mile from the boathouse the shore bent sharply around the tip of what I'd supposed, when I saw it on a map with no contour lines, to be a spit. However, the feature that enclosed Tulalip Bay was no spit, it was a drift peninsula 50 feet high, 500 feet wide, and nearly a mile long. I was geologically baffled.

It was not the first time beaches had baffled me. The alpine realm that originally stirred my scientific interest, when I was going on thirteen, is starkly simple—just about everything is naked, rawly new, and readily explained by "glacier." Ice was also the main shaper of the Puget Trough lowlands, but there the work was done longer ago and has been obscured by ups and downs of sea level, by water, by gravity—and by man.

Back in my University of Washington days, Professor J. Hoover Mackin drilled into us the method of the "multiple working hypotheses" whereby the investigator frames every imaginable explanation for a phenomenon and gathers evidence for and against all of them simultaneously and without favor. When one hypothesis at last outclasses the competition, it may be promoted to a theory, a step toward becoming a law. I earned an A from Dr. Mackin. In later years, though, removed from his rigors, I've developed a tendency to fall in love with every pretty hypothesis that comes along. As punishment I've been hounded by geologists—climbing and hiking companions, drinking buddies, chance acquaintances, total strangers bumped into on the street—who sneer that "Manning knows next to nothing about geology and half of what he does know isn't so."

My excuse is that despite my training by Mackin, the world was defined for me by my first textbook, inherited from somewhere, a treasure of my childhood library, the 1896 (fourth) edition of *Elements of Geology* by Joseph Le Conte. This is the language of *my* science: "Strewed all over the northern part of North America…is found a *pecu-*

liar surface soil or deposit…all sorts of material on all sorts of bed rock." It includes "*Stony clay* or *Bowlder clay* or *Till*" and "bowlders of all sizes, often of huge dimensions, sometimes even 100 tons or more." Le Conte comments: "We have said that the deposit is peculiar. Nothing resembling it is found anywhere in tropical or *low-latitude countries.*"

Le Conte continues, "When the phenomena of the Drift were first observed, they were supposed to indicate the agency of powerful currents, such as could be produced only by the most violent and instantaneous convulsions. A sudden upheaval of the ocean-bed in northern regions was supposed to have precipitated the sea upon the land as a huge *wave of translation,* which swept from north toward the south, carrying death and ruin in its course. Hence the deposit was often called *Diluvium* (deluge-deposit). *Now*, however, they are universally ascribed to the agency of *ice* acting *slowly* through great periods of time. Hence the name *Glacial epoch.*

"As to the manner in which the ice acted, however, opinions have been more or less divided, some attributing the phenomena to the agency of land-ice—*glaciers*—others to that of drifting *icebergs*…the decided tendency of science is toward the recognition of glaciers as the principal agent."

On publication of Le Conte's first edition, in 1877, the British geologist Charles Lyell was just two years dead and Charles Darwin had five more years to live. The air I breathe is of the dawn of geology. Catastrophism (the big-blast theory) versus uniformitarianism (ages-of-little-steps theory) is still a hot debate. At every garden party we enjoy scoffing at the Archbishop of Ireland, James Ussher (d. 1656) who after careful study of the Old Testament calculated the world was created in 4004 B.C., on October 23, at 9 o'clock in the morning.

Burdened by too much knowledge, my geologist friends get no joy from their science. In the early nineteenth century there was a world-rambling German scientist who in his travels picked up a bit about many fields of knowledge. I too go on tour innocent and cheerful, the Alexander von Humboldt of the Whulj.

Now I was baffled sociologically.

At 3:30, when I returned to the beetle via the bluffless, house-crowded bay shore of the peninsula, I noted that across the street from where I'd parked was the headquarters building of the Tulalip Tribes Utilities Department. The map showed that my whole route from Garbage Island had been on the Tulalip Indian Reservation. But not on Garbage Island, not on Priest Point, not at Mission Beach, nor on the peninsula had I seen a single non-European face.

I continued north along the mainland shore in twilight. Two lads I'd met earlier on the beach hailed me again.

"Hi, mister, where you goin' *now*?"

"Up the bay to Tulalip."

"Golly, what *for*?"

"To see if there are any Indians on this reservation."

Tulalip Bay

A spit thrusting from the tip of the peninsula nearly to the mainland shore cut off the south end of Tulalip Bay, forming a lagoon, into which bulged a meadow topped by a grove of fir trees. Within the grove stood a new building, a modified long house signed "Tulalip Tribes Potlatch Ground." Throngs of young and old were coming and going.

Throngs had been coming and going hereabouts some 10,000 years or more. Initially, in their Hunting Period, they used stone tools of the Old Cordilleran variety common from the Yukon to Mexico. The lances or spearheads of these people employed the characteristic Cascade Point, designed to kill big game. During the Early Maritime Period, they continued hunting land animals but also pursued sea mammals and began catching salmon. In the Intermediate Period, roughly 750-1250 A.D., they even-handedly exploited resources of land and sea. The growing sophistication of their spear points and fish hooks in the Recent Period, 1250-1750, evidences steady advances in the use of both sources of sustenance, and the erection of palisades to protect villages indicates an increase in political activity. After that came the Historic Period, defined as the arrival of the Europeans.

The Snohomish people had villages on Priest Point, Whidbey and Camano islands, and upriver a ways at Hebo'lb, their original home (where the transformer, Dok ibet, put them when he came and "changed everything"). But apparently they did not live at Tulalip ("almost landlocked") Bay—at least, Vancouver found no inhabitants.

The absence is baffling unless one realizes how many other equally attractive places there were to live in the region of North America that had the densest pre-European population north of Mexico. Nevertheless, a person likes to envision canoes snugly harbored in the protected bay between sorties out to Port Susan, where salmon swam north to spawn in the Stillaguamish River, and to Possession Sound, where they swam south to the Snohomish. In addition to five sorts of salmon—supplying eggs as well as flesh—there were sturgeon, smelt, herring, trout, flounder, cod, rock cod, and skate, not to mention seals, whose fat was a valued source of oil.

The lagoon was a giant crab pot and its mud and sand were acres of clams, and the stonier beaches were thick with mussels and oysters and—preferred because they were tastier—barnacles. The skies were darkened spring and fall by clouds of migratory waterfowl which rested at night on marsh and bay, easily netted or speared at night by torchlight. In summer, nests of grouse and duck were robbed for eggs.

The uplands were a nut farm (hazelnuts), an orchard (Indian plum, bitter cherry, crabapple), and berry patch (salal, Oregon grape, blackberry, salmonberry, serviceberry, raspberry, thimbleberry, strawberry, elderberry, gooseberry, currant, blackcap, red and blue and black huckleberry). Ground crops included leaves of nettle, fiddleheads, and bracken fern to boil; roots of thistles, lilies, and wapato to bake; and miner's lettuce, cattail hearts, and new shoots of salmonberry to eat raw.

The Snohomish did little hunting, mainly leaving rabbits, beavers, mountain beavers, raccoons, squirrels, cougars, bobcats, and bears to run free and unafraid. When they wanted the red meat and hides of deer and elk they bought them from their neighbors, the Snoqualmies. There was wealth to enjoy and wealth to ignore in one of the fairest homes man has ever found.

An 1854 census of the Snohomish counted 350 souls. In 1792, when Vancouver anchored three days in Tulalip Bay, and on June 4 landed here or in the vicinity to take possession for England, were there 1,500, or 3,500? How many before the sea otter brought Europeans to the Northwest Coast? Smallpox came to the Northwest in 1775 and reached the inner Whulj in 1785; Vancouver made particular note of the many pocked faces. In one estimate, by 1835 some 85 to 90 percent of the total native population of the Northwest Coast had died of "the fever."

The 1855 Point Elliott (Mukilteo) Treaty that established the Tulalip Indian Reservation gathered in the Stillaguamish people from the north and some of the Snoqualmie and Sammamish from Mount Si and the

Issaquah Alps. Though scattered individuals and groups did refuse to report to the reservations and somehow found isolated spots overlooked by the European invaders, one wonders if many survivors of the plagues were not just as glad to leave their depopulated, haunted villages. One also wonders how long, had they not been compelled to huddle together, the tribes would have preserved their identities. In view of such slaughters as the Mashel Massacre of 1856, one wonders how they survived at all. They barely managed that on the reservation. In 1865, 1,000 people were settled there. Two years later, 300 survived.

Germs were only one of their plagues. The European-Americans were another. In 1865 an Indian agent wrote (as quoted by Harry Majors in *Exploring Washington*): "These Indians are very peaceably disposed and if there is ever any serious difficulty it will grow out of abuse heaped upon them by unprincipled white men. Nearly all the difficulties grow out of giving the Indians whiskey, or white men cohabiting with their women....During the last six months four Indians have been murdered in my district by the hands of white men. In every instance these cases have been laid before the grand jury. The grand jury...cut off all investigation....It would seem hopeless to prosecute a white man under any circumstances for killing an Indian."

In 1869 the subagent in charge of Tulalip was reported to have stolen all the annuity funds and goods due under treaty terms, plus every dollar in the tribal treasury, and sold all the reservation's working oxen.

The 1911 map shows some eighty-five structures on the 23,000 acres of the reservation. A dozen are sprinkled along the shore from Ebey Slough to Priest Point (where a cemetery lies atop the bluff). Another dozen (and another cemetery) are at Mission and the mouth of Mission Creek; some two dozen and a church and a large pier at Tulalip and Tulalip Creek; and a dozen more two miles north at a place called Subeebeda, at the end of the road from Marysville. Who lived in the structures? A reservation continues as a legal entity even after every acre is sold off by the original owners. How much land did the Tulalips retain by 1911?

In the period when I was camping with Boy Scout Troop 324 at Carkeek Park, my friend Dick's troop frequently camped in the meadow of the Tulalip potlatch ground. At night they were invited into a building Dick believes was the famous old long house, said by anthropologists to have been the largest potlatch house of the Snohomish, 115 feet long and 43 feet wide. By firelight Chief Shelton, remembered by Dick as a person of great dignity, philosophy, and warmth, told the boys of times past. Born as he was in the treaty era, conceivably he knew elders who as children watched Vancouver claim their home for King George.

In the period that Dick was camping at Tulalip, I was on the Ronald Schoolboy Patrol, morning, noon, and afternoon escorting kids across Highway 99. We patrol boys passed the time between customers identifying cars as they came in sight. Far off we could spot an "Indian." Whites sped along at 40 m.p.h. and even their flivvers managed 20. Indians drove scarcely faster than a walk. The marvel was they moved at all, so decrepit were the cars and so incredibly burdened with humanity.

I had supposed that cramming themselves into junks was a culture trait, like eating fish-head chowder, until a winter night years later when I was rescued from a deserted highway by a woman who, I subsequently was told, was famed along the ocean coast for a heart as big as all outdoors. Another busted car appeared in her headlights, another castaway signaling for help. She braked—then hit the gas. The man shrugged. He'd only hoped her headlights might be Quinault, like him.

In the 1930s Highway 99 was lined by thumbs. Cars were few, gas expensive. Failure to give a ride was antisocial and immoral. We all relied on hitchhiking. But chances are that few of the thumbs were Tulalip.

One wonders why they would want to leave the reservation. We Europeans loved Will Rogers, who bragged that his ancestors didn't come over on the *Mayflower*, they met it at the dock. We admired the Mohicans, Sioux, Apaches, and the Indians of British Columbia, who were as bloodthirsty as the U.S. Cavalry. But we viewed our local Siwash as a degraded subrace, dregs of the continent.

If leaving the reservation was to suffer, so was staying. A University of Washington course informed me that "Siwash," derived from the French word for "savage," was an epithet as derogatory as "nigger." The course also instructed me how little, if any, less rich their Vancouver-era culture was than the culture of my ancestors in Ireland and England. Soon after that course I met a Tulalip girl. We walked around the campus and sat on the lawns, and she told me how it was.

Walking the shore in twilight I remembered her stories. *This was the place.* She was born and raised in one of the fairest homes man has ever found.

The potlatch ground was the social and business center. But where, now, did the Tulalips *live*? On the far side of Mission Creek I entered Totem Beach, with its houses, stinkpots and, apparently, residents all white as snow.

I paused at St. Anne's Church, built in 1904 to replace the earlier one on Priest Point. The steeple retained the 1858 bell. The National Register of Historic Places describes the church as "an example of the late Victorian Gothic style, an ornamented frame structure…a link to the historic mission period."

One doubts Chief Shelton ever considered himself a savage, and suspects that to the end he trusted his personal spirit, or *sklaletut*, acquired in the rites of puberty, to preserve his soul, both on Tulalip Bay and across the river in the land of the ghosts. But one wonders if the parents of my University of Washington friend had not been Siwashes so long they could be saved only by a powerful outside intervenor such as the God of St. Anne's, adopted by Chief Sealth. There must have been some exceptional support for a girl whose features were not those of a walnut-stained Hollywood starlet but of Northwest Coast classic. Here where she lived, few finished grade school, and some her age had died of alcoholism before she entered the university. From 1942 to 1945—years when the blacks were called Negroes and kept to their ghetto south of the Lake Washington Ship Canal, and the Japanese had been exiled from the Pacific Coast or herded into detention camps—I rarely saw a non-European face at the UW.

The mouth of Tulalip Creek, in 1911 the site of a large pier, was a turmoil of construction today. A worker, a Tulalip, told me a fish farm was being added to the salmon-rearing pond that since 1970 had produced five million juvenile salmon for release. The next addition would be a hatchery. Then the Tulalips might be self-sufficient in the salmon business, no matter what was done by Ballard fishermen, Weyerhaeuser pulp mills, and hydroelectric dams.

By the creek was another enterprise, the Tulalip Smoke Shop, selling tax-free cigarettes and booze. Not yet two years clean, still deviled by cravings for a nicotine fix, I wished the Indians didn't feel the need to deal in dope.

It was fun, though, to visualize the shades of the 1865 pioneers watching Indians sell cheap whiskey to the whites.

Past Tulalip, another apparently pure white village (where *do* the Indians live?), I rounded the bay to the north tip, Hermosa Point. I sat on an erratic and gazed over the bay under a crescent moon, the tide at the full, house lights glowing on the shore and rippling in the water.

The mind blinked. Electric lights snapped off. From within the long house on the potlatch meadow came flickers of flames, aromas of baking salmon and steaming clams. It was the last night of olden times. Tomorrow morning the sloop-of-war *Discovery* would sail into the bay, cannon would boom, and thousands would die.

16. Kayak Point

Friday, January 13, 1978

All I knew about Port Susan was what I'd read in the papers—that in the 1960s Atlantic-Richfield planned a refinery, bay residents hired a sharp lawyer named Ehrlichman, ARCO fled to Whatcom County, and the lawyer went to the White House as an aide to President Nixon and, after Watergate, to prison.

I set out for Bellingham and discovered an unsuspected body of water fourteen miles long and two to six miles wide, enclosed on the west by Camano Island, opening on the south to Possession Sound.

On June 1, 1792, anchored off Kayak Point, one thing he didn't name, Vancouver named Port Susan for the wife of the admiral for whom he named Port Gardner. In 1841 the Wilkes expedition charted a depth of 40 feet remarkably close off the point. The 1911 map shows a docklike structure jutting out to that deep water. Yet the area has no visible means of economic support for a mosquito fleet or lumber schooners. Two more structures jut from the shore in the two miles north. Salmon on the way from the ocean, rounding the tip of Camano and aiming for the mouth of the Stillaguamish River, would hit all three. Fishtraps, by golly!

The tide chart listed a high of 13.1 feet at 8:19 a.m. My 10 o'clock arrival was premature. While waiting for the beach to appear, I toured Kayak Point County Park. The bluff was only 100 feet high and gentle and stable enough to permit a road down to the water. Huge Douglas firs grew on the slope, old wolves too mean for the loggers who came by boat in the nineteenth century and by railroad in the twentieth.

In a field above the bluff I was eyed by a four-legged wolf that appeared to be on the lookout for a sleighful of Russians; a ranger later told me the park's coyotes are famously large and arrogant. On the beach I leaped high in the air at the "Gark!" of a pterodactyl; the ranger said a dozen or more great blue herons are resident and a nearby heronry is suspected. A bald eagle sailed above, a common enough sight in salmon-spawning country in winter; the ranger said they stay all summer, which means nests. The ranger added that sometimes one scarcely could see the water of Port Susan for the fleets of waterfowl. There were reasons not to want ARCO here.

The three-quarter-mile-long park beach encompassed the best-preserved spit of the mainland from Seattle to Bellingham. The lagoon had been sacrificed to picnic tables and parking lots, but the driftwood was intact, and there were even bits of dune. The lack of a row of picture windows puzzled me, until the ranger explained that when ARCO was driven out of the county by the Port Susan militia, it sold its 670 acres to the people. As prudently as Standard Oil at Picnic Point, it retained thousands of surrounding acres upon which to build a new city, bragged up by realtors as an especially nice place to live because of its handiness to one of the great parks of the Whulj.

Expressing thanks to ARCO would have risked a rupture of the spleen. Nonetheless, I was pleased to have so neat and easy a put-in, and was ready to put my boots in as soon as the tide made room.

Lake water is like a puppy that won't bite, just licks your hands. Saltwater plays war games. A person can spend hours building a sand fortification, raising ramparts ever higher, reinforcing slumps, throwing out walls to block flank attacks, and in the final melee raising-reinforcing-extending until the denouement wave overwhelms all. Or one can dig holes in the sand to erect a fence of driftwood poles running out from the shore and in the evening sit by the fire watching each pole in turn be lapped, ringed, undermined, and toppled.

A lakeshore is a still photograph. Where the water is this morning is where it'll be tonight. What lives there today is what will be there tomorrow. Saltwater is a movie. The shoreline is a continuum of ups and downs, at the highs invading the sand fleas, at the lows exposing the anemones. The flood casts up the shells of clams, crabs and snails and corpses of jellyfish and starfish. The ebb amasses a Sargasso Sea of green, red and brown weedery, and entrapped driftwood, beer bottles, milk cartons, thongs, and frisbees. At the high there's the bracing tang of salt in the breeze, at the low the planetary stink of primordial soup.

The tides were as familiar as the beat of my heart—and as mysterious, sometimes frightening. That comes of living inland, not sleeping beside the water enough for the blood to learn their rhythms. In the course of this journey I did a little reading on the subject.

I learned a tide is caused not solely by the moon but also by the sun (46.6 percent as effectful), gravity, centrifugal force, something called the Chandler Wobble, and enough other factors to make a total of some 250 forces. I found there is not, as I'd always supposed, a single species of tide all over the world, but several, determined by the shapes and sizes of individual sea basins and their surrounding land masses. Some basins have a single tide cycle a day. The Mediterranean is virtually tideless!

The Whulj has two high-low cycles in a period of approximately 24 hours and 50 minutes, that being how long it takes the moon to orbit Earth. Thus, each day's tides are about fifty minutes later than on the previous day. Ours is a *mixed tide*, with some highs higher than others, and some lows lower than others.

My notion of the tide had always been of a single bulge of water that dogged the moon around Earth. To make this hypothesis tenable I'd had to deliberately avert my mental gaze from the fact of *two* daily cycles. Now I learned from my reading that what really happens is two simultaneous bulges on opposite sides of Earth, one a pull-up by the moon's gravity, the other a pushing outward by Earth's centrifugal force. But there are 250 complications, including the sun.

A bulge that on an all-water world would at once encompass one entire side of the planet is broken by land masses into the separate bulges of *tide basins* of various sizes. (Tides can be detected in lakes, and conceivably in bathtubs, and surely are in the blood.) Because the basin of the Whulj is tributary to the larger basin of the Pacific Ocean, our tidal bulges (highs) and intervening troughs (lows) "enter" and "leave" mostly through the Strait of Juan de Fuca (complicated by #251, the Strait of Georgia), so that highs and lows, generally speaking, come earlier near the ocean. However, since in open water the direct influence of the heavens combines with that of the ocean basin, in the larger expanses of the Whulj the difference in high-tide times between places nearer the ocean and farther is minor—between Kayak Point and Seattle for example—merely several minutes. But where waters are constricted, notably on the sea-in-the-forest, the bulges and troughs cause *tidal currents* that gain and lose velocity in bewildering fashion, and cause such "pile-ups" and "holes" that the difference from one place to another may be a half-hour or even two hours. The difference between highs may be different from that for lows or even reversed, and von Humboldt is seen tearing distractedly at his beard and hypothesizing dragons.

Because of the 250 complications, no formula has been devised to predict the time and height of a tide. Tide charts are patient accumulations over the years of observations at fixed stations, tabulations of the time and height of *high water* and *low water* and the difference—the *tide range*. The tide range increases as the tidal bulge moves farther into a narrowing passage because the normal lifting up that occurs in the open ocean is made even greater by the constriction of the bulge in the passage. (Tide is the up-down motion of the water; *tide currents* are the in-out motion as water is forced into a passage.) In the oceanlike northern mouth of Admiralty Inlet the *annual mean tide range* is a meager 4 feet; on the sea-in-the-forest of Olympia an awesome 10.5 feet. The *daily tide range* at Seattle is, some years, nearly 16 feet during extreme tides, and less than 2 feet in other tides.

From the past the future is predicted. Complexly. Never the same one year as the next. Some years the highest highs, which come in winter and summer, run above 14 feet at Seattle—one source lists a record of 14.63 feet and another 14.8 feet. (*Mean low tide is* 0 feet.) The lowest highs, which come in spring and fall, drop below 8 feet. In other years the highs of every month may be around 12 feet. Some years the lowest lows may be under –3 feet in June and January; one source gives –4.7 as Seattle's record; another says –4.87. (Anything lower than the mean low is a *minus tide*.) Sometimes the highest lows are above 7 feet. In any one month Seattle highs may vary 5 feet or more, the lows 10 feet. In stone towers around the Whulj and the world sit little old

Chaldean astronomers, with owls on their shoulders, working up horo-scopes and tide charts.

The greatest difference between high and low is on a *spring tide*. I'd always imagined this to be a celestial celebration of the vernal equinox, a time when true believers gathered by the waters to chant "Evoe!" Now I learned it occurs twice every month, near (only "near" because of the 250) new moon and full moon, when Earth is in a straight line with the sun and moon; the straight line combines their gravities for maximum bulge. The Seattle tide range then may be 16 feet. The "spring" derives from the Indo-European root s*pergh-,* with meanings in the area of "has-ten."

The least difference is on a *neap tide,* also twice monthly, near the first and last quarters of the moon when it, Earth, and the sun form a right angle. The Seattle range may then be less than 2 feet. The diction-ary informed me the term was *népflód* in Old English, from the same root as *hnappian* ("doze, nap"), the Low German nibbeln ("nibble"), and Old Norse *hnögge* ("miserly").

The amateur runs helter-skelter to the beach whenever a Blue Hole calls, and that's well and good when there's a railroad to organize the shore. The professional, however, must plot strategy in advance.

> When water loiters at the neap,
> All day the feet can dare to creep.

For hours during a neap tide the miserly water lies napping lakelike, at most nibbling. The beach of morning is the beach of evening. No flood will send the walker to the wall, nor will any ebb expose broad plains of shining sand.

> When water rises in a spring,
> The frightened feet had best take wing.

Impossible to believe until witnessed is a tide range in a single day of 16 feet—the height of a three-high pyramid of standing humans. At the ebb one suspects a dragon has pulled the plug on the ocean. At the flood one worries for the mountain peaks. The hastening of a spring tide is fearsome. The water that lies so beauteous and benign at the low stirs to demonic vigor, attacks the land, and pursues the walker, chasing him up the wall into the hellberries.

Though Kayak Point came early in my education, already I was learning that except during a neap it was prudent to consult the chart for the *time of high water*. If it came at midday, better to skip the beach and go survey a river or a mountain. Today's tide was ideal—outgoing to a low at 2:30, and not enough hours of incoming after that to affect my return.

The *height of high water*, I'd learned, opens the subtler study of how much beach to expect in any given place at any given time. Virtually all beach-making—which is done by bluff-attacking—occurs in *storms at high water*. The waveless water of a calm day may fail to reach the base of a (stable) bluff even at a (forecast) high of 12 or 13 feet. In calm weather a high of 10 or 11 feet usually leaves a narrow (natural) beach, and at 9 feet or under the avenue is dependably wide.

The above parentheses are crucial. About "stable": Many bluffs are *not,* and when a chunk slides to the water the waves may take a whole winter to chew it away. There may, meanwhile, be no beach at that spot until the ebb nears 0, and the mass of muck up to the knees and the trees in a jackstraw heap may daunt any walker but a berserker. About "natural": Bulkheads and seawalls may so invade the wave-cut bench that at 9 feet of water a 6-foot walker may need a 4-foot snorkel. About "forecast": See below.

The *height of low water* often is significant. *Feeble-wave beaches,* even at low water, tend to be overhung by alders and maples that hang inches from the sand, a brushfight for any creature taller than a weasel. Fallen trees lie undisturbed for years, growing slimy with seaweed and crusty with barnacles. On the sea-in-the-forest, the only decent beachwalking may be on mud flats exposed at the low. (Between the inner, firm-graveled beach and the outer mud flat there often is a narrow band of soupy sand-mud that sucks the legs in and scares the novice beachwalker; further out the mud usually firms up. But not always.) *Strong-wave beaches* steepened by *powerful longshore currents* may be gravel sidehills where a pace of even one mile an hour is a weary plod; the only easy walking may be on firm sands of a wave-built terrace exposed at quite a low low, and then only for a few hours, a time to unleash the feet and let them triple the pace.

Now, about "forecast":

The morning of December 16, 1977, Dad glanced out the window of his house on Hood Canal—and stared. The dock had vanished! But there'd been no storm in the night, the water was quiet and glassy. As he marveled, the dock reappeared. It had been submerged by a high that at 9:40 a.m. had been 13.9 feet in Seattle, 1.2 feet above the tide chart's prediction. (So says one source—others of the little damn Chaldeans measured 14.6 and 14.8 feet and said it—whichever— was Seattle's all-time record.)

Today on Kayak Point I saw amid picnic tables a litter of small drift. Among the 250 factors is the weather. The Chaldeans chart only the theoretical *astronomical tides*, not the real-world *meteorological tides*. They do not try to forecast a "sunshine tide" with high atmospheric pressure that depresses the water level, causing tides lower than expected, nor the "storm tides."

On that December 16, there occurred a conjunction of three factors: First, a spring tide (twice-monthly event); second, heavy, warm, snow-pack-melting rains in the mountains that caused rivers to dump more water into the Whulj than it could quickly flush to the ocean (which happens two or three times during a normal winter); and third, a deep storm centered offshore in the Pacific, its extremely low pressure extending inland over the Whulj (an event of every other winter or so). This Conjunction of Three quietly raised glassy water over the driftwood of Kayak Point, over the dune, through the picnic tables and parking lots, into the restrooms.

What if there had been a Fourth—gales of a deep storm *not* staying out in the Pacific but blowing on in, stirring the Whulj to a fury of surf?

17. Kayak Point to Tulalip Mile 61$^1/_2$–54

Friday, January 13, 1978

Two hours after the high, the bay was as full as ever, nibbling at the driftwood, maddeningly neapish. Yet in the next four hours, said science—contrary to what any sane person could believe—it would drop nine feet. If it did, Port Susan would have to expel enough water to flood an area the size of the city of Seattle to a depth of five or six feet. Where would it all go?

Where had it all come from?

Earthquakes, volcanic eruptions, meteors, tornadoes, the flip-flop of the magnetic poles, things that go bump—these excite or awe or terrify us. But twice a day, every day, the Whulj undergoes a monstrous convulsion and we accept it as blithely as we do the sun's explosions that amount to many hydrogen bombs a day.

Pacing up and down the spit was jittering my feet. I'd once asked a friend who'd quit cigarettes before me how long it was until he felt free. He took a swallow of Scotch, pondered, and spoke from a darkness: "Two years." I had months to go. In the predawn of this Friday the 13th I'd been wakened by a sudden fright:

> Walking, lads, walking's the trick
> For fellows whom it scares to tick.

At 10:30 I began clambering southward over slid-down alders and washed-in logs between jungle wall and wavelets. To what end?

> spin mehitabel spin
> you had a romantic past
> and you re gonna cash in dancing
> when you are croaked at last

I said the hell with dry feet and waded knee-deep around a log jam to McKees Beach, a crudely unclassic spit, the tip bent against the shore. Inside the driftwood lay a half-mile row of old summer cottages converted to commuter homes. Strewn outside the driftwood was a litter of other homes whose residents had been boiled, scooped out, and eaten; offshore buoys marked crab pots waiting under the water to entrap centerpieces for Whulj bacchanals of tossed salad and garlic bread and the cry of "Wine, wine, more wine. Bring on the dancing cats!"

The village had been depopulated by some plague, and dogs had inherited the earth. They barked me along the half-mile, home dogs guarding hearths. Home dogs had sat by the pyramids and barked at the Hyksos. But rover dogs accompanied Mongol yurts across Asia and lifted their legs on the Great Wall of China. Often these winter days I, the only available human, accumulated a gang of walking dogs, conquering dogs, who were not humiliated to be led by a beard, umbrella, and a rucksack protected from rain by a plastic garbage bag. I would slink swiftly by houses, trying to dissociate myself from my rowdy companions who committed nuisances on doorsteps. Picture windows glowered at the ragged old khan and his mongrel horde. At McKees Beach I recruited a German shepherd who brought me a stick to throw, splashed far out into the bay to retrieve it, then shook himself dry and me wet, the immemorial ritual by which dog swears allegiance to man.

In leaving the spit I entered (said the map) the Tulalip Reservation. A wild bluff leaped to 320 feet and a bulge cut me off from Kayak Point. Ahead stretched miles of the unknown, lands and waters resembling my home waters, yet not quite it. There was a disturbing feeling of lakeness: unlike four-doored Possession Sound and multi-doored Puget, Port Susan had but a single door. Moreover, Camano Island, the land across the water, lay intimately close to the mainland, not at a haze-dimmed distance, as lay the Bainbridge-Kitsap shores opposite my Golden Gardens, Carkeek Park, and Richmond Beach. This was not where I came from and that was good for the adventure, but bad for the loneliness that made the sound of my voice, talking to myself, spooky.

My dog attacked the forest. Birds flurried in the bushes. A snow-white beast lept out and streaked across the sand, pursued by the Hun. Some cats sleep by the fire, some go hunting—and are hunted. Dogs chase cats. Coyotes eat cats; mehitabel knows that.

Two herons garked overhead.

For a mile the bluff showed no signs of man, then trails appeared. The 1911 map shows a path from the beach up the bluff to several houses and a logging railroad; the nowadays trails descended 80 feet from a fossil beach terrace perched above the water. The map calls its dozen houses "Sunny Shores." Today there was not so much as a bright spot in the gray sky and the "shores" consisted of boathouses that thrust out into chest-deep water, forcing me to climb a bulkhead to get by. My Teuton took revenge by assaulting the terrace and brutalizing the home dogs.

Three herons garked on high.

Offshore a line of floats supported nets spread across the route of salmon headed for the Stillaguamish River.

I rounded a bulge to wildness. The barking faded. Then, again, humanity snuggled up to the water, again on an unclassic spit. The 1911 map shows a scrap of lagoon, long since obliterated by the half-mile row of boxes on Tulare Beach, the name under which the developers advertised lots for sale.

The dog town mobilized to repel my solitary panzer. The bedlam was certain to bring riot police. When my Beast of Berlin came galumphing back from his raid to be kissed on both cheeks and awarded medals I commanded, "Go home!" He recoiled, aghast, then turned and slunk north, casting reproachful glances over his shoulder.

At noon I rounded the farthest-out bulge of the day to a mile of perfect solitude beneath a naked gravel cliff, the brink 220 feet above my head. I sat on a log to eat kipper snacks, an apple, and drink a Pepsi. Hat Island was framed between the tip of Camano Island and the peninsula enclosing Tulalip Bay. The Scott plume billowed from Mill Town.

I missed my dog. I'd no right to send him home in disgrace. It had been his expedition, too, and he'd been doing his duty brilliantly. In the 12,000 years since humans and canines came to an agreement, our dogs have fought our battles, shared our kills. When we descended from the North to destroy the Roman Empire, our dogs whipped theirs. When we chased the Celts out of England into Wales, their miserable curs tucked their tails between their legs and ran with them. When The People crossed the land bridge from Asia, did dogs come too? Or did humans and canines form their alliance only after the journey? Were North America's pre-Columbian dogs natives, or immigrants like the rest of us? Anyhow, after these 12,000 years it's not natural for a man to go walking without a dog.

In a blufftop snag perched an eagle. To become an Eagle Scout I'd hunted birds from winter to fall of 1940, armed with a book from the Seattle Public Library and binoculars obtained for two Wheaties boxtops and twenty-five cents in coin or stamps. I'd earned a bird study merit badge, required for Eagle rank, by identifying fifty birds. Over the years I'd lost some of those and gained a few others. These winter days on the beach, living more with birds than people or even dogs, I was thinking about buying real binoculars. Even lacking them, at this lunch stop the Audubon booklet let me identify the common murre, surf scoter, and goldeneye.

While stowing lunch garbage in my rucksack I reflected on the amazingly clean beach here, away from Main Street, the only traffic being play boats, fishing boats, and clamming dredges, a fleet that in a year can't generate the garbage of a single breakfast aboard a Korean freighter.

I walked on, the beach wide and tangle-free, to the end of the wild mile. Suddenly the air was full of flying children, swinging out from the bluff on a rope dangled from a Douglas fir that leaned over the beach. They let go of the rope and plummeted shrieking to the sand, ker-whump. High tide obviously would be more fun, ker-splash.

The bluff was indented by a bowl, result of some glacial antic. Cottages nestled in meadows and fir groves, old and grown-in. Beside the beach was a community park with lawn, picnic tables, boat-launch ramp, and the Stars and Stripes. The new map calls it Spee-Bi-Dah, whatever that means; the 1911 map has it Subeebeda, obviously a summer colony, with a half-dozen houses. Piling stubs remained; the ten miles from City Dock in Everett would have taken a steamer an hour or less. There was a new alternative in 1911: Subeebeda lay at the end of the road from Marysville, and though the auto route from Everett was a roundabout twenty miles, the drive would have taken little more than an hour.

Wild bluff resumed. A fishing boat passed close. After hours of lapping the bay awoke in a flurry of slapping. Nets were being tended by men in small boats. Tulalips? The shore curved out to a narrow strip of not-quite-complete beach in the lee of a bulge, scant space for the boxes of Tulalip Shores.

Again, past the bulge, solitude. The tide was rushing out, the sand avenue widening by the minute. I took a swerving route, now beside the wavelets and far from the bluff, now close against the wall. The bluff rose 200 very vertical and beautifully naked feet, a mural depicting millennia of meltwater streams (sand and gravel), lakes (varved clay), and glacial snout (unsorted till, some of it studding the beach with boulders).

Hermosa Point at the mouth of Tulalip Bay drew close, Hat Island beyond the mouth of Port Susan grew large, the industrial hum of Everett loud, the aroma rich. A train horn linked me to Mill Town. Yet I was on the longest, lonesomest beach of the day, one and a half pristine miles, the purest wilderness of the walk.

In Howard Zahniser's definition, embodied in the Wilderness Act of 1964, wilderness is an area where "the earth and its community of life are untrammeled by man, where man himself is a visitor who does not remain."

There isn't any, not anymore.

There was in that 1938 sunset when I gazed west from Marmot Pass. Since then man has trammeled the planetary air and water with the ingenuities of chemists and physicists. He has so trammeled the peace with the roar of exploding hydrocarbons that God's thunder often goes unheard, so trammeled the darkness with the glare of electricity that His lightning goes unseen. He has trammeled with motorcycles that burp and fart along the trail of Daniel Boone, snowmobiles that whine and belch where Peary and Amundsen sledged, airplanes that reveal to every See-Europe-in-Two-Weeks traveler the mysteries of the Greenland Ice-cap, swamp buggies that churn through the Okefenokee where Pogo's friend Churchy commented as Albert's cigar fell in the lemonade, "We have met the enemy and he is us."

Though the individuals may be visitors, when they form an unbro-ken parade the species *does* remain. In 1950 I was in a small group that doubled the number of humans who in all history had entered Luna Cirque in the Picket Range of the North Cascades; nowadays nobody bothers to count the numbers who climb the peaks there every summer. In 1951 two other snowshoers and I likely were the first ever to traverse the blue Blue Glacier on Mount Olympus in winter; nowadays hardly a snowflake falls that is not quickly squashed by the skis of scientists who commute from universities across America. Zahniser wrote in the 1950s, when genuine, pure wilderness was still abundant. In a single generation we've trammeled it all.

Something survives: In the Glacier Peak Wilderness and Olympic National Park, because not every meadow swarms with Kelty packs and the skies are not constantly racketed by Navy hooligans breaking the sound barrier. And in the vacant lot down the street where after-school safaris explore scotchbroom-and-alder jungles of the Dark Continent. And in the marsh next to the garbage dump where Sunday voyagers pad-dle rafts in search of the Northwest Passage, because though the whole world be tamed, the inner man (boy or girl) may yet be wild.

The mood is the thing—a mood never attained on machines or in simian crowds, and easily shattered, yet sure to prevail if you've got it in you and the apes will just let you alone for a minute.

It's not necessary to go to the Himalaya or Antarctica. Bluffs of the Whulj are as virgin as any land on the planet, and when molested have the power to renew their virginity, a mystery deep and true enough to be Eleusinian. I didn't know on this Friday the 13th, but would learn before I got to Bellingham, that the most virginal long stretches of the mainland shore north of Seattle are on Port Susan, climaxing in these one and a half miles of bluff-guarded beach, wilder for sure than the trekkers' garbage dump at Everest Base Camp or the scientists' winter resort at the South Pole.

White head nobly white, a mature bald eagle sailed close over the sands.

The afternoon darkened, winds stirred. Trammeling began with the old houses of Arcadia tucked in creases of the bluff. Bulkheads forced me far out in cold water, up to my hips. Emerging on steep, green-slimy cobbles I fell and banged knee and head. Stars exploded in my eyeballs. It was still Friday the 13th and I'd miles to go to the beetle parked at Kayak Point. But first I limped to Hermosa Point and looked into Tulalip Bay. A German shepherd ran up to say hello. Was it mine? He seemed confused. He ran south, the wrong way. A different dog, I hoped.

In the final minutes of the ebb, the current was racing south, sluicing driftwood navies with it. The bay was pitted by raindrops. I raised my umbrella and turned north in the glooming, electric lights already winking on Camano Island. Through the rain came the smell, as old as my nose, of burning driftwood. I'd not reach Kayak before night, a night perhaps as dark as the one in the week after Pearl Harbor when the U.S. Army suspected me of being a Japanese spy. The flood might cut me off, leaving me to beg for mercy from the picture windows. My knee throbbed, my head was light, my feet were wet and my hips too, and it was raining hard and cold and my dog was lost.

At the end of Arcadia I began the wild mile and a half. Beneath a jungle with no trace of trail, a broken shack sagged on rotten pilings. Somewhere there must be people of my age for whom these shores held memories of leaping from bed at dawn to make barefoot tracks on tide-cleansed sands, and sitting around a beachfire under the stars singing songs, toasting marshmallows, and crying from the smoke.

> my youth i shall never forget
> but there s nothing i really regret
> wotthehell wotthehell

there s a dance in the old dame yet
toujours gai toujours gai

18. Kayak Point to Hat Slough   Mile 61½–68

Tuesday, November 22, 1977

The temperature was 30 degrees, the sky a heavy, pregnant gray, and it was rash to leave Cougar Mountain at all, but innards were awry and far to the north shone a band of blue. At 10 o'clock I set out from Kayak Point, casting a long shadow forward in gleaming sand. Briefly, until the edge of darkness caught up with me.

The north end of the spit, outside the park, had a half-dozen houses; in 1911 there were three, connected up the bluff to a road from the Stillaguamish River. Then commenced one and a half miles of beach intruded on only by staircases and paths. From the outlet of one trail, where there had been a fishtrap in 1911, jutted a dock. A sand slope below a cliff was pitted with craters exploded by small bodies jumping from the brink.

The small bodies were not abroad today. It was an hour to nail up the shutters, batten down the hatches, bugle patrols back to the fort. The blue retreated farther north; the snows of Komo Kulshan, two miles high, still shone rosy-bright—but cold, cold as in that winter dawn when we cramponed the Coleman Glacier. The south grew darker; the Olympics were as grim as in that winter twilight when we snowshoed the Blue Glacier. From mainland to Camano Island, Port Susan was deserted, silent, the water dead on the beach, the air still as a tomb. Ducks swimming, gulls wheeling, hawk sailing, killdeer running, me walking, all were watching for the first snowflake.

At 10:45 I rounded a bulge (in 1911, a fishtrap here) to bluff's end; the slope was suddenly so gentle that not a single but a triple row of houses paralleled the beach. Hip to hip they fronted the shore—old summer cabins remodeled for year-round living, and new picture-window cedar boxes. They bellied out bulkheads and boathouses, and from these pricked out iron-rail and concrete-ramp boat launches. For a solid-built mile I walked by windows and saw not a single human and just one dog, a shivering mutt too dispirited to go walking, too miserable to bark.

The rows of houses curved inland around a soggy meadow recognizable as a filled lagoon. In 1911 Birmingham was here, a cluster of two dozen structures. A logging railroad switchbacked up the slope inland. Not shown on the map but still upright in the water were old pilings where the railhead used to be. Booming grounds, obviously. The pilings couldn't have been for a mill, nor a dock to load lumber ships. I *knew* that.

I knew that because I *knew this place.*

On a Saturday evening in 1938 my Troop 324 made camp in the lagoon meadow. The tide was high, waves rattled a shingle beach, and we anticipated a bracing swim before breakfast. Sunday morning the bay was gone! From the narrow strip of shingle a vastness of mud sprawled a quarter-mile to water's edge, and once there we had to wade another quarter-mile to a depth sufficient for legs and arms to flail and even then it wasn't proper swimming—not with toes and knees, elbows and bellies squishing mud, stirring a thick, warm soup. Warm.

Though the temperature of Elliott Bay, enclosed and industrialized, rises from a February average of 46.7 degrees to 55.8 in August, open waters of the Whulj, such as at Richmond Beach, are substantially the same in summer as winter. Temperatures of the sea-in-the-forest climb higher, which is why a respectable native no more will swim there than in a heated pool, lewd as a hot tub, or a lowland lake, incubator of loathsome diseases. However, most of the Whulj most of the time, summer as well as winter, is as clean and decent as an alpine tarn ringed by snow.

When Troop 324 swam here, it no longer was called Birmingham, but Warm Beach. The mud-bottomed, scarcely watered waterway was warm as a pool, infested as a lowland lake. Shuddering, I waded ashore, microbes creeping all over my body. Afterward, I so completely erased the place from the history of my life as not even to remember where it was.

I'd felt foreboding this morning when leaving Cougar Mountain. I knew, then, the blue was simply the bait.

A person who is recovering from an addiction to dope and has had a bad night's sleep and drinks too much coffee and then goes walking a lonesome beach, studying a 1911 map and watching for snowflakes, and who unexpectedly finds himself in 1938, may lose track of the direction of time's arrow and find Troop 324, Indians, booming grounds, woolly mammoths, logging railroads, fishtraps, glacier, and snowstorm all higgledly-piggledy together.

A person too much alone may wonder if he has a hole in the seat of his britches and start feeling around back there as he walks. Or he may talk to himself—not a cause for worry until he starts talking back. He surely will talk to the birds and the beasts, and, after a few days in the wilderness, to the rivers and trees and rocks as well—no cause for worry until he starts lying awake at night listening to them talk about him.

On a day of the previous winter I'd climbed alone through silent fog in virgin snow, enveloped by a dense whiteness above, below, and all around. It struck me that this was how it must have been at the end of the first day, when God had decreed that there be light and divided it from the darkness but had not yet made the firmament, much less Earth. In all this raw material that later would become Creation, the sole evidence of form and being other than my body was the line of my boot tracks. Returning along them that afternoon I had nothing else to look at, nothing else for my eyes to fix upon. Whatever a hypnotic trance may be, I had walked myself into one. It came to me that I wasn't sure who had made the tracks. I glanced over my shoulder—tracks were there, following. I stared ahead into dimness—tracks were there, approaching. Tracks were ahead and behind in the fog, coming and going, the thens were tangled with the now, and I was fragmented. Shadows coagulated in white void, dissolved. There he *is*. No, *there!* Who?

He was on the beach.

Never on a winter midweek had I seen another beachwalker. It was a thing that I, peculiarly and uniquely, did. It was the definition of me. Today was winter, midweek, and he was on the beach.

Swiftly we converged, impelled north and south by our mutual fate. In passing I glanced at his face—and saw my fear mirrored.

At the end of the one-time bay the bluff resumed, but in leaping upward, it left the beach to swing far inland—not to curve around another bay, but for some new, large, dread purpose. Not so much as a bank edged the shore, only a willow swamp. My right flank, secured by solid bluff the length of Puget Sound, Possession Sound, and, until now, Port Susan, was exposed. A mystery: the beach was littered with shattered ice. Another: it was dotted with tufts of grass.

Now the willow swamp swung inland and I was even more exposed on a narrow beach of grassy sand and shingle, between reedy marsh on my right and frozen bay on my left. The panes of ice that crackled underfoot were fragments of a sheet that had formed atop the high tide, been left unsupported by the ebb, had collapsed under gravity and shattered, and been washed in by the new flood.

Boots flipped out from under, knee smashed on a sharp boulder, head thumped frozen sand. After lying a while on my back in the ice I sat up to watch the blood welling from the rip in my pants. I stood and almost fell again. I wondered how saltwater could *freeze,* and how a *sharp* boulder came to be on the beach.

The beach ended. Ice to the left, reeds to the right. Giddy and ill I reeled from bunchgrass hummock to hummock, leaping ditches bottomed by terrible black muck.

In 1792 Vancouver sought to land here but could find no land. In 1841 the supremely methodical Charles Wilkes became so disoriented he failed to locate the mouth of the Stillaguamish River.

The *river:* That's why the bay was frozen—mountain water diluted the salt. That's why it was a mud flat—the silt of ground-up mountains filled the deeps.

The edge of dark had advanced north beyond Twin Sisters; Canada alone lay under the blue. Its turn would come. Everybody's turn would come. The sky to the south was homogeneous gray—a snow sky.

The tide was on the rise. The flood was oozing through reeds and around hummocks, filling the ditches. I'd known at the outset that a retreat to Kayak Point would be impossible and had planned to return overland by road. Now I was cut off even from Warm Beach. Sick at stomach, light in head, throbbing of knee, and shivering to the bone, I leaped through cattails, retreated in panic from cul de sacs, looped witlessly this way and that. The final ditch was wider than the world's record for the standing broad jump, but I flew across on wings of terror, clambered up a mysterious slope of boulders (not wave-rounded, but sharp as those blasted in a quarry, like the one that had sliced me to the blood). From the secure crest a dozen feet above muck and ice, I looked down the far side to cows chewing cuds.

I hobbled onward along the elevated causeway, pasture below to my right, marsh to my left. When the dike turned right I side-tripped left on a finger of marsh grass that led out to the open waters of Port Susan, here swollen to a gulf five miles wide. A mile inland behind me, steadily dimming in the thickening air, rose the bluff. I felt the horror that grips the vitals of a mountain man strayed out on the Great Plains.

I returned to the dike and followed it to the river—Hat Slough—a "slough" because as late as the 1911 map it was a secondary outlet of the Stillaguamish, though by the time of the 1956 map it had become the main outlet. My second river, thirty miles from the Everett Massacre. How far to my third? Would I like the delta? There were reasons to think not.

The dike and farm lane led up the slough to Marine Drive. A thumb in the air took me partway to Kayak Point. Feet finished the job at 3 o'clock. At Everett I drove into the snowstorm, and at 5 o'clock I abandoned the beetle in a churchyard at the foot of Cougar Mountain, shouldered my rucksack, and amid jackstrawed commuters' automobiles, and snowflakes dancing as smartly as an alley kat, limped bloody-legged through the night, climbing to the 200-meter hut.

> dance mehitabel dance
> caper and shake a leg
> what little blood is left
> will fizz like wine in a keg

PART THREE

The Northern Isles

ENDLESS SUMMER

THE WHITE CLIFFS OF WHIDBEY

THE WHIDBEY LEE

THE WEST COAST OF WHIDBEY

THE DEATH TRIANGLE

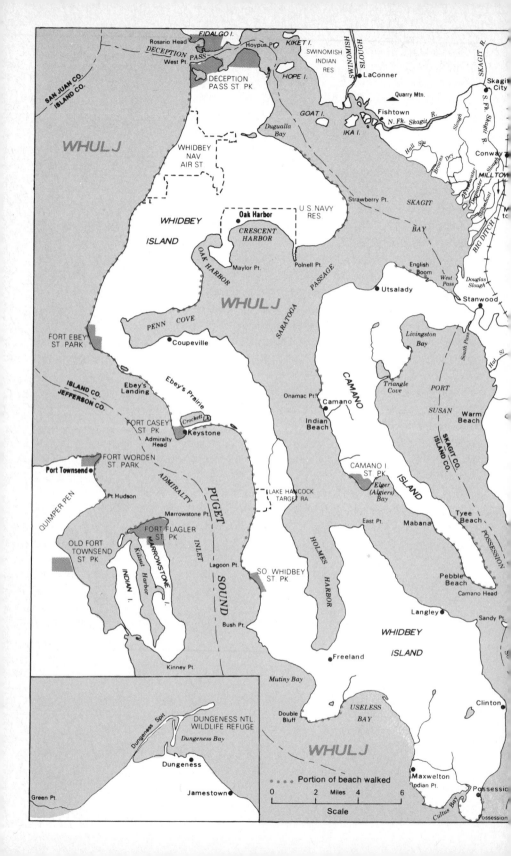

19. Camano Island

Thursday, February 9, 1978

During the Joint Occupation that ended by agreement in 1846, the United States and Great Britain disputed ownership of the area between the Columbia River and the parallel remembered in history for the cry of the war hawks in Congress, "54-40 or fight." Charles Wilkes, in 1841, campaigning for the Stars and Stripes, filled maps with names of American victories and heroes, among them, "McDonough's Island." In this case he was defeated by a British cartographer who chose to honor Lieutenant Jacinto Caamano, commander of one of the five Spanish ships exploring the Northwest Coast in 1792. Caamano's realm lay far north of the island in question but even American geographers agreed he was more relevant to the area than the hero of the Battle of Lake Champlain.

"Camano." Penetrating through the Indian and the Anglo-Saxon, the wet and the cold, it was a breath of southern sun, hidalgos, armadas and gold, senoritas, castanets and orange blossoms.

Were my feelings borrowed from forgotten stories told me by forgotten friends, or were they seeping up from my own submerged memories? "Camano" to me was joy and love and endless summer.

Summer was on the other side of the world as I walked the spit of Point Lowell (named for a Wilkes crewman) on a Thursday morning all bluster and melodrama. Waves spanked along by an eighteen-knot wind rolled the two miles across Saratoga Passage (named for the lead ship in the Battle of Lake Champlain) and smashed to white smithereens. Beyond the waters, and the forest of Whidbey Island, a turmoil of sky framed the ice-bright Olympics. Low clouds raced north. A sunburst suddenly electrified whitecaps and picked out a pair of eaglets. Pussywillows were budding!

I rounded the bluff of Point Lowell to the baymouth bar and lagoon marsh of "Elger Bay," as modern maps call it. Surely the map of 1911 is correct in calling it "Algiers Bay." In 1815, just twenty-six years before Wilkes arrived here—and in the very year that he, as a lad of seventeen, entered the Merchant Marine Service—Commodore Decatur whipped the navy of the Dey of Algiers and proceeded to humble Tunis and Tripoli, concluding the War Against the Barbary States and solacing a young country whose national pride had been recently mortified by the Englishmen's burning of the White House.

Sunday, February 12, 1978

Since Thursday, I'd talked to Dad about Camano and knew there were memories to be found. He couldn't remember the name of the exact place; it would be a matter of feeling my way. My wife, Betty, joined me for a day of searching.

We began on the north end of the island, drawn by the oddity on the map, "English Boom." Why "boom?" Were the English any more percussive than any of the island's other visitors?

The woods road descended a hillside to driftwood and a lagoon in the zone of combat between the longshore currents pushing east and the silts of the Stillaguamish delta pushing west. We walked a mile east to the end of the beach in marsh grass, and a mile west to glass-and-cedar ticky-tack piled on the spit of Browns Point. Much of our way was paralleled offshore by a forest of pilings. Of course! The log booming grounds of the English Logging Company, property of the famous Mr. English, who here assembled logs from the Stillaguamish and Skagit valleys for rafting to the mills.

Thursday had ended in snow squalls. Today the sky was frozen blue, beach logs frosted white. Skagit Bay, fifteen miles long and five miles wide, merged with the vaster sea of the Skagit delta—what appeared at first to be islets were clumps of farmyard trees. From the edge of the great Skagit flat the Cascade front rose 4,000 feet up to the twin humps of Cultus Mountain and Woolley-Lyman, gateway peaks facing each other across the Skagit valley. The ice mound of Komo Kulshan was near enough to chill our bones. North over the border in Canada were white giants, unknown to us. Amid this geography on such a gigantic scale a little Bonaparte's gull chased a great blue heron around the bay.

From Browns Point we walked south under the bluff to Utsalady ("land of berries"). Here in 1853 Camano Island's first white settler began logging. He shipped pilings to San Francisco; loaded the first full cargo of spars from the Whulj, some for the French and Spanish navies; and in 1857 started a sawmill. The Paris Exhibition featured an Utsalady flagpole 150 feet high and 24 inches around at the base. A railroad was schemed, a college planned, and a canal envisioned through Whidbey Island to the Strait of Juan de Fuca. But in 1870 the Hall Brothers Ship-yard moved to Port Blakely, in 1896 the mill closed, and the 1911 map shows barely a dozen houses.

Our 1978 eyes saw houses by the hundreds—on baymouth bar, bluff terraces, blufftop—thousands of glowering picture windows. We retreated, and none too soon, as we looked back to see that we were being pursued by a rich lady brandishing a rake. It was Sunday and sunny, and poor people were forbidden to go near the water.

In olden times there were so few people, and so much waterfront, there was room on the beaches for the rich and the poor, and plenty to spare. Anyone could afford to buy a lot and throw up a shack or at least rent one for the summer. Cabin colonies were clustered around the steamer docks at Fletcher's Bay, Indianola and Lemolo, the places where Mother and her family summered, and at Richmond Beach, Pic-nic Point, Subeebeda, and hundreds of other spots from the sea-in-the-forest to the San Juan Islands. As soon as school let out in June, the mothers and the kids would head for the cabin and settle down to relearn how to live without electricity, gas, ice, central heating, and indoor plumbing; how to dig clams, whittle driftwood sticks, sing around the beachfire and mess about in boats. The fathers would "bach" in town during the week, arrive by steamer for the weekends.

Other families were strictly weekenders, staying at their own cabins or with friends, or with aunts and uncles and cousins, by whose dozens there were sure to be enough beach properties to accommodate the whole clan, not to mention the whole population of Seattle.

The golden age of summering-on-the-beach ended with the death of the mosquito fleet. Car ferries were more expensive and never so care-free. A hungry, sunburnt, played-out family desperate to get back to the city might very well watch the ferry pull out, full, leaving them stranded on the dock. Camano, however, has not really been an island since the Stillaguamish silted in the seaway between Port Susan and Skagit Bay.

Engineers finished the job in 1912, by replacing the cable ferry with a bridge. Old summer colonies and new came within easy weekend reach of Seattle, and families that once rode the mosquitoes to Bainbridge and Vashon now took highways to Camano.

Betty and I drove the east shore alongside Port Susan, the sheltered lee, passing by weaknesses in the bluff that let roads down to the baymouth bars, spits and fossil beaches—Lona Beach, Driftwood Shores, Cavelero Beach, Camano Country Club, Mountain View Beach, Cornell, Sunny Shores Acres, Tillicum Beach, Tyee Beach. No memories for me here.

Our search then turned to the west shore, Saratoga Passage, the weather side of the island. The bluff here also had many weaknesses and the settlements were as old as the mosquito fleet: Maple Grove Beach, Rocky Point, Camp Grande, Camp Lagoon, Madrona Beach, Sunset Beach, Rockaway Beach, Woodland Beach, Camano, Indian Beach, Cama Beach, Saratoga Shores.

A developer's road, not yet signposted "PRIVATE," gave us access to a splendid spit newly named Onamac Point (presumably to repeat the success of Serutan). We walked south to Camano, a village with a 1920s flavor, then north under a 280-foot bluff, a fine and lonesome mile. On a small terrace a derelict cabin sagged, windows broken but roof intact, the handsome fireplace crafted of beach cobbles. The privy still stood. The well held water. The trail was overgrown.

A bit further north by a creek, another terrace held a much-used campsite, fresh ashes in the fire ring, the bluff trail well trampled. Campers had come here by foot and boat for decades—or, for centuries. In the brown humus of the wave-cut bank gleamed a white layer of clam shells—a kitchen midden.

The sun had fallen by now into western clouds. In twilight a silent canoe passed close, cleaving oil-smooth waters. We hadn't found the place, but it was nearby. Sometime during the afternoon we'd been there.

If two people are properly small, they can both fit on the window shelf behind the seat of a Model A coupe. Between 1941 and 1947, the years I owned my A, I often regretted growing up to a lummox.

Once upon a time there was a place where the sun was always shining on the waves and sands at the edge of the forest camp where two Model A's were parked. One was our sedan, but I preferred Aunt

Ruth's and Uncle Mort's coupe and sharing the shelf with Patsy. Born the same summer, more twins than cousins, we were on the beach together all day and whispering in bed long after we were supposed to be asleep. In our special spot for which we were just the perfect size, we rode back and forth to the perfect place—Camano, where summer never ends.

20. Camano Head

Friday, February 10, 1978

It was from Mukilteo, far to the south, that the tall bulk of Camano Head first caught my eye. Through the salt haze it had the look of a great ship, a super-galleon, its high, blunt bow cleaving the blue plane of Possession Sound sailing south. Relative to the north-flowing currents it truly *was* sailing south, over the year averaging several knots, and had been doing so for maybe 5,000 years, the equivalent of 5,000 circumnavigations of the globe. The millennia of bow-battering waves had shaped Camano Head into one of the tallest, steepest bluffs of the Whulj.

The problem for a walker wanting to get there was the put-in. The uplands of Camano's south end are empty, the second-growth forest broken only by scattered fields of old starvation-acre farms. The shore is another story—of the post-World War II fulfillment of the American dream of life after work. Every road to the water was sternly signposted "PRIVATE."

Except at Mabana (a word seeming Spanish but actually named for the initial letters of a settler's daughter, Mabel Anderson, with the "a" tacked on for euphony). Of the six structures noted south of Algiers Bay on the 1911 map, two were here, where a flaw in the bluff made a way for farm wagons to descend to the water. Though the steamer dock is long gone, the Port of Mabana lives on as a public boat-launching ramp.

At 10:45 I turned south from the ramp, just as the sun burned through a morning fog. Umbrella, sweater, and stocking cap could be left in the beetle. The tide was ideal, dropping to a low at 1 o'clock. A cliff of naked sand footed in clean blue clay stood 100 feet tall, and the map showed miles of dense brown contours, meaning miles of solitude.

The cliff was low enough the first mile for blufftoppers to descend on trails and staircases and electric contraptions; but except for pilings to protect staircases and picnic terraces, the shore was scarcely bothered. Then a boulder bulkhead forced me up on the rocks to skulk between back doors and bluff jungle. It's these beach invaders who need that lesson "by which God teaches the law to man." Back down, another lonesome mile led to a beautiful large spit curving out to enclose a lovely lagoon that emptied through dune grass and driftwood to a beach-trenching creek. The 1911 map shows the buildings and dock of the logging camp that operated here until 1916. Time had repaired the damage but barbarians had returned—southward from the spit ran a mile of boxes-on-bulkheads.

At the end of the line, I found an elderly naval man, obviously retired from the crew of H.M.S. *Pinafore*. He displayed for my admiration his home-made cableway for hoisting firewood logs to his blufftop cabin, and the wooden cockleshell of a kickerboat in which he regularly rounded the island coast from Saratoga Passage to Skagit Bay to Port Susan to Possession Sound. He informed me that he'd chosen this spot as the island's best. He told me he was the last man—beyond lived only birds and barnacles. He promised me that I stood at the gates of delight. It made him happy that I was going to be so happy.

In a scant mile I came to the island bow, sat on a log, and opened my rucksack for kipper snacks, apple, and Pepsi, and took off my boots to wiggle my toes in the sand. Ferries shuttled from Whidbey to Mukilteo. Fishing boats loitered to ambush the salmon making the turn around the island tip on their way to the Stillaguamish River. At my back rose 320 vertical feet of green alder, white till, gray clay, and tan sand.

Far to the south, Tahoma was breaking free from clouds; its cliffs wedged into the white sea of the Emmons and Winthrop glaciers, pointing upward to Columbia Crest. With Port Susan to my left and Saratoga Passage to my right, I was pointed straight out into Possession Sound. Holding my course for nine more miles I'd pass Hat Island to starboard and Priest Point to larboard, tack through Port Gardner's rafts of logs and Everett's plumes of steam, and enter the Snohomish estuary.

A few steps more took me around the corner—from bright summer to dark winter, warm calm to chill wind, from a quiet in which the loudest sound was the distant drone of Mill Town to choppy little waves rattling gravel.

The bluff reared now to an astounding 420 feet, a glorious sweep of wildwood. The beach was narrow, even at this low-tide hour, a slender 20 feet, because the storm waves that pound Camano Head slide by here as powerful longshore currents that slim the beach instead of battering the bluff. A bald eagle launched itself from a snag.

Man had been here recently, excavating cedar logs from the forest wall, splitting shake bolts, loading the treasure on small boats, probably at night.

Man had been here not-so-recently. A gully sliced the bluff in the fall line, too straight to be natural. Bullteams and horses in the nineteenth century or donkey engines in the twentieth had dragged logs to the high brink and turned them loose down the chute, who could say when. Sometime between the start of island logging in the 1850s and the end in the early 1920s.

From the foot of another unnatural gully jutted a pair of iron rails rusted nearly to nothing, set in concrete weathered to a surface of jewel-like pebbles. Precisely here the 1911 map shows a structure, the only one anywhere near Camano Head.

An eagle circled close above, its meat-hungry eyes examining me intently. I wished it wouldn't do that.

The shore curved gently in, gently out. I looked across Port Susan to Tulalip Bay, north to the poplars on Kayak Point, north farther to a tall chimney marking the near edge of the Stillaguamish delta, and onward north to Chuckanut Mountain marking the far edge of the Skagit delta. A pair of eagles flew by and a hawk.

At 2:30, three miles from Camano Head, the shore bent slightly to form a subtle lee where longshore currents had been dropping loads, building a longshore bar. The map showed the next three miles to be solid people.

I stole past the bulkheads and picture windows of Tyee Beach to escape from the flooding tide, expecting a lookout to shout, "Stand by to repel boarders!" and ticky-tackers to pour from boxes waving cutlasses. Except for one fellow puttering with a gasoline mower and another gloating over a bale of peatmoss, the place was deserted. I climbed onto the PRIVATE road and followed it up the bluff.

Walking back across the island, here less than a mile wide, I passed a pair of headstones in roadside woods, marking where Dorothea and George Nelson rest in endless summer.

THE WHITE CLIFFS OF WHIDBEY

21. Possession Point, Scatchet Head, Indian Point

Friday, March 3, 1978

From West Point in Seattle they seem to be faraway clouds, tricks of the eye, or inventions of the imagination. From Richmond Beach, when sunset rays set them glowing, they become the white cliffs of Whidbey, the northern boundary of my childhood.

By telescope on crystalline winter days they could perhaps be seen from Maury Island, south of Seattle, though the sightline would be narrow between out-thrusts of mainland and islands and peninsula. However, the bulges that block the eye do not stop the currents of air. Over fifty miles of open water, all the way from Tacoma, the stormy winds blow and the raging waves roll to attack Possession Point, Scatchet Head, Indian Point, and Double Bluff. If islands were mortal and glacial drift were flesh, this would be the bloodiest battleground of the Whulj.

And if islands were warships, Whidbey would not be a lone galleon, as is Camano, but a Great Armada.

We (today I was accompanied by friends Dick and Grace) parked on a street-end where piling stubs remained from the steamer dock at the hamlet of Possession and walked south past cottages that had the belonging look of inhabited driftwood. (A pity they'd not survive the tidal onslaught of the Conjunction of Four, but the drift people could be trusted to accept God's Lesson as gracefully as the gamblers of Perkins Lane.)

Cottages ended, the bluff leaped up at the end of the terrace in vertical, naked till. We were aboard.

Poplars stood airy-faint on the distant mainland shore. Two years ago, I asked the fellow where I was and he said "Picnic Point." Silver tanks on Edwards Point and pastel tanks on Point Elliott marked Edmonds and Mukilteo, the one periodically spitting ferries out in Main Street, the other spitting them into the alley.

The bluff rose higher, to 380 feet. How it must heave and groan in a forty-knot wind on a 13-foot tide! Even now, the tide at 10 $1/2$ feet and the waves mere ripples, the beach was scarcely wide enough for boots.

A kickerboat was anchored offshore. This was the Possession Hole where the ebb once captured Dad in a rowboat and carried him away to Double Bluff.

Our morning walk ended at the mouth of Cultus Bay. "Cultus": Chinook jargon for "useless"—wide open to southerly blows, no shelter for vessels, made shallow by a creek that dumped silt from island heights and by currents that dumped the debris of wrecked bluffs. The map characterized the entire bay, a mile long and nearly that wide, "MUD." We stopped at a spit that had been augmented in the 1960s, its lagoon dredged. The assembly line had spewed out gaudy plastic houses and stinkpots and people to fill them up.

Our afternoon walk began across the bay on Scatchet Head, where a bar terrace had been riprapped and platted. Beyond the subdivision the beach crunched underfoot, gleaming white in shells. The bay wasn't "cultus" to the folks who used to live here.

The bulge of Scatchet Head was greenly forested. However, beyond the spit at its base began a mile-long wall 300 feet tall, composed of sand with lobes of clay, capped by till that had been tumbled to the beach in big chunks, mingling with granite erratics weathered from the cliff.

I traced the mainland shore from Picnic Point to Edmonds, the Kitsap shore from Appletree Point to Foulweather Bluff, and far south made out Magnolia Bluff. From *there* and *there* and *there*, from beaches and ferries, I'd marveled at this cliff under which I was now standing.

It was a mile that would endure in wildness, the brink too scary for picture windows; the wall too tall and unstable for electric elevators, trails, or rope ladders; the base too menaced by sea and bluff to permit a sound sleep in a box on a bulkhead.

We rounded Indian Point, high but wooded, to the mouth of Useless Bay. The bluff swung inland from a beach terrace, and we walked into the village of Maxwelton. The 1897 map calls it "Island," two buildings and a trail, isolated by a mile-long tidal lagoon behind a baymouth bar. Maxwelton became the central settlement of Useless Bay in the summer cottage–mosquito fleet era. Much of the town retained the homely old style, though new glass-and-cedar boxes lined the terrace and bar.

The Maxwelton Grocery was unchanged, said Dick, from hot summer days of the 1930s when he stopped in with his folks for bottles of pop kept in a water-filled cooler with a block of ice. We spent a half-hour browsing the shelves before buying ice cream bars. By our next visit this driftwood-looking store would probably be boarded up and the glass-and-cedar people would be shopping at a 7-11.

22. Double Bluff

Tuesday, February 21, 1978

Wilkes judged the broad scoop five miles from Indian Point to Double Bluff as cultus as Cultus Bay and straight-out named it Useless Bay; no Britisher contradicted him. Lacking a safe anchorage or much else to attract European interest, by 1897 its total shore population required only a half-dozen structures, of whatever sort. Early in the twentieth century farmers descended the gentle slopes to the lagoons and salt marshes, primevally two miles long and up to a mile wide (among the largest wetlands of the Whulj) to dike them off and dry them up enough to serve as pastures. After midcentury the developers arrived to riprap and fill and dredge.

The 1953 map shows half a hundred buildings on beaches and dikes; the 1968 map double that; the 1978 eye saw three miles of unbroken habitation. (The 1981 eye hungrily read a report by scientists of the Goddard Space Flight Center that they believe they have detected a 100-year-old warming trend, probably caused by the greenhouse effect, the result of the burning of fossil fuels, which increases the carbon dioxide in the atmosphere. They predict the warming will reach an "almost unprecedented magnitude" in the next century, perhaps enough to melt the ice of west Antarctica, which would raise the sea level by fifteen to twenty feet. That would "flood 25 percent of Louisiana and Florida, 10 percent of New Jersey, and many other lowlands throughout the world.")

Beyond the site of a vanished boathouse I walked past the far end of the three miles to lonesome beach. In a few steps, unready and confounded, I was aboard the co-flagship of the Great Armada, nameless as its companion. Composed mainly of sand in Grand Canyonlike alternation of vertical strata and sloping talus, naked except for patches of grassy meadow, the summit 367 feet above, the front more than a mile long. It surely was a Noble Eminence to gape at from below, as I had done for some time from afar.

As I continued walking, the bluff's height lowered to 160 feet but the steepness grew, strata steps yielding to a single cliff. The bluff had a peculiar look and I turned in from water's edge for closer study.

The sand was brown, stained by the iron oxides that weather out chemically from gray minerals. In the drifts of the Vashon Stade of the Fraser Glaciation I grew up on north of Seattle, this stain extends down from the surface a couple feet, below which the color is unweathered gray. Here, however, the brown was complete from top to bottom. Moreover, the sand wasn't loose but was *sandstone*—not hard stone (it readily let the fingernail scratch away grains) yet truly rock. What originally had been blue clay had become brownish-to-whitish *claystone* or *shale,* and crumbled off in small fragments. The till capping had become *conglomerate* or *tillite.* The strata were not merely weathered to a different color and compressed to a greater hardness but *folded*: I passed a complete little *anticline* of rumpled strata. The folds were *tilted*: gulches revealed a dip of 70 degrees inland.

All in all, it was very different drift from the stuff we dug post holes and ditches and blasted privies in. Of course, "our" drift was on the ground surface, left there by the retreating glacier, and thus was thousands of years younger than deposits made during the advance, and it never was crushed under the weight of some 3,000 feet of ice. But could such metamorphoses as I was seeing here have taken place during any portion at all of the Fraser Glaciation, or in the 12,000-odd years since? Was I, rather, looking at drift of the Salmon Springs Glaciation of 30,000-odd years ago?

The tilted formation was sliced by an erosion plane, an *angular unconformity* marking the end of a period of degradation and the start of aggradation. Atop the plane rested a horizontal stratum of sandstone 25 feet thick, capped by a foot-thick layer of black peat, source of the black driftwood I'd been seeing on beaches hereabouts and had supposed to have been colored that way from soaking in a swamp a few years or decades.

I'd supposed right except that the soaking had been in the swamps of the Pleistocene—swamps perhaps of 30,000 years ago. The contents of the peat indicated that our region could not have been entirely subarctic-like tundra during the whole of glacier time. I examined one of the ancient logs, 20 feet long, that except for its dark color was identical to fresh logs beside it on the beach. (Near Scatchet Head, Dick, Grace, and I dug into a layer of peat varved in the exact pattern of enclosing clays. Pulling apart layers of pressed fragments of wood and twigs we found recognizable cedar bark and alder leaves—and Douglas fir cones that appeared tasty enough for a squirrel's lunch.)

An eagle sailed overhead to join another in a snag leaning out from the brink. A great blue heron flapped by, fleeing a gull. I turned a corner, the first of the twin points of Double Bluff—reduced here, actually, from a bluff to a mere bank. At the second point, I looked into Mutiny Bay, saw boxes without end, and retreated to the solitude of a comfortable log to eat kippers and apple.

Foulweather Bluff, three miles across Main Street on the Kitsap Peninsula, at the mouth of Hood Canal, hulked dim in the haze-fog. The Point No Point light to its east winked through the murk hanging above the glassy water. In olden times the Edmonds-Ludlow ferry passed close by both, carrying the Model A and Trapper Nelsons toward the high Olympics. My memories of alpine flowers and whistling marmots are interwoven with views north to the Noble Eminence and Double Bluff and the thin slice of water horizon.

Double Bluff is momentous to a seaman. Obeying a light atop the bank and a buoy offshore, ships from the ocean make the turn from Admiralty Inlet to Puget Sound. Here, Suibhna the Sailor Man sets his mouth for buckets of steamers. Dad remembers it well. Here is where he was carried willy nilly in a rowboat from the Possession Hole. Here the *Standard Service*, homeward bound to Point Wells from Alaska, rounded the corner. Here, on his first entry into the Whulj, he neared Bremerton and the rendezvous at Fletcher's Bay, concluding the voyage that began when he rode his motorcycle to Boston and joined the Navy, continued over the Atlantic and through the Panama Canal on the *Pyro*, an ammunition ship, and after a tour on the *Tennessee* proceeded on the *New Mexico* to South America and Australia.

Traffic was light today. Two jaunty little Navy craft. A tug and a barge. Commercial fishing boats—one, passing close, set smooth water slapping the beach, waking me from a nap.

I climbed the bank to a pasture, remembered from ferry views as a green field above blue water. Cows were grazing as they had since the land was homesteaded a century ago. But survey stakes were in place.

The physicist and philosopher Sir Arthur Eddington taught me to ask: Are we moving forward or backward in time? How do we know the direction of the arrow? He taught physicists to knit their brows to figure out a means of determining which of two moments occurring very close together comes first. Whulj walkers readily solve the problem: What is better is the past. What has the most garbage is the present. The agony beyond endurance is the future. That's entropy.

I'd come to the island in the morning on the *Rhododendron* (built at Baltimore in 1947, 12 knots, 65 autos); in the afternoon it was gone, returned to its usual run elsewhere. The *Vashon* (built at Houghton, on Lake Washington, in 1930, 10.5 knots, 50 autos) was tied up, on standby for weekend crowds. The last wooden ferry in the state's fleet, it was nearing the end of its days. By the luck of the draw I escaped the miserable *Kulshan* and caught the *Nisqually,* sister ship of the *Klickitat,* featuring an upper promenade deck and a cheeseburger galley.

At 5:13 we pulled out from the island shadow into the orange-pink spotlight of the low sun, about to bury itself in the Olympics. A full moon was rising from dark Cascades toward the gray-yellow clouds that ringed my day's Blue Hole. I walked the whole way to Mukilteo, around and around the promenade, gazing from Komo Kulshan to

Camano Head to Tahoma, eating a cheeseburger and drinking a can of Tahoma (Rainier) beer.

THE WHIDBEY LEE

23. Columbia Beach to Ala Spit

Saturday, March 4, 1978

The lee of Whidbey Island is the history side, where mariners could find safe anchorage in bays not cultus, where settlers could build homes out of the wind.

The name of Freeland, at the head of Holmes Harbor, recalls the socialist colony of 1901. The forest of rotten pilings tells of old booming grounds, perhaps a mill.

From May 28 to June 2, 1792, Joseph Whidbey, master of the *Discovery*, explored northward through Saratoga Passage as far as Penn Cove, which Vancouver recorded as "very excellent and commodious." Whidbey wrote of "a delightful prospect consisting chiefly of spacious meadows, elegantly adorned with clumps of trees, amongst which the oak bore a very considerable proportion....In these beautiful pastures, bordering on an expansive sheet of water, the deer were seen playing in great numbers. The country in the vicinity of this branch of the sea is the finest we had yet met with."

The Skagits lived here in a village fortified against Clallam raiders. In 1840 Father Francois Blanchet arrived to instruct them in Christianity, a faith adopted by many natives in expectation it would save them from the plagues. Here in 1853 came Thomas Coupe from New England in his full-rigged ship, a vessel my great-grandfather might have hailed while sailing off Nova Scotia. In Coupeville I walked by Coupe's house, still inhabited, as are others of the period, and the 1853

Methodist Church, and the Alexander Blockhouse built for the troubles of 1855.

If Joseph Whidbey had continued north a bit past Penn Cove, he would have seen the green meadows and groves of oak that slope gently down to a broad bay, divided by a parklike tombolo into Oak Harbor and Crescent Harbor. Settled in 1849, the town of Oak Harbor (called Taftsonville on the 1866 map) perhaps could have outcharmed Coupeville, but most of its history went up in flames during the Great Fire of July 1921. Then the Navy came to spawn "Hooligan City," an agglomeration of fast-food franchises serving a transient population of the good ol' boys who "palmed the gooks in Nam" and keep in practice for the next such diversion by harassing Americans. I've read in the papers of a baby's heart stopping three times as the Blue Angels three times jolted a city. On the wilderness ocean I've seen anemones snap shut, hermit crabs leap out of their shells, and clams piss by the thousands when a dragon roared over the breakers. In the mountain wilderness I've damn near made all these responses simultaneously and on one occasion was knocked cold—very nearly stone-cold since I happened to be alone on a cliff.

Hooligan City concentrates a third of the island's 37,000 residents. Most of the rest live on the beaches, and most of those on the lee, where the quiet-wave bluffs are largely low and much-broken, and where longshore currents have built miles of spits and bars.

I spent more time driving than walking, searching for ways to the shore through the defenses of private-property zealots. Once, when I succeeded and went walking the beach, I returned to find my retreat cut off by a barricade of bales of peatmoss defended by a home guard armed with spades and pruning shears. What especially alarmed them, investigating the beetle while I was away, was a stack of Geological Survey maps in view on the seat. Only after I convinced them I was not a developer or tax assessor did they release me. I thought it just as well not to mention I was writing a book about the area.

I also spent more time on Whidbey reading maps than walking. From tip to tip thirty-six miles, from side to side one to nine miles, Whidbey is only surpassed in size in the old forty-eight states by New York's Long Island and Michigan's Isle Royale. Whidbey is perfect for the Sea-Level Game taught us as undergraduates by Dr. Mackin. In this game one imagines the shoreline lowering as the continental glaciers withdraw water from the oceans, exposing broad shore plains; and rising as the icecaps melt, flooding the tulips of Holland and the subways of London and New York. In Western Washington we play a variation, the Lake Russell Game. The detailed history of Whidbey in and after the age of Lake Russell—the body of fresh water dammed by the Canadian glacier between the Olympics and the Cascades—is beyond the ken of this von Humboldt. He can, however, spread out the contour maps and move the water up the slopes to see what happens. To keep the game simple enough for him to play, he ignores the uplifting of the land when released from the burden of the ice.

At a level 40 feet higher than at present, Mutiny Bay and Holmes Harbor join to lop off the south end of Whidbey, "White Cliffs Island," and at less than 40 feet the Strait of Juan de Fuca and Dugualla Bay connect to lop off the north end, "Hard-Hearted Island." At 60 feet two more channels fill: from Admiralty Bay to Saratoga Passage, creating "Cousin Al's Island," and from the Strait to Penn Cove, dividing "Prairie Island" from "Hooligan Island." At 100 feet "Scatchet Head Island" secedes and both "Prairie" and "Hooligan" split in two. At 200 feet a half-dozen more islands join the Whidbey Archipelago. At 500 feet only several hillocks remain for icebergs to bump against.

Maps are as bloodless as aerial photographs and computer printouts. To know the land one must feel it out inch by inch with the feet. When the after-church stroll in the park gave way to the Sunday drive, Americans began losing their roots. I was in danger of losing mine on the Whidbey lee, insulated and isolated by wheels. In the late afternoon, this Saturday was salvaged by a walk from Penn Cove to Blowers Bluff. I gazed across Saratoga Passage and Skagit Bay to the distant delta and the white Cascades. I turned and gazed over tawny fields to Coupeville and—to my surprise, uprising beyond the island crest—the white Olympics.

Waiting on the *Nisqually* to head back to the mainland, can of Tahoma in hand, I watched latecomers race through Clinton and rumble dock planks. At 6:02 the bell rang, gates fell, engines throbbed, and propellers churned; two cars were left on the dock for the *Kulshan,* then simultaneously leaving Mukilteo. Poor bastards.

I rounded the promenade to the easterly outlook. Everett glared electric-bright between blue evening on the water and pink sunset on Cascade snows. Cheeseburger from the galley in one hand, a second Tahoma from the beetle in the other, I rounded the promenade to the westerly outlook. The water reflected the banding of the sky: brilliant rose on the horizon, then yellow-green, then slate-gray dimming upward to black. Far south on the dark mainland shore a train's Cyclops eye rounded Picnic Point.

Tuesday, March 14, 1978

North of Hooligan City a superb, large lagoon marsh had recently been gridded with dredged channels for stinkpots and riprap ridges for boxes. The mile-long baymouth bar as yet had only two such dwellings; the gaps defended solely by surveyors' stakes permitted easy put-in. In the cold drizzle of noon I set out north, joined by two romping dogs. The rain beat harder and I stopped to get into costume, draping a garbage bag over my rucksack and hoisting a red umbrella. The dogs ran home whimpering.

The bluff leaped up and bulged out to Strawberry Point, where Saratoga Passage opens into Skagit Bay. Dimly seen far beyond Camano Island's English Boom, the nine-mile front of the Skagit delta was as awesome as Montana.

Ancient pilings and weathered concrete supported a boathouse built of 8- by 14-inch timbers, ax-squared and notched and laid up log-cabin fashion. A faded sign advertised "Apples For Sale 50¢ a Sack." Now, as when that was the price of apples, fishing boats passed, bound north for LaConner or Anacortes, south for Stanwood or Everett.

A scurrying caught the corner of my eye—a weasel or mink, perhaps a river otter? A heron flew over. Alders and maples leaned a hundred feet out over slimy-green gravel insufficiently rattled by waves to be mineral-clean. The bluff was brightened by white blossoms of coltsfoot and Indian plum, red of currant, and yellow of Oregon grape. An eagle flew over. Creeks gushed from wildwood ravines. Erratics as big as beach cabins were crowned by forests of ferns. Ancient pilings provided perches for cormorants. Every mile or two the wildness was interrupted by a house, usually appearing not much younger than the 1855 Alexander Blockhouse. At 2 o'clock, on a lonesome sandspit six miles from the put-in I turned around. Emerging from cold clouds, the Big Scoop in the side of Cultus Mountain was outlined by fresh snow.

Enough of the day was left to drive north. At Dugualla Bay I paused on the baymouth bar to sniff things dead in tidal muck and things dead in tidal marsh, cow shit and bird shit and clam shit, the soul of the Whulj. A pair of deer dipped their snouts in seaweed and slowly stepped away—and took wing as two boys on jet motorcycles razzed through Clover Valley on the way to Ault Field.

In waning light I walked out on Ala Spit in the northwest arm of Skagit Bay, a cozy sub-bay harboring a miniature archipelago of islets sized to scale. South lay Goat Island, Seal Rocks, and tiny Deadman Island and Little Deadman. Close enough east to hit with a stone was Hope Island, once the site of a boathouse famed among sports fishermen for bringing in lunker kings. North were Kiket Island, where in the youth of nuclear power Seattle City Light naively proposed to build a reactor to keep The Towers simian-brilliant, and Skagit Island, at the mouth of Deception Pass, whose tidal races separate Whidbey from Fidalgo Island. This archipelago's bald mounds of ice-polished rock, tawny fields of grass, groves of oak and madrona, and shrub-size fir and pine, these were of the matter of the San Juan Islands and not—so far as the journey in hand was concerned—my business.

At the ferry dock I drank a Tahoma to whet my appetite for the cheeseburger. A screen of pilings hid the vessel to the last minute. The *Kulshan*! At 6:30 the bell rang and propellers churned. I sat shivering in the beetle and opened my emergency can of kipper snacks.

THE WEST COAST OF WHIDBEY

24. Ebey's Landing

Monday, February 25, 1974

The highway curved down through pastures to the largest lagoon of the Whulj, enclosed by its longest baymouth bar. I drove by a marsh-lake where ducks swam, herons waded, blackbirds flittered, and two snowy owls from the Arctic sat wondering where all the lemmings had gone.

The way rounded a fortified hill to an alluvial plain, a checkerboard of black and green squares.

The road ran off the brink of the plain and plunged to the beach, to ocean-size waves exploding in the sun, spindrift flying over the drift-wood to fleck brown grasses of the bluff. Ringed by blackness, the Great Blue Rainshadow Hole glowed; beneath, whitecaps of a great blue sea stretched westward to a planet of waters.

So I first came to Ebey's Landing.

25. South of Ebey

Tuesday, February 21, 1978 and Thursday, March 2, 1978

In the fifteen miles north from Double Bluff are three useless (except to developers) bays—Mutiny, Admiralty, and one that is nameless—and two ruined spits: Bush Point and Lagoon Point. Twice I walked to Lagoon Point, first from South Whidbey State Park on the south and then from Admiralty Bay on the north—for old times' sake, because this was where I first knew the island, a quarter-century earlier.

The 1953 map shows a dozen houses on the spit, aptly named, its lagoon marsh a mile long and a third that wide. Soon after it was mapped, Cousin Al bought a cheap lot, scrounged junkyards for lumber and plumbing and basements for furniture, and nailed together a cabin tight enough to keep out summer drizzles and spring breezes. Betty and I and the kids came for a weekend of beachcombing and pottering about in Al's kickerboat, trolling for salmon. We didn't know then the time was ending when anyone who wanted to live by the water could.

Early settlers, seeking shelter from the winds and never building near the water except after careful study of high tides, left abundant space for the mosquito-fleet summerers and ferry weekenders. These vacationers and holidayers were content with weather shores (when stormy winds blow, stay in the city) and cheerful about risks (should the cabin be smashed to driftwood, it's back to the junkyards and basements). That was the way of the Whulj during our visit to Cousin Al's Island.

In the 1960s Seattle erected its Space Needle and all Kansas came to Oz and never went home. The new arrivals lugged carpetbags of money to bid up the land, assessors tacked on zeros, and the swollen taxes supported a bureaucracy that swarmed over the cabins to condemn the wiring and the plumbing. The Cousin Als sold out to folks who could afford to pay the taxes and meet the inspections. When all possible living room by the water was full, developers began riprapping spits and filling lagoons. Old settlers watched from the bluffs and wondered if anyone had told these Kansans about tides.

The 1968 map shows fifty-four houses added to Lagoon Point since 1953, most behind a seawall guarding a boat basin. My 1978 eye saw uncountable more dwellings on flattened duneline and filled lagoon.

Up jumps the Devil.

"Which of us is the *real* Enemy of Mankind?" says he. "Me, I'm a sociable sport, fun at parties, but *you*—whenever you find a row of nice, neat, comfortable houses you snarl and rant. If you can't stand the people, why don't you get out of the world?"

"Old chum," I retort, "invigorating as is your company, on occasion I yearn to commune with—you'll pardon the expression—God, and I find that difficult while breathing gasoline fumes in the front yard of a fellow who is looking out his picture window and picking his nose."

"So you look in his window and dream of a Conjunction of Four, the Great Cleansing, the Manning Tide that will depeople the Whulj."

"Malignant Deceiver, your brain is as twisted as your tail. When I seek depeopled beaches I go to the wilderness ocean in a storm. The Whulj is what it is *because* of Coupeville and quirky little driftwood fantasy castles, fishing boats and ferries, beachfires and beer busts and ukeleles in the moonlight. I don't want it to be a wilderness. It is a place to trammel up a little, a place to *live*."

"Why, then, these prayers begging me for a tsunami?"

"Because the situation has gotten out of hand and we need to start over from scratch. *Some* men—and women and boys and girls—should be permitted to sleep with the water and hear it in their dreams, and at dawn step out barefoot on the clean-washed sand and squish jellyfish in their toes, and at noon and eve hear blackbirds in the lagoon back yard and waves in the shingle front yard. To make that opportunity potentially available to *all* man, *some* should be allowed on *some* spits and bars—not *all*—not *many*."

"Hmmm....You may be right. But my business is the *wrong*. I confess there's an appeal in a great stormy night of shrieking and moaning, carports and Winnebagos crashing into lanais and Chriscraft, and there *is* a traditional association of Hell and high water. But you see, I have a conflict of interest. These new people—they're *mine,* you know."

"Yes, We do know. In them We see your plan. But Our plan is different. When your people are eliminated—or let Us say, relocated atop the bluff—Our people will resettle certain permitted beaches. They will live holy lives according to Our commandments:

Thou shalt build minimal shelters that resemble driftwood and shalt grow gardens of reeds and sedge, shells and agates and sand dollars.

Thou shalt garb thyself in clothing that looks like it's made of seaweed and sand, and in manner and behavior shalt emulate the seals and coots and oysters.

Thou shalt row, row, row thy boat.

Cometh the Next Cleansing, thou shalt climb the bluffs and cheer the waves.

"Shalt me no shalts, you son of a ————."

(Thunder and lightning and high winds. A giant furnace appears from a cloud and sucks in the Devil.)

26. Ebey

April 1976 to February 1982

The Skagits, accustomed to digging camas roots on the island prairies, welcomed the Hudson's Bay Company's potato. In the 1840s envious Clallams began paddling over from the Olympic Peninsula to cultivate the tuber, stimulating the Skagits to keep their Penn Cove stockade in repair. In 1848 Thomas Glasgow sought to hoe a row but was dissuaded by the established residents.

After the Donation Land Law of 1850 legalized squatters' rights, Isaac Ebey filed a claim and became Whidbey's "first permanent (sic) white settler." He served as delegate to the territorial legislature, collector of customs, prosecuting attorney, and colonel of a company of volunteers in the Indian (White) Wars. In 1856 the Haidas, paddling 600 miles down from the Queen Charlotte Islands on their regular summer raid, chanced on a ship of the U.S. Navy and lost the Battle of Port Gamble—and a chief. "A chief for a chief" being the rule, on the next tour, after asking around the northern Whulj, they learned Colonel Ebey had the biggest head in the neighborhood, and on August 11, 1857, chopped it off.

"Ebey" starts on Admiralty Bay. Part of the primeval lagoon—remnant of the ancient sub-bay that was closed off millennia ago by the three-mile-long baymouth bar—has been ditched dry for pasturing and in effect is now an extension of Crockett's Prairie, named for a colonel who kept his head while Ebey was losing his. The eastern third of the bar is a solid glass wall of picture windows, "Admiral's Cove," and in 1974, the rest was staked. Crockett's Lake, a wetland more than one and a half miles long and a half-mile wide, was to be dredged for stinkpots. The Friends of Ebey's Landing mobilized and Save Whidbey Island For Tomorrow sued the bastards.

From Keystone, on the west end of the bar, the ferry crosses to Port Townsend, a run sometimes as sporting as rounding Cape Horn. A favorite local entertainment in breezy weather is watching the green-and-white ferry unload passengers of the same color scheme.

All this is "Ebey," and so is Fort Casey State Park on Admiralty

Head, and it is possible to walk for hours and never reach the landing. However, there at the landing begins our family's customary Ebey Day.

Ebey's Prairie, at its north edge near Penn Cove 100 feet above sea level, slopes imperceptibly southward one and a half miles to a low point of 60 feet, and then runs out in the sky. Ebey's Landing Road slants down to the beach, close to a gulch that has the look of having been dug to provide a wagon ramp. On our Ebey Day we park by the driftwood and walk northwesterly beneath the bluff. This is uniquely "Ebey," not the standard Whulj mix of drifts, but almost all sand, mainly meadowed, freshly green in spring, and in other seasons the color of the deer which feed there. We're rarely alone, and on fine Sundays expect a crowd. Ebey was saved by fame—if it indeed proves to *be* saved.

Here in the rain shadow of the Olympics the annual precipitation is 18.64 inches, compared to 25 inches on the White Cliffs and 36 in Seattle. Often, under Ebey's Blue Hole, the violence of storms to the west can only be guessed at from the fury of the waves on the shore here.

Seals poke long whiskers and watery eyes above the waves. Bald eagles ride the wind above the blufftop forest. Once I heard a frightening turmoil and looked up to a bird that chilled my marrow, until I recognized my son's Chinese dragon kite being harangued by gulls and crows.

A mile from the landing the bluff is cut off from the waves by the bar that encloses mile-long Perego's Lake (Lagoon)—brackish water, tidal muck, reeds, saltgrass meadows, sandpipers, and rafts of logs washed over the dune ridge, stranded by storms.

From the end of the lake we climb grass and flowers 240 feet to the top of Perego's Bluff and turn back toward the prairie, following the meadow path between the brink and the thicket of Douglas fir and Sitka spruce. Outpost trees sculptured by the winds of centuries are giant bonsai, nature's inspiration for the art form that was perfected in the lands where the west winds come from.

We look down amber grass to the lagoon's thousands of bleached logs, from this height seeming just of a size for pick-up-sticks, and to the dune line (reed-and-grass tan), driftwood line (brown-white), shingle beach (gray), breakers (white), and the sea (gray-green), flecked with (white) caps.

We look to four mountain ranges: on Vancouver Island, in the San Juan Islands, and the Olympics and Cascades. We watch the ferry thread through the Main Street parade of ships from far oceans, tugs and lografts and barges, fishing boats and stinkpots—and white sails that seem little suns on the wide sea. Here I'd have turned my tiller to steer out of the Whulj toward the end of flat earth and the start of the round globe of water.

We descend from the forest to the floor of what presumably was, in glacial times, a lake—Ebey's Prairie, a green billiard table patched with the black of fresh plowing. No land in the Northwest has been continuously farmed so long. The Skagits and Clallams began it. Since the 1850s Europeans have been working the land, at one period trying sheep, at others potatoes or grain. The soil, Ebey Sandy Loam, produced 117 bushels of wheat an acre in 1894, claimed then as a world record. Nowadays vegetables and hay dominate.

Houses and barns dot the prairie, many dating from pioneer times, as do the blockhouses, where Ebey should have been the night the Haidas came calling. Beyond a wooded rise lie Crockett's Prairie and, largest of all, Smith's Prairie, three miles square.

In 1974 I saw billboards advertising lots at Ebey's Landing and on Ebey's Prairie. A spokesman for the Friends summed up: "To build houses along this strip of land would completely destroy the picture and its message. Cropland—with a footpath along its outer edge—is all that is wanted here."

In 1977 the state legislature appropriated funds to purchase an eight-mile beach-and-bluff trail corridor from Fort Casey to Point Partridge. In 1978 Congress established Ebey's Landing National Historic Reserve, twenty square miles of prairies and Whidbey's west coast and Penn Cove. As late as 1979 we saw prairie lots freshly staked. In 1980 Congress appropriated funds to buy some of the land and purchase development rights on others. The Friends dare not relax. If the developers win one battle they win the war. We Friends have to win 'em all.

27. Point Partridge to Perego's Lake

Friday, February 24, 1978

At 10:30 in a dull-sky morning I hoisted my rucksack and descended the vale of Point Partridge County Park, the only breach in the bluff for miles in either direction.

My "Whulj"—the saltwater *I* know—is cloistered: Puget Sound by Bainbridge Island and Kitsap Peninsula, Port Susan by Camano Island, Possession Sound and Saratoga Passage by Whidbey Island, and Admiralty Inlet by Marrowstone Island and the Olympic Peninsula. These are homes, safe, where a person can sleep.

On the shores of the wilderness ocean we adventure in the sense of Vilhjalmur Stefansson's definition: "an adventure is a sign of incompetence." We never can be truly competent there. Every night that we lay ourselves down and zip up the bags, we know the world may end before sunrise.

Point Partridge, the westernmost jut of Whidbey Island, is somewhere between wilderness and hominess. I looked out over the thousand square miles of open sea between the Olympic Peninsula and San Juan Islands, from the Strait of Juan de Fuca to the Pacific Ocean, the Bering Sea, the Mindanao Trench—and shrank back.

I turned south under an amber-sandy bluff, while small waves lapped. High tide was in late afternoon, giving plenty of beach going and coming. A small Blue Hole fought through clouds to the northwest. Front ridges of the Olympics stood clear of rain billows. Snow peaks of the British Columbia Coast Range shone. I was lulled.

At 10:50 I rounded Point Partridge, its offshore bell buoy silent in the glassy sea. The shower-washed air was so lucid that two promontories of the far shore were sharply three-dimensional—Wilson Point Lighthouse at the tip of the Quimper Peninsula, and Marrowstone Point Lighthouse at the tip of Marrowstone Island. Protection Island marked the mouth of Point Discovery. The Dungeness valley's deep gash in the Olympic front pointed to Sequim Prairie. The tall bulk of Mount Angeles gave the location of Port Angeles at its base.

"GONG! GONG!" yelled the bell buoy. Waves crashed around my knees. I waded to the bluff wailing, "No! Not *now*! *I'm* on the beach!"

he come up once before he
drowned toujours gai kid he
gurgled and then sank for ever

I started to crawl up the bluff, wondering if the tsunami would beat me to the top.

The landsman loves the water in a different way from a seaman; even in a rowboat near shore on a calm day, when the limeade is too deep to see bottom I make out faces—cold gray faces, dull staring eyes. The waves already were tamely lapping again. The freighter was almost out of site, the jolly comrades of Suibhna the Sailor Man laughing at the havoc of their passage. On the horizon were other ships, and I'd be sure to watch for them.

Five oystercatchers went all to pieces at my approach, couldn't decide whether to run or fly, and scrambled south, a group hysteria of "EEP EEP EEP."

At 11:10 the rounding of a bulge brought Fort Casey in view on Admiralty Head.

Two cormorants and a German imperial eagle rode a floating log. A hawk sailed out from the bluff, hunting. I caught up with the five oystercatchers and they threw another EEPing fit.

I passed Cedar Gulch, the odd valley that lacks a creek (as Ebey's Prairie lacks a lake) and runs out in the air at about the same height above the beach as the prairie. Von Humboldt began to hypothesize hyperactively.

At Perego's Lake two deer ran up the deer-colored bluff—stopped—vanished. Their eyes were watching me. I'd also been watched here by seals and eagles, but never by a picture window. In the three miles north from the lake to Point Partridge, and in the four miles south to Admiralty Bay, never a human dwelling breaks the wildness, and that's one of the things that makes Friends.

On the return I climbed a new trail, just beyond Cedar Gulch, 220 feet above the beach to the road-end parking lot of the Point Partridge Recreation Area of the Washington State Department of Natural Resources. The path led to campsites carved from salal and scrub fir. I expected to come out on the edge of a drift plateau—and instead found myself on a strange ridge above a strange valley—rather, a pit. I'd seen others like it along the road at Penn Cove and supposed them ancient gravel pits. What in Whidbey's human past ever could have demanded *this* much gravel?

A fresh litter of feathers on the beach said the hawk had lunched. At 1 o'clock so did I, sitting on a log to eat kippers and watch the parade: on the water, a fishing boat and a bare-masted sailboat running on the auxiliary; in the air, a mysterious flurry of small craft, fixed-wing and choppers, and an unusual number of floatplanes. Proceeding north I met my five oystercatchers, who decided I had them surrounded and EEPed out to sea.

A shower recleaned the air and moved on. The pulp mill plumes of Port Townsend and Port Angeles fixed the positions of those cities. Even Dungeness Spit, fifteen miles distant and hardly higher above the water than a man is tall, could be made out; binoculars would have picked up the lighthouse.

To the north the Smith Island light winked. Beyond, above the low profile of the nearest San Juan Island, Lopez, rose the apex of the archipelago, 2,409-foot Mount Constitution on Orcas Island. When the winter air is particularly crystalline I can see it from the heights of the Issaquah Alps. On May 31, 1933, *"Old Ironsides"* sailed (actually was towed by a minesweeper) under the peak that Wilkes named in its honor. On the way to Elliott Bay, one of ninety ports in the grand tour, the forty-four-gun frigate passed the island named for Commodore William Bainbridge, its 1812 commander in the victory over the *Java*.

West of Lopez lay San Juan Island. I spotted the hills we've climbed above American Camp and English Camp, where the two armies sat down in 1859 after an English pig ate some American potatoes and the American farmer killed the pig, bringing near to a boil the dispute about the proper boundary between the United States and Canada. In 1872 the arbiter, Kaiser Wilhelm I, accepted the American argument for Haro Strait, west of the San Juans, and rejected the English case for Rosario Strait, east.

Haidas in canoes laden with plunder and slaves. The superstar frigate of the War of 1812. English and American armies (and potatoes and pigs) in confrontation. It seemed a great lot of war for so serene a scene. There was more—concrete slabs on the beach, reels of rusty barbed wire and stacks of rusty Army cots, and hundreds of uprooted stumps that had been dumped down the bluff near Fort Ebey.

Nearly returned to the county park, at the small scoop of a little lagoon, I climbed a path to the blufftop and there found a trail newly trenched south in head-high salal and wind-stunted spruce and fir. Beyond the miniature automated lighthouse and a concrete observation bunker, I came out at a gun platform. The adjacent ammunition vault, a dark, dank cave, had large letters inset in the concrete of the entrance, "USED 1942." The bluff slope was patched by thickets of a shrub with yellow blossoms much like scotchbroom but with formidable thorns as well. (Did I hear bagpipes skirling?) I descended to another oddity, a wide bench 30 feet below the 212-foot blufftop. Evidently Lake Russell had been up here, but why had I not seen evidence of this phase of the lake elsewhere?

I climbed to a second gun platform and then, exploring old military roads inland, met a ranger staking out a campground for the new Fort Ebey State Park. Why, I asked, with three other forts so near, was Fort Ebey added? Later, someone told me this fort was pre-World War I, to cover a blind spot of the others, but the ranger's explanation was that by 1942 the others forts' obsolete guns had long since been sold for scrap and, in any event, this was a better location for modern guns, permitting down-the-throat shots far west in the strait. Two six-inch guns were thought sufficient. The military did not expect the super-battleships *Yamato* and *Musashi* but merely a suicide flotilla of destroyers and light cruisers. He confirmed the bagpipes—the thorny thickets were gorse, planted to supplement the barbed wire. The bench was cut not by Lake Russell waves but Army bulldozers that uprooted the stumps and scooped the earthworks to emplace the machine guns that would defend the six-inchers against the assault of the Imperial Marines.

Fort Ebey would be hard to explain to a person who had not been detained in 1941 on suspicion of being Japanese.

I continued north in woods and fields, passing pits with no outlets, ridges with no connections. When science falters, spooks are hypothesized—I saw ancient astronauts flinging themselves across the cosmos, greedy for gravel, rare as gold and precious jewels on their steaming, gassy-liquid planet that never knew a glacier. At the largest pit, filled with water, Lake Pondilla, I remembered: *kettles.*

While messing about in graylands in the Cascades and Olympics, Canadian Rockies, and Selkirks, I've observed the kettle process: Stagnant ice of a dying glacier melts into separated blocks. Sand and gravel slough off the surfaces of the blocks to form ridges between what become, when the blocks melt away completely, pits. The pits I'd previously seen in the making were a few feet across and deep. Here there was a far, far greater glacier than I had ever known.

Some 12,000 years ago the ice front had melted north to the vicinity of the Canadian Gulf Islands. Isolated chunks lingered to the south half a millennium longer. Lake Russell had emptied and the shore of the Whulj-to-be lay some distance west. Caribou and bison roamed amid blocks of ice, nibbling the willow and wild rose, sedge and cattails, alder and buffalo berry. On the moraines of Sequim Prairie, Manis Man cracked open the mastodon's skull to get at its brains.

Returning to the beach I realized the little scoop-and-lagoon also was a kettle, broken into by the waves.

Haidas paddled north, the colonel's head in a basket.

James McMillan of the Hudson's Bay Company passed in a hired canoe, running an errand (December 1824) for Governor George Simpson (our distant relative on my father's mother's side) from Fort George on the Columbia River to the Fraser River.

Large, loud waves were rolling in from the China horizon. Within Olympic clouds an eerie glow told that our sun was dying again, already at 4 o'clock.

Hard rain battered the beetle. At 5:12 the *Nisqually* pulled out. As I drank my Tahoma and ate my cheeseburger, a shaft of sunlight pierced the clouds to paint Pilchuck and Big Four—but only these two among all the hundreds of night-dark mountains—brilliant orange.

28. Point Partridge to Ault Field

Wednesday, March 1, 1978

Komo Kulshan shone two miles high in air so still the steam plume rose a third mile before bending east in the jet stream. On Labor Day of 1948, friends and I contoured slopes of the crater, vapors curling up from the black pit in the white snows, but not until 1975 did geologists come a-flapping from all over the world, filling the air with helicopters, grants, and dissertations about vulcanism.

Day hadn't penetrated to Mukilteo, buried deep in dense fog. The crossing of Possession Sound on the *Nisqually* was a voyage through the mind. Foghorns of our ferry, of the unseen other, and of unseen Point Elliott told sad stories. A tugboat not-quite-materialized, towing a dead ship, stripped to a hulk and loaded with Seattle's dead cans, bottles, TV dinners, and mehitabels.

> i know that i am bound
> for a journey down the sound
> in the midst of a refuse mound
> but wotthehell wotthehell

The beetle climbed the hill from the ferry dock into bright day, leaving below gray billows creeping over glassy water.

As I set out north from Point Partridge, Smith Island shone in warm spring sun. My beach lay in chill shadows of the bluff, the driftwood frosted winter white.

The swale that crosses Whidbey from Point Partridge County Park to Penn Cove divides Prairie Island from Hooligan Island. My way north wasn't "Ebey" anymore. The West Beach Road ran atop the bluff, fences and shrubs were sometimes visible from the beach, and paths descended from homes. In two and a half miles the bluff was breached by Hastie Lake Valley and a row of cottages; in another two and a half miles, by Swantown Valley and a mile of picture windows on a baymouth bar; in a final three miles by what used to be Clover Valley and now is hooligan headquarters, Ault Field.

It wasn't Ebey but it wasn't bad; anywhere else on the Whulj these three long stretches of waterside wildness would be the joy of walkers near and far.

The bluff wasn't Ebey either, but was equally, if differently, impressive. Often as high as 250 feet, it was sometimes formidably vertical, other times Grand Canyonlike, the sloping ledges of brown sand alternating with risers of clay, the whole topped by till eroded to battlements and pinnacles. Much of the drift was the nearly-rock I hypothesized was Salmon Springs, 30,000-plus years old. At least, so I hypothesized until the geologists who pursue me like so many harpies denied me Salmon Springs and scornfully declared I didn't know the difference between *advance outwash* of the Vashon Stade (laid down 16,000 to 14,000 years ago—the period from the glacier's crossing the border to its reaching Olympia, depositing much of the material I'd been viewing in beachside bluffs) and the *melt-back drift* from 13,000 to 12,000 years ago (the period of the glacier's retreating north past Seattle to the Gulf Islands, depositing other material I'd been viewing on the beach, and also dropping the stuff I grew up on).

In 1983 I came upon a journal article with a photograph captioned, "West Beach on Whidbey Island. Bluff is about 200 feet high." The author identified the elements of a vertical section, from the top:

1. Sand dunes (postglacial). Cows grazing on the flat pasture of the brink.
2. Till (Vashon drift).
3. Gravelly sand (Vashon advance outwash).
4. Massive silt (loess). "First recognized along the bluffs of West Beach in the fall of 1979." Wood in the base of the loess dated at 34,000 to 30,500 years ago. It is thought the loess was deposited between 28,000 to 33,000 years ago, marking the change from nonglacial to glacial conditions. As Canada's glaciers pushed south, their meltwater sprawled out deltas of sand and silt that, in the absence of anchoring plants, were picked up by the "cold high-velocity winds generated by glaciers" and deposited here—and elsewhere around Whulj country.
5. Stratified pebbly sand (pre-Vashon).
6. Stratified silt with some sand and peat (the Whidbey Formation). Perhaps 30,000 years old.
7. The beach upon which I walked.
8. Von Humboldt thumbing his nose at the harpies—but then growing thoughtful, wondering if he and his friend Joseph Le Conte, that nineteenth-century writer on geology, ought not have a long talk. There is not only *drift,* there is *outwash…*

Returning in the hot afternoon I met a beachwalker who proved to be an ex-climber. We sat on a log to discuss North Cascades peaks, Whulj beaches, and whether prayer might hurry along the Cleansing.

He was a blufftopper, retired to a spot selected with judicious care. As a mountaineer he'd rejected the lee shore of Whidbey as too tame, yet as an *old* mountaineer felt no more need for foolish discomfort.

Many years he walked the bluffs in storms, feeling the winds at this point and that, aware that on the Whulj the huffings of the dragons are distorted by mountains and islands, hills and inlets, bluffs and straits—whitecaps and water smooth as glass may be seen yards apart in different microwinds.

During his studies he watched immigrants buy lots in spring, build glass-and-cedar mansions in summer—and in winter call back the contractor to install triple-pane glass in picture windows, steel beams in walls, cable anchors for roofs, and extra oil tanks to keep furnaces roaring as loud as the winds—and after another winter call the realtor to find another sucker fresh off the Winnebago from Kansas.

He found a "dead spot" in a crease of the bluff, built his mountaineer's snug hut, and as next-door foreigners quailed in the gales, he snuggled between the eddies and exulted in the surf.

Resuming the way southward, my thoughts were of great winds:

A 1930 evening on the *Bainbridge* when Granny, who ran the food concession, dished up ham and eggs and hashbrowns from the griddle just as the ferry heeled over. It was a scene from a Charlie Chase comedy—Granny running downhill to the counter and throwing the plate in the customer's lap.

The Sunday morning of October 21, 1934, when our neighborhood was a carnival, the air full of flying shingles, our fathers up on roofs trying to nail them down in the winds of 75 to 90 knots that were tearing ships loose on Elliott Bay and all around the Whulj were hurling boats up on beaches and smashing them to driftwood.

Columbus Day of 1962, when Typhoon Frieda hit the Northwest, killing forty-six people and blowing down fifteen billion board feet of timber and closing the World's Fair. At our hut in the lee of Cougar Mountain, we never heard the wind. Very early, however, the power went out. Betty transferred the roast and potatoes to the fireplace, and we lit up the house with candles, wondering if our dinner guests would arrive. They did, just before the Floating Bridge was closed lest it suddenly cease floating. Suibhna the Sailor Man was amused by the surf breaking over the bridge. He compared Frieda disparagingly to a typhoon in the South China Sea he hadn't thought the least funny.

Descending to Columbia Beach I witnessed a thousand suns blazing in Everett windows. Pilchuck, on the Cascade front, was a shocking pink; Glacier, deep in the range, a pale rose. At 5:50 I drove off the *Kulshan* (I hate that rotten scow) in winter twilight.

29. Deception Pass to Ault Field

January 1978

The San Juan Islands, native home of the Blue Hole, are a mountain range of hard rock that has been rounded and plucked, polished and scratched, by Canadian ice, but only dressed lightly with drift. Due to dry sky and hard rock they are sea meadows in the Spanish sun, clumps of oak and juniper, gardens of seablush and blue-eyed Mary, chocolate lily and miner's lettuce, grass widows and California poppy and cactus.

The little archipelago in Skagit Bay, east of Whidbey, is geologically "San Juan." So is Fidalgo Island, north of Whidbey across Deception Pass. And so too is the northernmost segment of Whidbey itself.

From the middle 1950s on, "San Juan" was our family rite of spring. Every Easter we came to sunny Rosario Beach near Deception Pass to hide and seek eggs. We stopped on the way at a truck always parked at the turnoff from the Anacortes highway, bought a sack of shrimp, and peeled away in the microbus. My kids remember Fidalgo's shrimp man as I do Washington Fish and Oyster.

Rosario was so good we never found time to explore more of Deception Pass State Park.

Become a professional pedestrian with a book to write, I spent four days in the park and concluded that were I a Napoleon sent into exile, condemned to live out my days on a mere 2,600 acres—of my choice—this would be the spot, and here I'd never miss Paris, or the Grand Army, or Wellington, or Josephine, or the wine.

Nevertheless, this was not the way to Bellingham. On the North Beach of Whidbey, where the trails over rock points connected separate arcs of gravel, I realized that were it not for glacial drift carried by currents and dumped in lees of coastal juts these hard-rock islands would have no beaches at all. San Juan shores are for boats, not boots.

Dick and Grace and I walked south, one Wednesday, on Whidbey's (and the park's) West Beach. The rainshadow sun was fighting it out with squalls. A wild west wind was driving a Pacific-size surf. The Panamanian-Liberian-Taiwanese merchant marine passed in review, carrying containerized cargo south to Seattle and billions of quarts of oil north to refineries. In a scant mile a sign announced "Surf Crest Beach Private" and behind the driftwood line fluttered hundreds of plastic ribbons. In another long mile we halted at the runways of Ault Field.

Something was radically wrong. Unlike every other part of the Whulj I knew, there was *no bluff* here. Examination of the map showed that longshore currents had smoothed every indentation in the shore for an astonishing eight miles and built a continuous bar that had cut off a string of superb lagoons, culminating north of Ault Field (Clover Valley) in the park's Cranberry Lake. Why had not this vigor, during a preceding age, carved a bluff in what were, instead, gentle slopes rising to the island crest?

Clover Valley (Ault Field) is just barely above today's sea level, and a water level 50 feet higher would connect Cranberry Lake to Deception Pass, cutting off still another member of the Whidbey Archipelago, "Goose Rock Island." Lake Russell could be fitted into this picture. But there should then be *lakeshore* bluffs. And there aren't. There are no bluffs at all.

Professor Mackin cautions von Humboldt against overworking the lake hypothesis. Can one be sure the Juan de Fuca Lobe of the glacier continued to wall off the ocean and dam in the meltwater while the lake followed the retreating Puget Lobe this far north? Was the lake ever here at all? Does one *need* it? In the multiple-working of the hypotheses, don't neglect the ups and downs of *isostasy*.

Archeologists at the Sekiu Shelter, west of Port Angeles on the Strait, estimate the dig, 25 feet above sea level, has been waterfree 3,000 years. All around the Whulj a beachwalker comes upon wave-built fossil terraces perched 6 feet or 20 feet or more above today's beach, and on some of them are kitchen middens buried under centuries of accumulated soil. Von Humboldt is seen tearing his whiskers.

For the return we crossed the driftwood line—to dunes that the Bedouin legions of Lawrence of Arabia could lurk behind to ambush the Turks. The outer line, close inside the driftwood, was naked and active, though only several feet high. But inland across a sand-filled lagoon rose a line 20 feet high, relic of a drier past, anchored on the windward slope by grand fir, shore pine, and Sitka spruce, on the lee slope by fir and hemlock. The dunes retained the classic marching profile, a few actively advancing, smothering alders. Primevally the line was continuous for perhaps three miles. The hooligans flattened one mile, Surf Crest Beach Private another. The remnant preserved by the park remains the greatest dune show of the Whulj.

At the north end of the park lay Cranberry Lake, bordered on the east by a tight-woven forest, on the west by the wide Pacific sky. Scarcely a dozen yards separated the surf crashing on beach sand from lake waves lapping dune sand. The shore trail burrowed through head-high salal, and the lake water was "ocean tea," colored by bark tannins, reminiscent of Ozette Lake on the wilderness-ocean strip of Olympic National Park. A rib of ice-polished rock thrust out in the water, a shore-pine bonsai on its tip.

We sat for lunch on the hard rock of West Point, at the mouth of Deception Pass, and ate our sandwiches and carrot sticks, kippers and apple. Our views were out across the mouths of Rosario Strait, Haro Strait, and Admiralty Inlet, and out the Strait of Juan de Fuca to the ocean.

Had we been sitting here June 18, 1841, we'd have seen Charles Wilkes's brig *Porpoise* at a stone's-throw distance as it exited Deception Pass, the first craft larger than canoe or launch to transit that violent canyon. If we were here in 1841 on other occasions, other vessels of the United States Exploring Expedition might have come in reach of our glass: sloops-of-war *Vincennes* and *Peacock*, store-ship *Relief*, and tenders *Sea Gull* and *Flying Fish*. It was a splendid squadron, and Wilkes felt patriotically justified in striving to make the San Juans a memorial to his shipmates and to the War of 1812. He named Perry's Island (previously and subsequently Fidalgo), Chauncy's Island (Lopez), Rodger's Island (San Juan), Hull's Island (Orcas), and Ringgold's Channel (Rosario Strait). He succeeded in permanently celebrating a few American naval heroes and victories and ships—among islands, Decatur, Blakely, and Shaw; among mountains, Constitution and Erie.

As has been commented on by historians, the martial and the esthetic coincided for Wilkes: "Nothing can exceed the beauty of these waters, and their safety: not a shoal exists within the Straits of Juan de Fuca, Admiralty Inlet, Puget Sound, or Hood's Canal that can in any way interrupt their navigation by a seventy-four-gun ship. I venture nothing in saying there is no country in the world that possesses waters equal to these."

During Wilkes's 1841 visit and any time after 1836, we might well have seen the *Beaver*, second steamer to cross the Atlantic and first to enter the Pacific, on an epic voyage from Blackwell, England. What did the Indians think when they stopped digging clams to gape at the mosquito and its plume of wood smoke, paddlewheeling south to Nisqually House or north to Victoria and Fort Langley?

The year of the history feast was 1792, climax of the Nootka Incident that for three years had been stirring talk of a general European war that would have pitted Britain and Holland and Prussia against Spain and France, these latter two expecting support from the United States in payment for having won their Revolution for them. That spring Nootka Sound, on the west coast of "Quadra and Vancouver Island," harbored five Spanish ships, eleven English, eight American, two Portuguese, and one French. George Vancouver and Juan Francisco de la Bodega y Quadra negotiated the sort of ending the Spanish were getting used to. In 1795 the Spanish quit the Northwest Coast forever.

From May 2 to 18, 1792, Vancouver anchored at Port Discovery to repair his ships—the sloop-of-war *Discovery,* 400 tons, and the armed tender *Chatham*, half that size. His purpose was to make spruce beer for treating the scurvy that had developed on the long voyage from England, and to explore the Whulj in small boats, of which he had a cutter, a longboat, and a pinnace. From West Point we'd likely have seen the *Chatham* sometime between May 18 and 23 as it toured the San Juans, captained by W. R. Broughton. The *Discovery* turned south, the first European vessel to enter Admiralty Inlet, and it anchored May 18 off Bush Point and May 19 off Restoration Point, on Bainbridge Island. Turning north, Vancouver anchored May 31 off Camano Head. From that vicinity, during May 28 to June 2, Joseph Whidbey took a small boat up Saratoga Passage as far as Penn Cove. On June 4, Vancouver landed at (or near?) Tulalip to take possession of New Georgia. The June 6 anchorage was off Point Partridge, and on June 7 in the mouth of Rosario Strait. We'd have seen his ships with the naked eye then, six miles off West Point. On June 9 we could have exchanged hails with Peter Puget and Whidbey as they traversed Deception Pass in a launch, on that trip learning the land mass to the south was not a peninsula, as they had originally thought, but Whidbey's Island. On August 28, after explorations northward, Vancouver was at Nootka to negotiate with Quadra. During his visit (and later, at his desk in London) he put some seventy-five enduring names on the Northwest map.

In 1792 the Spanish hadn't yet given up their claim. While Jacinto Caamano explored north from the Strait of Juan de Fuca to the Queen Charlotte Islands, Dionisio Galliano in the *Sutil* and Cayetano Valdes in the *Mexicana* toured south. On June 10 we'd have seen them anchor in Rosario Strait just off the tip of Lopez.

Proceeding backward in time:

In the years before 1792 the Spanish gave the appearance of meaning business. In 1791 Francisco Eliza, prior to sailing north to the Gulf of Georgia, which he thought was the Northwest Passage, an-chored at Port Discovery from June 29 to July 26. We'd have seen his officer, Jose Narvaez, sail past Boca de Flon, as he called Deception Pass, and become the first European to navigate the Gran Canal de Nuestra Senora del Rosario la Marinera. This was the year Eliza named the San Juan Islands.

In 1790 Eliza led an expedition to Nootka, occupying the site with 200 Spaniards and Peruvian Indians. One of his officers, Salvador Fidalgo, cruised north to Alaska. Another, Manuel Quimper, in the sloop *Princesa Real,* explored the east end of the Strait, saw Komo Kulshan, and named Canal de Lopez de Haro for his pilot. On June 29 his man Juan Carrasco discovered San Juan Island and, on July 5, Dis-covery Bay, Point Partridge, and Rosario Strait, which he called Boca de Fidalgo. The same day he discovered Lopez Island and landed on the southeast tip. We'd have seen him then with the glass, though his report fails to mention Deception Pass.

Those were the European beginnings on the Whulj. Earlier, West Point witnessed the work canoes of Skagits and Clallams going about their routine pre-holocaust business of earning their daily fish, and the war canoes of Tlingits and Haidas on routine Viking-style raids for goods and slaves. No tall ships. However, local conversation must have been full of news from the Pacific coast.

In 1789 Don Esteban Jose Martinez sailed a fleet to Nootka and seized the English vessels anchored there, igniting the Nootka Incident.

He did so because the growing traffic on the Northwest Coast irritated his government, which had a charter from the Pope making Spain the sole proprietor of most of the Pacific. In 1788 John Meares established a post at Nootka and loaded a cargo of furs for China—and mast timbers as well, making him the first Northwest logger and timber-exporter of record. In 1787 Charles Barkley found and named the Strait of Juan de Fuca. In 1785 La Perouse sailed by on his way to Alaska. All this and other traffic came in the aftermath of Captain James Cook's third and final voyage in 1775, when a few sea otter pelts picked up by chance at Nootka brought a fortune in China, and a few European germs dropped off in passing began pocking faces, as Vancouver noted seventeen years later.

Earlier mariners did not enter the Strait. From West Point we'd have had an indirect connection with Juan Perez in 1748, the first European to see the snowy mountain he named Santa Rosalia (renamed Olympus by Meares).

1592? Might we, sitting here, have seen the galleon of Apostolos Valerianos, a Greek serving Spain under the name of Juan de Fuca, who said (or is said to have said) he found a broad inlet where the fabled Strait of Anian, the Northwest Passage, was expected to be, and went "sayling therein more than twentie days"? The weight of opinion is, probably not.

In 1579 Sir Francis Drake reached as far north in the *Golden Hinde* as—by one calculation—the latitude of Everett; by another, perhaps to that of the Columbia River. In 1543 Bartolomé Ferrelo may have coasted north to the latitude of the old Oregon Territory.

In the eleventh century the Chinese invented the compass and not long afterward the sternpost rudder and watertight compartments, and so began the golden age of Asian exploration. Gigantic ocean-going junks, far larger and more technologically refined than European ships would be for centuries, sailed to the East Indies and India and Africa. The epic voyages of Chung Ho covered the years 1405 to 1433. Can it be doubted that his associates—accidentally or on purpose—went out on the dragon seas, their voyages never recorded because they were unable to battle home against the prevailing westerlies?

Before closing its door and retreating into feudalism, Japan, too, was at sea, from the late 1100s into the 1500s. Sitting on West Point in, say, 1242 or 1442, might we have seen Japanese sails approaching on the waters where, 700 or 500 years later, the U.S. Army expectantly trained its pair of 6-inch guns?

THE DEATH TRIANGLE

30. The Phantom War

During one dark week, surveying the mountain front, I daily walked the forests of Ohop Crick, Mashel and Deschutes rivers, and daily heard a great thunderstorm and got out my garbage sack and umbrella to rig for rain. But the rumbling never chased me, never stirred from an area I eventually triangulated as Fort Lewis, where doughboys (including Uncle Bill) once prepared to chase Kaiser Bill up and down Unter den Linden, and GI's to "p-TUI in der Fuhrer's face." Troops now training there on the South Puget Plain, which so uncannily resembles the North German Plain, fire 50,000 rounds a year from 105-mm and 155-mm howitzers and 8-inch guns.

During the same period, while ascending Wheeler Mountain, between the forks of the Stillaguamish, I felt an inexplicable urge at each mudpuddle to DIVE DIVE DIVE. A bit away, miles-long wires, draped over Jim Creek valley from Wheeler to Blue Mountain, were sending superpowered messages to submarines poised in several oceans, awaiting the signal to obliterate Moscow.

On a drear winter day I followed the Hood Canal beach north to the moldering mosquito-fleet wharf of Bangor and saw earthmovers rearranging the planet for a new generation of Moscow-blasters. Having lost my beach to the tide, I returned overland on the road paralleling the Navy fence, garbage bag over rucksack and umbrella over head against the icy rain. On the Navy road inside the fence a gray Navy jeep kept pace, while gray Navy eyes watched me all the while—why I couldn't imagine, until on TV I saw the gray police hauling fence-climbers off to jail.

These are scenes from the War-in-Becoming, another embodiment of the Second Law of Thermodynamics, which stipulates that the future is always worse than the past. The old wars of the Whulj seem by contrast comfortable, with a childlike charm. Moreover, they gave us some of our finest parks.

During World War II, Cougar Mountain was armed with anti-aircraft guns, until the Army decided Japan probably meant Issaquah no specific harm, and in the Cold War with Nike missiles, until the Army was informed no Russian aircraft could fly this far. Sites of the silos and the command radar now are King County parks.

In 1976 the World War II airplanes and the weekend warriors who flew them wore out, forcing the Navy to relinquish much of the Sand Point Naval Air Station on Lake Washington; the Army, informed that the Haidas hadn't beheaded a colonel in ages, disgorged the bulk of Fort Lawton; thus Seattle gained two superb parks.

A child of the 1930s who grew up celebrating the duels of "*Old Ironsides*" with the *Guerrière* and *Java,* and thrilling to Lawrence's dying command to the crew of the *Chesapeake*, "Don't give up the ship," cannot but empathize with Wilkes. His itch to put guns at the mouth of the Tacoma Narrows in order to "bid defiance to the navies of the world" caused President Andrew Johnson to reserve the site for coast artillery and thus make possible Point Defiance Park, Tacoma's pride and one of the supreme city parks in the nation. The possibility that Wilkes's *Porpoise* might be followed through Deception Pass by seventy-four-gun ships resulted in another military reservation that became one of the supreme state parks in the nation.

The Pig and Potato War gave us American Camp and English Camp of San Juan National Historic Park.

At the Battle of Port Gamble, in 1856, the coxswain of the *Massachusetts*, Gustav Englebrecht, poked his nose over a bulwark for a better look at the Haidas and became the first U.S. Navy man killed in a Pacific Ocean war. The battle caused the loss of Colonel Ebey's head and the construction of Fort Townsend. Years later, describing the Army's persistent efforts to rid itself of this chunk of pork, General William Tecumseh Sherman said, "Instead of Fort Townsend protecting the town of Port Townsend, the town is protecting the fort." The Army won in 1895, when the barracks accidentally burned. The people won when the site became Old Fort Townsend State Park.

The War of 1812. White (Indian) Wars. Pig War. World War I. World War II. Cold War. World War III. The Whulj knows them all, as well as my favorite, the Phantom War.

"The period from 1870 through to 1885 is one of the most humiliating periods in the history of the United States navy, for during these years the navy was allowed to go practically to decay. Every other nation on the globe had not only learned the lesson taught by the battle between the *Monitor* and the *Merrimac*—that the day of the ironclad had arrived—but they were busily putting in practice that lesson. England, France, Italy, and Russia were striving to replace their wooden walls first by iron ones, later by steel ones, while the United States, whose naval battles had changed the warship building of the world, was content to peacefully doze and dream of past glories. Even Chile's two modern men-of-war were more than a match for our obsolete navy."

So wrote a Navy chronicler who went on to tell how the New Navy was born in 1883 when Congress authorized four steel ships, three of 2,500 tons and one of 4,000. In 1885 four more were added, including the first without sails auxiliary to steam. Its keel laid in 1888, in 1895 the first American battleship was completed, the *Texas*, displacement 6,315 tons, speed 17.8 knots, armament two 12-inch, six 6-inch, and twenty-two smaller guns. Soon followed the similar *Maine*. America was getting ready.

For whom?

In 1860 Brigadier General Joseph Gilbert Totten, Chief Army Engineer, looked at a map and saw that if a hostile Britain wished to do so, it easily could close the Whulj to American ships. He proposed to close the Whulj against British assault with forts.

In 1866 President Johnson set aside twenty military reservations on the Whulj. The Board of Engineers, however, wondered about forts. Relations with Britain had so much improved, it was virtually an ally, and even should it turn surly, what reason could there be for attacking a virtually uninhabited wilderness?

In 1892 the U.S. Navy obtained a base on the Whulj, in Port

Orchard, and in 1895 a Navy board recommended the Whulj be fortified at Admiralty Inlet, Deception Pass, Agate Pass, Rich Passage, Magnolia Bluff, Dash Point, and Point Defiance.

Against whom?

Despite the War of 1812, the Pig War, and the Union's outrage at the British-based Confederate merchant raider, the *Alabama*, by century's end no rational American, and few generals and admirals, expected the British to sortie south in anger through the inlet named after their own admiralty. The most powerful navy in the world had other business, such as Germany.

Kaiser Wilhelm II, huffing and puffing himself into a sea lord out of envy for his cousins across the North Sea, cocked pickelhaube and twirled mustaches at the British Grand Fleet. Except for token cruisers the Pacific never saw his battle ensign.

France was preoccupied with the Mediterranean, Italy with the Adriatic. The Black and Baltic seas were all Russia could hope to handle. Japan, though it took Taiwan in 1894, wasn't recognized as a world power until 1905, when "it crossed the T" and blasted Russia's Baltic Fleet at the Strait of Tsushima.

So, whom?

A review of the navies at the end of the nineteenth century leaves a solitary possibility: the oppressors of "our little brown brothers" in the Philippines, the tyrants against whom Cuba was in full revolt by 1897, "women and children and the helpless the chief sufferers" of the misrule, the dastards who in 1898 blew up our battleship *Maine,* anchored peaceably in Havana harbor for humanitarian reasons, and murdered 266 of the crew and two officers as well.

Easy enough, wise enough after the victories of Dewey at Manila, Schley and Sampson at Santiago, to sneer at the Spaniards, but in 1898 American warriors pointed with alarm to the ship gap—our 86 vessels confronting the 137 of Spain.

While the New Navy was being built, new defenses were erected for the Bremerton Navy Yard, established 1892, and for the cities of Puget Sound not much older. But the critically strategic point was the mouth of Admiralty Inlet, where a nearly equilateral triangle, roughly three and a half miles on a side, is defined by Admiralty Head on

Whidbey, Marrowstone Point on Marrowstone, and Point Wilson on the Quimper Peninsula.

Construction began in 1897, was completed after 1900. Too late for Spain, too early for Japan. In good time only for the Phantom War.

Force requires counterforce—*national defense*. That much is accepted as widely among civilians as among the military. The subtler truth is that the *rumor* of force must be met by the *reality* of counterforce—even though this *national offense* converts the rumor to a reality because the Enemy's warriors think exactly like Our warriors.

On an alternate time track, the construction of the Death Triangle *caused* Spain to invade Puget Sound. A fortress is built to be shot at, and must be, and when the gun is ready for the job, it must be used. The Spaniards came because they were expected, and if the world's militaries disappoint each other, they're soon all out on the street in threadbare uniforms, clinking medals and selling apples.

Spain had older reasons to invade, as well. The military not only enlarges its appropriations but inflates its glory by magnifying the Enemy. The English remember 1588 as the year of what their historians insist the Spanish called the "Invincible" Armada. In fact, Elizabeth's ships—her official navy and her swarm of ravening merchants-pirates—far outnumbered the Armada. An objective historian has written, "To the Spanish leaders it was a desperate adventure against overwhelming odds—a forlorn hope, almost." The grandees and hidalgos were extravagantly gallant far from home in the northern storms—storms being the most damaging English weapon, and the decisive one.

Rankling nearer in time was their defeat by negotiation in 1792, on the shores of the ocean their own enterprise, valor, and the Pope's justice had given them. The Spanish, feeling themselves sinking beneath the surface of history, could not have been blamed after 400 years of Anglo-American contumely for taking to the seas in a final desperate gesture. Whenever the band struck up "Rule Britannia, Britannia Rules the Waves," a latter-day fife mingling in a strain of "Yankee Doodle," the shades of Quadra and Eliza and Quimper must have been heard murmuring, "Recorda la Nootka."

They would have come to the Death Triangle because it was there. Admiral Cervera's attempted dash for freedom through the blockade at Santiago tells us they'd not have slunk in by night, as our Dewey did at

Manila Bay, but in broad day, their arrival announced hours in advance by columns of black coal smoke. Would it be madness to run a gauntlet of forts? At Manila Bay Dewey not only destroyed the enemy fleet but silenced the shore batteries and the field artillery!

They'd have been met by American ships. The Asiatic Squadron commanded by Dewey, in 1898 based at Hong Kong, surely would have been here, including the four protected cruisers *Olympia, Raleigh, Baltimore,* and *Boston,* 3,000 to 5,870 tons, with 8-inch, 6-inch, and smaller guns. (Out the time slot I saw the Commodore's flagship, the *Olympia,* named for our state's capital city. Launched in 1892, she was a beauty, the sleek hull gleaming white, the gun turrets grim gray on bow and stern, two rakish stacks and two masts for hoisting sails to save coal on long cruises.)

What other ships? Schley's flagship at Santiago, the armored cruiser *Brooklyn,* would have been useful. Completed in 1896, 9,215 tons, it made 21.91 knots and mounted eight 8-inch, twelve 5-inch, and twelve smaller guns. Of America's first line in 1898—the battleships *Iowa, Indiana, Massachusetts,* and *Oregon*—the last surely would have been on hand, because to join the Atlantic Fleet at Santiago it had to steam 14,700 miles from the Pacific around the Horn. At 10,288 tons, 16 knots, with four 13-inch, eight 8-inch, and sixteen smaller guns, the *Oregon* was one of our first three modern, seagoing (as distinguished from coast-defense) battleships.

Spain could have sent against us the squadron that Dewey shattered at Manila: *Reina Christina, Isla de Cuba, Isla de Luzon, Castilla, Don Antonio de Ulloa,* and *Don Juan de Austria* (marching to the war). The squadron that left Cape Verde Islands for Cuba on April 29, 1898, under Admiral Cervera, and was shot to hell at Santiago, could have gone the other way through the Suez Canal (as did Admiral Cawara's squadron, too late for the war), coaled in the Philippines, and been shot to hell here instead: the flagship *Maria Teresa, Cristobal Colon* (yes, him), *Vizcaya,* and *Almirante Oquendo.* Though the largest ships were nine armored cruisers of 6,840 to 9,900 tons, the massing of 11-inch and 8-inch guns would have been nothing to sneeze at.

What year?

Forget the *Maine,* assume no pots overboiled in the Philippines or Cuba and that Spain took the offensive. ("Recorda la Nootka!" howled the crowds in the avenues of Madrid and Seville. "Tambien la

Armada!") To be a credible Imaginary Enemy it would have had to strike before 1900; by then America was racing toward the big leagues.

On December 16, 1907, the sixteen battleships of the Atlantic Fleet—the Great White Fleet—left Hampton Roads, Virginia, and returned February 22, 1909, having steamed around the world.

By 1916 (so swiftly!) America had ten first-line battleships of 20,000 to 27,500 tons, twenty-two battleships in the second line, 11,500 to 16,000 tons; ten armored cruisers and twenty-one cruisers of the first, second, and third classes; fifty-six destroyers, six monitors, thirty-seven submarines, three transports, twenty-two gunboats, four supply ships, twenty fuel ships, five converted yachts, forty-eight tugs, six tenders to torpedo vessels, twelve "unserviceable for war purposes," and eleven "special types." These all were in full commission or reserve; still more were "in commission in ordinary" or "out of commission." Finally, under construction or authorized in 1916 were seven first-line battleships of 31,400 to 32,000 tons, including the *New Mexico* (which with its speed and gunnery and armor and fire-control could have, all by itself, brushed aside the Death Triangle as so many popguns). In 1916, ten years after the British launched the *Dreadnought,* and the same year in which, on May 31 at Jutland, two battle lines of the new steel behemoths met for the only time in history, the Navy's spokesman called these "the great floating fortresses....Were our battleships destroyed, a landing on either coast could be accomplished easily."

I look out the time slot and see columns of black smoke round the corner from the Strait. Guns of Fort Worden speak to their right, guns of Fort Casey to their left, guns of Fort Flagler in their front—and, ambushing out of Rosario Strait, guns of Commodore Dewey. The heirs of the Great Armada, of Balboa and Magellan and Cortez, of Bodega y Quadra and Martinez and Eliza and Quimper, stagger and list, riddled with holes, aflame from stem to stern, magazines exploding. They run up on the beaches of Ebey and still the guns guns guns hail down shot and shell.

And a day or two later half the mosquito fleet arrives, loaded with half the population of the Whulj, come to see the wreckage of what Teddy Roosevelt would have called "a bully show, a lovely little war!"

Only in this phantom history book is described the climactic engagement of the Phantom War, ranking with Santiago and Manila Bay, if not quite Trafalgar and Midway—the Battle of Admiralty Inlet.

31. Fort Casey State Park

Thursday, March 2, 1978

The first time our family parked on Admiralty Head my son, years short of draft age and thus very warlike, burst from the microbus and dashed across the quarter-mile of parade-ground lawns to worship the massive concrete ramparts two stories high, the shiny-black iron stairs connecting magazine caves to ammunition lockers and walled bays of the gun emplacements.

Today, alone and peaceful, I parked at Keystone Harbor and climbed the other side of the hill, the one hidden from an approaching enemy, and there discovered the mortar pits. These were the fort's main firepower, the "ultimate weapon" of the age. For three decades, sixteen of the monsters, each weighing 250 tons, lay waiting to fire 12-inch, 1,000-pound shells on a trajectory so high they'd hurtle vertically down on decks.

The gun batteries on the brink of the 40-foot beach bluff seemed at first glance more sporting—out in the open and exposed to enemy fire. However, the seven 10-inch guns and those of smaller caliber were the then new DC (disappearing carriage) cannons whose recoil flung the barrel back and down into the concrete bay, where the crew could reload, safe from any but the luckiest enemy shot.

Atop the concrete I reviewed the tactical situation. From Mount Constance to Mount Angeles the blue-sky tier of Olympic summits shone high and bright. Below, in the green-forest rank, were the peaks of Walker, Zion, and Big Skidder. At the base of the land mass, the Main Street waters were thronged: Navy grays, NOAA whites, merchant motleys, tugs towing barges and log rafts, fishing boats and play boats, and the ferry threading patiently through.

Hold your fire until they sheer off toward Whidbey to escape Worden's tongues of flame. Then POW the guns and THOONK the mortars. Rake 'em fore and aft as they approach, hole 'em broadside as they pass, hit 'em in the arse as they scuttle away....

32. Fort Flagler State Park

Sunday, November 20, 1977

In crackling-cold blue-sky morning we (Betty and I and the two dogs) began on the spit that pushes prairie grass and gray sand from Marrowstone Island out in the waters of Port Townsend. The Olympics were gleaming shards, the pulp mill billowed gorgeously, and a church steeple two miles distant on city heights was cheerful as jinglebells.

We walked into shadow under the 100-foot bluff of naked sand and till that reminded Vancouver of an English rock, occasioning the name, Marrowstone Island. Frost crystallized on the driftwood, icicles dripped on the wall. The mongrel, Buffalo, chased shore birds. The Shelty, Cailin, primly heeled. A Navy gray sped by. The ferry shuttled. White sails flamed just beyond the edge of our shadow. A narrow slot between the Quimper Peninsula and the tawny bluffs of Ebey gave us a glimpse of the San Juan peaks warming in the Spanish sun.

Beyond a curve in the shore, the Cascade front with its dark forest valleys and brilliant snowy summits came into view. Deep in the range the volcano of Glacier Peak was so hugely radiant we marveled that Vancouver missed naming it. A covey of sailboats flurried by.

From bluff shadow we walked out into spit sun, from finger-chilling breeze to bone-freezing wind. We looked fifty miles over waters and lands to the Issaquah Alps—and beyond. Exactly as did Vancouver on May 7, 1792, from very near this exact spot, we saw to the south "a very remarkable high round mountain, covered with snow."

At two and a half miles from the western spit we crossed prairie grass of the eastern spit to Marrowstone Point. By the lighthouse, beside the frenzy of the rip, we paused for lunch. Northwest a long four miles lay Point Wilson. A clump of trees near the tip had the look of palms on a tropic atoll. North-by-northwest three and a half miles lay Admiralty Head.

Fingers, toes, and noses numbing, we hurried south along the beach to the fort's abandoned, sagging dock, in views to Point No Point and Foulweather Bluff, past dozens of gulls recently killed by hypothermia and drowning.

We returned west atop the bluff, exploring concrete walls and caves of the batteries. The 10-inch and 12-inch guns and 12-inch mortars were removed in 1933 and sold for scrap. These, "the ultimate weapons," were useless against a new generation of large, fast, heavily armored and heavily armed ships. We investigated an odd knoll in the meadow near the bluff brink and found a fire-control bunker, the top sodded over, a ladder descending to the concrete vault. We looked out the narrow slit on the broad waters where the Strait of Juan de Fuca and Admiralty Inlet were one.

A Marrowstone Island pioneer recalls that earlier in the century the troops practiced monthly on the guns, shooting at a moving target towed by a mosquito chartered for the occasion. Fort Flagler gunners were rated superior marksmen, splintering the targets amid geysers of spray, the projectiles then skipping on over the Inlet and finally sinking in the Strait. In Port Townsend the "reverberations shook windows, rattled dishes, and caused a general feeling of nervousness."

33. Port Townsend to Point Wilson

Sunday, March 11, 1979

The completion of the Hood Canal Floating Bridge in 1962 didn't kill the Ludlow ferry, already dead a decade and a half, but I hated it nevertheless for its part in destroying the isolation of the Olympic Peninsula. It was sheer happy luck that my *Footsore 3*, in whose pages I predicted the bridge would sink, was distributed to bookstores several days before February 13, 1979, when in a storm it did. By such happenings are hopes justified for the likewise predicted but still awaited Conjunction of Four.

In full family muster we parked at Edmonds and walked on the ferry to Port Townsend—a hastily scheduled replacement for the temporarily defunct bridge—in company with hundreds of boot-wearing, rucksack-carrying others celebrating the serendipitous return of the olden days.

Our vessel was the *Yakima,* 18 knots. Even so the trip was one hour and forty minutes, nearly as long as the old Ludlow run. Sightlines were reversed, the walker's land seen afresh through seaman's eyes. The whole hundred minutes I spent rounding the decks lest starboard views be missed while I was larboard. Passing in review on one side were Appletree Point, Point No Point, Foulweather Bluff, mouths of Hood Canal and Port Ludlow, Marrowstone Island; on the other, the railroad shore, the alley of Possession Sound, the White Cliffs, Double Bluff, the useless bays and ruined spits of the Whidbey West Coast.

At the Port Townsend dock the jumbo elbowed aside the little Whidbey ferry, and at 11:07 the pedestrian horde elbowed vehicles aside and stormed ashore. Most had come to poke about the gingerbread town that once jailed Jack London and in which sailors were shanghaied for outgoing sailing ships. Our way led beyond the Victorian business blocks to Point Hudson, thence on to the beach under the bluff, one and a half miles to the spit of Point Wilson, and three-quarters of a mile along its driftwood and dunes to the lighthouse. There we crept out of the wind into a driftwood-dune nook for lunch.

In the Phantom War the Enemy steams past guns guns guns. The real-life Main Street has a danger equally great to mariners—the land. In night and storm the ships are guided by lights lights lights.

Eastward in order from the Pacific: New Dungeness Lighthouse, earliest in the state, 1857. Point Wilson, the earlier installed in 1879, the present *Pinafore*-picturesque structure erected in 1914. Still in use is the original French lens that glared out 60,000 candlepower from a burner that utilized sperm-whale oil, coconut oil, lard oil, or kerosene. Admiralty Head on Whidbey, the 1860 light replaced in 1902 by the buildings that now are a park museum, the light gone dark. Marrowstone Point, the lighthouse completed in 1888; a fog bell failed to keep ships off the sands and was replaced in 1913 by a fog *gun.* Blinkers, not houses, at Bush Point and Double Bluff on Whidbey. Point No Point Lighthouse on Kitsap, 1879. At the turn for Elliott Bay, West Point Lighthouse, 1881, equipped now with a 1000-watt quartz lamp but still using the 1860 French lens that sends out a white beam visible at night for nineteen miles which alternates with a red beam visible for sixteen miles.

Ships turn Point Wilson so sharply that many a little tsunami jostles the driftwood. Nobody complains; beachwalkers find it exciting, once they understand what the hell is happening. At Point No Point the driftwood is cuddled by rows of boxes, and when bulkheads groan and picture windows rattle and porcelain gnomes topple on lawns, the government hears a chorus of whining from retired Kansans. Suibhna the Sailor Man loves to cajole his skipper into piling on the knots and cutting the corner tight, then lean on the rail and grin at the shaking fists and shout, "If you can't stand the waves, get off the beach."

May 7, 1792, was foggy. Vancouver landed on Point Wilson to wait for an opening before entering Admiralty Inlet and discovering Mount Rainier. To while away the time he walked the beach to Point Hudson.

Presumably the Society for the Preservation of the Memory of Wooden Ships is planning to recreate in 1992 his 1792 exploration, day by day from April 30, when the young third lieutenant, Joseph Baker, called attention to a snow-capped peak to the northeast, through the May 19 anchorage off Restoration Point and the June 4 taking of possession at Tulalip, to Jervis Inlet and finally Nootka, August 28.

There might be time enough to fund and build a *Discovery* and *Chatham*, but probably not to train crews of respectively one hundred seamen and forty-five seamen competent to navigate without charts, radio, radar, or auxiliary engines, and willing to breakfast and sup on biscuit and bully, "sauerkraut, portable soup, wheat malt and spruce beer, dried yeast, seed mustard..." A more practical plan is to recruit a handful of Whidbeys, Pugets, and Menzies to man (and woman) a cutter, longboat, or pinnace. They would be permitted fish and clams, though not potatoes.

34. Fort Worden State Park

Thursday, February 16, 1978

Lieutenant Worden commanded the *Monitor* the morning the "cheesebox on a raft" dueled the *Virginia,* née *Merrimac,* inaugurating the age of the ironclad. His namesake fort was the most elaborate of the Triangle because after 1904, when Flagler's shortage of potable water forced it to yield the honor, it was headquarters of the Harbor Defense of Puget Sound, with appropriate brass bureaucracy, band, chapel, and cemetery. I walked the parade ground, a quarter-mile greensward bounded on one side by military-yellow clapboard, the buildings now a conference center, and on the other by Officers Row, three-story mansions freshly painted in cheery pastels and kept in excellent repair because they are leased out, for a holiday weekend or a summer vacation.

I drove to Point Wilson, parked at Battery Kinzie, far out on the tropic atoll beside the grove of palms, and stepped from the beetle into a twenty-five-knot wind as cold as the glaciers of Tahoma. The longshore currents flowing from there through Puget Sound and Hood Canal into Admiralty Inlet were hard at work today extending Point Wilson into the Strait of Juan de Fuca. Rounding the corner into shelter from the southerly I was hit by a westerly no less energetically impelling currents from the Strait to extend Point Wilson into Admiralty Inlet. They met at the lighthouse in the fury of the riptide. The visible compromise of the millennia of uproar was a spit jutting a half-mile from the bluff. Though the lagoon was mostly paved, the dunes survived, surpassed on the Whulj only at Whidbey's West Beach.

As magma furnaces are to volcanoes, so currents are to spits. I thought back to my discovery of the wild side of Meadow Point two years before, and to West Point, Point Wells, Kayak Point, and others of the mainland shore, my home waters.

The currents there—and thus the spits—in the main are distinctly lesser than at Point No Point and Scatchet Head, Lagoon Point and Perego's Lagoon, Marrowstone Island and Quimper Peninsula. These, in turn, are distinctly lesser than at Dungeness Spit, the longest natural sandspit of the forty-eight states, and Ediz Hook, which makes Port Angeles a port.

From inner to outer there's a progression. The spits of these thousand square miles between Point Wilson, Ebey, Spanish Isles, and Vancouver Island are on a scale far larger than where I came from.

So are these thousand square miles of water.

Why is there no unifying name? Gulf of Vancouver? Gulf of Eliza? Vancouver y Eliza? Or Middle Whulj, the space between Home Whulj and Dragon Whulj?

PART FOUR

Crossing the Delta

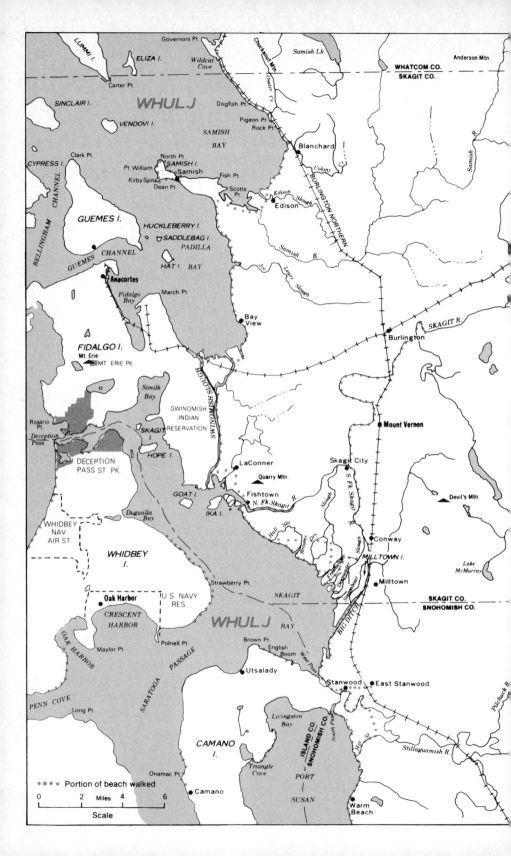

35. Hat Slough to Stanwood Mile 68–77

Thursday, December 1, 1977

Lower branches of the firs around our house on Cougar Mountain sagged under the rain, upper branches moaned in the wind, and to go out was madness. To stay in was worse.

> Walking, lads, walking's the act
> For fellows when their bells get cracked.

At 10:30 I parked beside Hat Slough, southernmost outlet of the Stillaguamish River. The gale had dwindled to breezes, the deluge to spatters, and though the day hadn't lightened past a dusk, the night was far behind and far ahead. Had my way been a jungle of thorny vines, a beach of jackstrawed driftwood, a tundra swept by a blizzard, or the flaming plains of Hell, I'd have been a contented pedestrian. But my route was beside a sullen river that had forgotten mountains and sky, remembered only sewers and cowflop.

The map said the air distance from Hat Slough to Blanchard was twenty-seven miles. I was no crow, I was a poor damn walker, and via the zigs and zags of dikes, the miles I'd be walking were beyond guessing. Nobody I knew ever had thought Bellingham worth it.

The river's green-brown surge frittered into muddy oozings through islets of cattails and willows, grass and reeds. Beyond Port Susan, the bluffs of Camano Island to the west were drizzly-dim. The bluff of the mainland, far across the fields to the east, was dissolving in cloud. I kept cleaning my glasses but it didn't help.

A grown-over unmaintained dike turned north, serving no apparent purpose because the maintained dike continued west, enclosing cultivated fields. I decided the inner dike was of an earlier frontier and wondered if yet another chunk would some day be taken from the tidal marshes still "unreclaimed." (On the Seventh Day the whole of Creation was sweet and arable, but Eve seduced Adam and so Mother Nature was given back the Garden for wildwood and desert and marsh. The task of Christians is to *reclaim* the unholy wastes, led by the friars of the Bureau of Reclamation and the warrior monks of the Corps of Engineers.)

My dike left the river and turned north. A pump sucked water from the fields on the Christian side and spewed it out in the saltgrass on the pagan. Both sides remained equally wet. Low spots in the dike had been newly heaped with sand, yet the dike's crest still rose barely higher than the cattails.

It was a day to make a bird lonesome. A flicker joined me, flying ahead a bit and perching to wait, then flying ahead again. A great blue heron lifted itself ponderously from the reeds, garking. A beelike bird-swarm swirled close overhead, eddied and soared and dove, massed on driftwood logs, and erupted in a flurry that faded to a twitter, then nothing. Sparrows scooted. Gulls wailed. A large hawk circled high. A pair of small white-rumped raptors swooped low through the dry cornstalks. From far out in the bay came such a sound as I'd never heard, like the yelping of a thousand hounds, a very great mystery.

Inland from my dike, a lesser rampart enwrapped a pond. Privy-size shacks had windows and stovepipes, more elaboration than seemed necessary for any apparent purpose. In the distance I could hear a dull *plut plut*. A mallard half-ran and half-flew through reeds and driftwood. Now I remembered: this was a pothole and those were warming shacks, the *plut plut* I'd been hearing was from shotguns, and I'd just met a half-shot duck.

Another mallard gabbled and I thought what a silly duck it was to announce where it was hiding. Then, recalling the gabbling that used to go on at feeding time between Uncle Bill and his tame mallards, I realized this was no true gabble, it was a silly hunter blowing on a patent gabbler.

I was the only visible human atop the dike and felt enormously conspicuous. A city boy might well be afraid to stand so tall amid reeds full of hunters in ambush. But as a country boy I'd loosed enough birdshot into rats terrorizing my chickens, and into packs of wild dogs trying to steal Mother's pies from the back-porch cooler, to know the limited killing range of shotguns.

Four small raptors were closely patroling the reeds and cornstalks.

It was a dangerous day for ducks and mice but probably not for a pedestrian under a red umbrella.

At 12:30 I came to South Pass.

In 1841, two years before the wagon trains of the Great Migration entered another South Pass, through the mountains to Oregon Country, Charles Wilkes failed to find this one—or West Pass either, or Hat Slough, or the Stillaguamish River. From Port Susan he took soundings of "2 2 2 1½" and quit, and from Skagit Bay of "8½ 5 5 4 3 (etc.) 3 2 1 1" and quit. Presumably based on Scatchet information, his map shows a narrow lane through the marshes, connecting the bays, but nothing of interest to the *Porpoise,* much less a seventy-four-gun ship.

The 1973 USGS map saw infinitely more than did my diketop eyes. Blue tussocks (the symbol for a marsh) extended three-quarters of a mile south from my rampart, there yielding to black-dotted blue (labeled "MUD") that in two more miles gave way to the solid blue that signifies open water. Through "MUD" ran a clear blue lane marked with "Piles," these to guide boats along the channel of the Port Susan shore of the Stillaguamish River.

The symbol that became more significant by the hour was the brown hatching labeled "Levee" that divided the white fields from the varied blues of bay, marsh, mud, and river. (Within that Christian white was *another* blue, a network of lines whose meaning I was yet to learn.)

The map saw all this plus roads, houses, section lines, benchmarks, and political boundaries. What I saw from the banks of South Pass was a gray plasma waiting for God to give it form and substance.

East in mist the vague bluffs were broken by an emptiness. The map said it was the valley of the Stillaguamish, one and a half miles wide, debouching on the delta.

In 1833 young Dr. Arthur Tolmie walked from Steilacoom up the Puyallup River to Mount Rainier, the first European to connect Puget Sound saltwater to Cascade Mountain icewater. A century and a half later I walked the Stillaguamish from Stanwood to Darrington, at the foot of Whitehorse Mountain, and having previously climbed that peak's glaciers, thus completed a parallel of Tolmie's journey. Today, walking where the lowland-fouled snowwater flowed into the saltwater,

I felt connected to the highland of hard rock and clean glacier—my land, as the delta was not.

Granted, I am presumptuous to call that highland "mine." A thousand times it has thrown rocks at me, avalanched me, frozen my bones and addled my head. But, after all those years of harsh lessons, I can still be warily comfortable there, in the manner of a Viking grown old raiding Ireland and Northumbria.

Here on the delta I was a Mongol bumpkin on his first conquest, having encountered the Chinese armies with their paper dragons and fire-crackers, and now riding a pony through a Chinese city. There was treasure, but I didn't know where or even what. And I wasn't sure in my mind that firecrackers were the worst I had to fear.

A chill gust goosed me north along South Pass, now distinctly a river flowing south in the ebb tide.

The dike path ended in a tangle of hellberry. A barbed-wire fence ran down one slope into fieldwater too deep to wade, down the other slope into marshwater deep enough to drown in. It was not a cow-fence rigged slack to be crawled through; it was a *mean-it* fence, the posts rigidly anchored by deadmen, the strands strung close and singing-taut.

Just like that, was the trip over?

I took a tentative first step. One foot up on the tightwire, then the other, both hands gripping the post. Now the step of no return: Bouncing, bouncing on the lower wire, I swung a leg over the top wire, now a dire menace, and balanced—bouncing, bouncing, where a gust of wind or burp of stomach might wound me most grievously. Swing the second leg over and it was done. And pray not to have to do it again.

The trail resumed, well beaten by the cows eyeing me morosely from green islands in the lakes. At 1 o'clock I attained a Momentous Spot, the splitting of what was once the main Stillaguamish into two channels: South Pass flowing to Port Susan and West Pass to Skagit Bay. For the Scatchets the junction of the three water roads had always been a key link in their travel network. For the Europeans it became so after dredging and channel-marking permitted the mosquitos to shortcut from bay to bay rather than taking the long way round through Saratoga Passage, and let river steamers paddlewheel upstream to Arlington. The 1911 map shows Stanwood as the largest town between Marysville and Mount Vernon, a trading center for reclaimed farmland of essentially the present size, and the meeting place of steamers, railroad, and automobiles.

One wonders what sort of person began the Stanwood settlement in 1866. One hundred and ten years later, after thousands upon thousands of man-years of hauling in bargeloads of fill, wagonloads of fill, trainloads of fill, truckloads of fill, helicopterloads of fill, the highest Stanwood ground shown by the map is "BM 6" (Benchmark 6 feet) at town center—six feet above mean high tide, a goodly number of feet *under* a high high at flood time, a Conjunction of merely Two. The dikes, shown by the map at 9 and 10 feet, seem like the Great Walls of China. In 1866, dikeless, there would have been long spells in three seasons of the year when only cattails and willows broke the sea that was continuous from the mainland bluff to Camano Island bluff.

I see Huckleberry Finn's pappy tying a raft to the willows here at the crossroads, one and a half miles from dry land east and just as far from dry land west, ladling out Injun whiskey to customers who don't know tobacco juice laced with cayenne pepper and turpentine from genuine rotgut. Despite endemic ague, grippe, and rheumatism, not to mention mold, mildew, and wet rot, the generations thrived. One marvels. Surely the living-room rugs of Stanwood must squish underfoot, the closets harbor man-eating fungi, and upstairs rooms have ropes handy for tying around the neck and jumping out the window.

Downtown Stanwood was separated from my dike only by the width of the river, but there was no bridge. I turned upstream and walked northeast, east, southeast, south, southwest, south, southeast, east, northeast-by-north, east-by-northeast, south, southwest, south, southeast, and east—five river miles to do two air miles. So the map told me later. On that grim afternoon I only knew I was haunted. From the great distance of Port Susan I'd admired the tall brick stack of Hamilton Lumber, relic of the vanished mill, the delta equivalent of the Space Needle, Washington Monument, Eiffel Tower, and Cleopatra's Needle. Now the damn thing kept circling around, leaping out at me from every willow grove.

River, sloughs, lakes, clouds, farms, and town had no color except darkening grays and browns. The spatters of morning had built to a steady hard rain. New cold water in my boots never let my feet warm up the old water. The sideways drift under the umbrella never let me clear my glasses. My underwear was soaking wet, notebook, map and the money in my wallet; nothing on my body or in my rucksack was dry. Nothing in the whole damn delta was dry and solid, the gradations of density ranging from fully liquid rain to bootsucking muck. If a person stood in one spot too long he would sink from sight.

Then an apparition materialized: a tall old house in a grove of tall, very old shade trees, three stories of gingerbread and gables, three brick chimneys, and a veranda. Hellberries blockaded the windows and doors, but they were not needed to keep me out. Delta structures float on silt, and if left untended settle unevenly; this derelict was so tilted from the perpendicular as to tip my mind over an abyss. I felt chills, glanced up, but not quite quick enough to catch the faces at the upstairs windows.

The 1911 map shows the house standing alone at the outermost thrust of a diked peninsula between South Pass and the undivided Stillaguamish, overlooking the steamer dock and the town. It obviously was one of those ambitious and belligerent lords granted a fiefdom on an empire's frontier who dared this arrogant invasion of the bay. What stories might the leaning castle tell? What tales are whispered in Stanwood of the Blank Mansion and the tragedy of some dark and rainy December night in Nineteen Hundred and Blank?

I hurried away, up the river. On the town side were moored houseboats, play boats and fishing boats. On my side derelicts rotted in the mud.

Suddenly—

Barbed wire was strung tautly atop a locked gate and down along both dike slopes. To the rear was that mean-it fence, where, if I retreated, I would have to repeat my high-wire act in weariness and night.

In the mountains, when one comes to a glacial torrent and sees that to study the situation will be to find the crossing impossible, one grips the ice ax in both hands, takes a deep breath, and *leaps*. So now. I slithered down riprap to where the wires were submerged in ugly brown water, clutched barbs in my bare hands, gritted my teeth against the bleeding, and leaned out in space, my fanny hanging inches above a churning abyss. "Damn the torpedoes. Four Bells, Captain Drayton. Go ahead—full speed."

A riverbank road led me to a bridge—a drawbridge, dating from the age when steamers paddled up to Arlington. Stanwood lay a road mile north; I turned south. My route to the bridge by dike had been eight miles. My return by Marine Drive was one and a half—a lesson in the geometry of Flatland, a warning of how very far it was to Blanchard.

Walking the highway in the night I reflected that today I'd passed the enterprises of the poor (sagging shanties with moss roofs, antique machinery and broken trucks rusting in the rain, and swaybacked barns missing half their shingles), of the middling (modest-cozy homes beside barns of sturdy old red-stained wood or shiny new tin), and of the rich (Twin City Foods, largest processor of frozen peas and corn in the world, its fleets of trucks and machines tended by factory gangs). Now in the night I walked by the Old Delta Empire as it was in the Golden Age. Beside the highway, spic and span and freshly painted with out-buildings to match, stood a three-story farmhouse with three brick chimneys—the sort of house nobody could build anymore because lumber of that quality hasn't been milled for decades and craftsmen with those skills are extinct. The map of 1911 shows the house. As I could tell walking by, it was the sort Grampa Clark was building then in Ballard. Happiness spilled into my sodden gloom. Within those fortunate walls were neither mildew nor squish nor despondency. These nobles—not driven by overweening pride to desperate invasions of the bay but prudently content with the delta's inner edge—were warm and dry and serene.

Walking in the night I savored the nose-stunning, stomach-wrenching reek of cowshit, horseshit, pigshit, chickenshit, synthetic shit—the palpable cloud that hangs heavy over fields, dikes, ditches, and roads, the geist of the delta. The nineteenth-century manor was warm and dry but surely stank of manure.

No doubt when Ole and Sven come home from the sea to Ballard there is, in Grampa Clark's houses, the stink of halibut.

36. Stanwood to Milltown

Mile 77–84$^1/_4$

Friday, December 2, 1977

Rain had poured for days, the mountain snowpack had melted, rivers were rising, and looters and ghouls and gawkers were being warned to stay away from the delta. At 10:20 I parked in East Stanwood—not on the delta but not at the top of the bluff either, only just above the railroad tracks. An elevation of 20 feet above mean high tide seemed amply cautious.

I descended to the plain and walked through downtown Stanwood, expecting to have to skulk past a police barricade. The police force was having coffee. The citizenry was getting and spending as usual. Where were the sandbag crews, Red Cross, helicopters, National Guard, TV cameras? Several winters ago the papers had run front-page photos of this very street flowing deep in brown Stillaguamish water. Were folks here so accustomed to floods that they went about their business to the very last minute? Would they all, at a given signal, casually evacuate their homes, businesses, and schools, the town and the delta, leaving me a solitary alien, perched on a dike as the waters rose to 6, to 9, to 10 feet, poured into the fields and filled them up and rose still higher, till at 15 feet above mean high tide it was chucking my chin?

At 10:50, having passed the Hamilton stack and the Twin Cities factory on the west edge of town, I studied the concrete arch vaulting over West Pass to the delta marshes of Camano Island. (When the signal came, would sirens whine, churchbells ring, and cannon boom?) Perhaps I could flee there and await rescue by a TV helicopter. I'd put extra apples, kippers and Pepsis in my rucksack.

I climbed onto the dike, unhappy to see West Pass flowing at a level many feet higher than the fields. But the tide was ebbing, and so too, I hoped, was the crisis. The gloom had lightened, the wind fallen, the Olympics were emerging. Clouds were solid and swift but thin and empty. No need today for the red umbrella. Of course, one must take into account the possibility that the sun might be shining here, the birds singing and the children playing on the teeter-totter, when the mountain cloudburst of the day before yesterday comes thundering down the river in a brown wall of mud, trees, houses, and National Guard jeeps.

A farmhouse adjoined the dike. To avoid walking impolitely through the yard, I detoured onto the railroad spur that served the Twin Cities factory, to my rear. When the spur bent east to the main line I continued north on the farm lane, and when I noted the dike was diverging northwest, struck off over the fields to intersect it.

The first rude lesson of the day was that it is not necessarily easy to romp about in the white Christian fields of the map. The muck sucked down my boots, ankles, calves, tried for my knees, lusted for my hips and lips and eyes. I struggled nearly to the dike and to a second lesson: what the map shows as a thin clean blue line may be a drainage ditch as wide as a river and the color of homogenized shit.

I followed the bank north, hoping for a bridge, since many dikes are used as access roads to fields. The best bridges I found were slimy hunters' planks that sagged toward the vile soup of dung, chemical fertilizer, pesticide, herbicide, and coliform bacteria. I did not cross.

My progress was halted by a tributary ditch, merely a jump wide had I been able to make a running start. I did not jump.

By noon I was slinking humbly past the farmhouse windows, an hour wasted, feet soaked, pants mucked to the knees, but my education advanced: Those innocent blue lines on the map, some curving in and out of lakelet remnants of old sloughs, others simple and straight and unrelated to Mother Nature's primeval dispositions, were in real life corrupt and potentially lethal.

West Pass empties into Skagit Bay. As Balboa stood on a peak in Darien, I stood on a dike (elevation 11 feet).

Beyond the half-mile-wide band of salt marsh lay a hundred square miles of water, so enclosed by Camano, Whidbey, and Fidalgo islands as to seem a lake—a very, very great lake. The delta on the reclaimed side of the dike was greater, nearly twice as great as the total of all the Whulj's deltas to the south of here.

In 1911 Douglas Slough, an ancient channel of the Stillaguamish, was a third "pass" that together with West Pass ringed a diked island. Now I was walking the former island, and the slough was a dredged ditch. The map's little blue lines led into this remnant of Douglas Slough, then oozed north to the Skagit River.

I'd crossed a divide, lost my connection through Port Susan to Possession Sound to Puget Sound—my Whulj. The homiest thing in view was that damned Hamilton Lumber stack.

Except that the delta in the transition zone was at its narrowest, less than a mile from dike to bluff, the route was the same mix as before. The dike was a partly well-mown truck road, partly weedy and mean with fences to climb over and crawl through. Fields were lakes or fresh-plowed black-brown earth, or green pasture, or rows of dead cornstalks and rotting cabbages.

How did the pioneers know what to grow here? Were their pappies Mississippi dikers, their granddaddies Holland dikers, and so on back to the Tigris and Euphrates? How did they go about the reclamation? The North West Boundary Survey map of 1866 shows the primeval undisturbed; the USGS map of 1911 shows the job essentially complete.

Douglas Slough passed through the dike, from fields to marshes, via a "Tide Gate" (so labeled on the map), a plank dam with a movable closure that was opened on the lowering tide to drain away soup, closed when the tide rose to bar the salt.

I walked by a little box on stilts, out in the reeds, a blind in the sky reached via rowboat and ladder.

I met a "jump-shooter," a hunter who scares up birds by walking, as distinguished from a "blind-shooter" who lurks in ambush. The weather being pleasant enough for the prey to sit safely in the bay, not driven by storm winds toward the waiting guns in the bushes, I greeted him with the traditional, "Great day for the ducks!" He smiled wryly, gestured to mountains and sky, and said, "What the hell, where else would we rather be?"

A Blue Hole over the Cascade front lit Little Mountain and Devils Mountain, marking the east boundary of the delta. Beyond Whidbey another Blue Hole shone above the unseen Gulf of Vancouver. Massive in cloud-shadow, Blanchard Hill and Chuckanut Mountain marked the north boundary of Flatland, far away. Yet close at hand rose Mount Erie, visible on clear days from the Issaquah Alps. I was again connected. I might yet prevail.

A hellberry horror blocked the dike top and slopes. But here no drainage ditch prevented my descent to fields, and these fields were well drained and solid, the fences easy, and the blue lines sturdily plank-bridged. Shortly I came to a public road that took me west a few steps to a parking lot signed "Big Ditch Access, Skagit Wildlife Recreation Area, Washington State Department of Game." A concrete tidegate controlled a *very* big ditch, big as a river but too straight to be one, and not shown on the 1911 map. A quaint old wooden bridge crossed to an odd sort of dike that did no reclaiming but merely hemmed in Big Ditch so its waters couldn't seep through the tules to join Tom Moore Slough. Why the dikers wanted to keep the two apart was for the Mesopotamians to explain.

I turned downstream on the dike. Far ahead I saw pilings, labeled "Jetty" on the map and shown extending more than two miles from "Beacon" at its outer tip to a marsh island at the mouth of Tom Moore Slough. Booming ground? Fishtrap? The location seemed wrong for either. Whatever, it was built after the 1909 surveys for the map of 1911. Only much later did I find the explanation in a memorandum of the U.S. Army Engineers, "Condition of Improvement, 30 June 1972."

> The project, adopted 25 June 1910, and modified 2 March 1919, provides for obtaining a reliable channel of entrance through the delta by means of a dike at the mouth of the South Fork; regulating dikes and a mattress sill near the head of the North Fork; and closing subsidiary channels at the delta; and for increasing the available depth at Skagit City Bar by combining dredging operations and training walls. The length of the section included in this project is 9½ miles.
>
> The project is 46 percent complete. Construction of the mattress sill and closing dikes, and of the training dike to a length of 10,450 feet, was completed in 1911. All of the completed features are in very poor condition...project has been classified inactive.

Later I would deduce that "closing dikes" blocked off river channels at their upper entries, "regulating dikes" confined their flow, and "mattress sills" had something to do with manipulating the bed of the river. The "Jetty" of the pilings was a "training dike" to make the river scour a channel deep enough for steamers to paddle upstream via Steamboat Slough, South Fork, and Skagit City Bar to Mount Vernon. The project was "inactive" because there weren't any steamers to paddle there anymore.

I walked off the downstream end of the hemming dike and into "MUD AND SAND."

The map showed nearly two miles of this midworld reaching out to the start of open water. A Blue Hole poured out a flood of light that set the wetness shining, a sky beneath my feet.

Peep!

A cloud of wings, thousands of little birds that flew inches from my face, peeping, never laying a wing on me, ran over the sand inches from my feet, peeping, dipping their needle noses in the wet, peeping, and never touched a boot. As one cloud, they ran the sands, peeping, exploded aloft, peeping, set out for Canada, peeping, wheeled toward Mexico, peeping, plummeted to the sands, peeping, peeping, peeping.

The ragged V's and company fronts of migrating geese and ducks, the rabbles of bushtits and grosbeaks and crows, these are "human"— this is how *we* would fly (how we *do* fly). But the peeping cloud moved always as one.

Or almost always. A cloud from Canada would meet a cloud from Mexico and the two would seamlessly become one. A cloud would divide, not in a confused dithering but decisively, the one cloud becoming two.

Scientists haven't decoded the peeping, haven't guessed the means of instant mass communication and decision, or located the group mind that functions through an extra sense. They will. As in World War II the scientists learned sonar and radar from the bats in order to win battles under the sea and in the air, a crash program on the scale of the Manhattan Project will be mounted the moment the Soviet Union is detected peeping.

At home I pored over books to try to sort out the sandpipers I was meeting on the delta. An Audubon friend laughed, "Just call them peep!"

The hemming dike was the first public dike of my route. I felt—if not at home—at least welcome, and on my way upstream from Big Ditch Access lengthened my stride—trackwalker-beachwalker becoming dikewalker. The *plut* of distant guns didn't bother me, nor even the *blam* of close explosions in the cornfield across Big Ditch; some of my best relatives have been birdbusters.

The map showed, a few yards left of the dike, a row of black-outlined white boxes, the symbol for derelict structures. The map was wrong. These were *duck shacks*.

From the pagan side of the dike the plankwalks-on-stilts crossed reedy marsh to a dozen shacks on pilings or anchored floats, beside and partly in the roiling brown of Tom Moore Slough. Surely a person could not *sleep* here? Fresh driftwood on the dike slopes showed the water very recently had risen over the walks and reeds and come within two or three feet of surging over the dike into Christendom. Nevertheless, though some of the shacks were squalid and tumbledown, places where Huck's pappy might snore in a drunken stupor, most were snug warrens cunningly crafted of salvaged lumber and gifts of the river and bay. Some were neatly painted, ornamented with rope, fishing floats, and nets, embellished with flower pots and planter boxes, more home than home.

The dike path dwindled to a meager track in willow woods festooned with hellberry vines poised to claw a walker's eyes out. A black something darted along a plankwalk and I followed, not catching up, to a second village. The slough was not the blandness in my 1930s memory, it was a wide and scary turbulence. On the far side was the mouth of an even larger waterway, Steamboat Slough.

My eyes saw two brown avenues through the monotony of reeds and the gray of tanglewoods. The modern map saw five square miles of the same, but with names: Tom Moore Slough, Isohis Slough, Steamboat Slough, Boom Slough, Old River, Crooked Slough, Deepwater Slough, Brandstedt Slough, Freshwater Slough, Wiley Slough, and a dozen more without names. In their midst were Milltown Island, Ericson Island and countless nameless others. The 1911 map surveyed the maze and named the only feature that mattered, Steamboat Slough. There in the 1930s, Dad, crouched in the cattails, would hear strange chuggings and clangings. When he stood up to find out what was happening, he'd see either the *Gleaner* or the *Harvester*, twin sternwheelers, carrying freight to and from farms and markets, appearing to be giant plows preparing fields of tules for cultivation. In 1866, 1911, the 1930s and 1970s, it all was willow-tangle swamps, grass-reed marshes, brownwater lanes. It was boat country, where the *African Queen* chug-a-chugs around the bend, Huck and Jim drift by on a raft, the gunboat *Carondelet* leads the Union flotilla past the batteries of Island No. 10, and Dad and Uncle Bill and their Irish water spaniels float by in a rowboat.

A kickerboat, outboard motor laboring, bow dangerously dipping, was working its way upstream, barely making headway. The two hunters and their Labs aboard it looked my way and turned in to shore. Their shack was up the river and they were keeping an eye out for people who didn't belong. But I *did*.

They were in no rush, so I told them that Dad and Uncle Bill and several friends used to have a shack hereabouts, on school land leased from the state for a couple of bucks a year. And that they'd also had a pothole, possibly along Steamboat Slough. A fisherman who lived year-round in one of the shacks scattered corn in the pothole on weekdays to draw the ducks, a favor repaid on weekends with jugs of corn liquor. In black predawns of the weekends the hunters would row from the shack to the pothole and tie up at their blind, an old scow mounted on pilings and concealed in the brush. They'd put the spaniels in a kennel at one end of the scow to keep them dry and warm. They'd uncrate Uncle Bill's tame mallards, fit them with harnesses, and anchor the attached lines, taking care to position their living decoys in a natural-seeming formation. At stormy dawn (assuming it was a bad day for the ducks) hunters elsewhere on The Flats would start banging away. Frightened flocks would head for their weekday restaurant, see it was safe because mallards already were settled in and gabbling back and forth (with Uncle Bill, who gabbled so expertly that mallards came to him to learn how). The .12 gauges would *blam-blam-blam,* four or five shells in the magazine and one in the chamber, five or six rapid-fire *blams* per gun, and the spaniels would leap from the scow and swim out to retrieve. And all too soon each hunter would bag his day's limit of twenty. On opening day, when targets were so plentiful that Dad might shoot five boxes of shells—125 rounds—Mother and Aunt Grace would drive up to The Flats at noon to haul away the dead ducks that had been retrieved (which despite the efficient spaniels, were never more than a fraction of those shot). Then each hunter could shoot another twenty that afternoon, and, with similar teamwork, another twenty on Sunday.

My visitors, not a duck between the two of them and their Labs, hung on every word of this tale of the good old days when, on a bad weekend for the ducks, a hunter might take home sixty dead, and kill or cripple another hundred or two. My audience had to be moving along to beat the night or I'd have told them more. Like: How after a great day for the ducks Dad often came home without ever having pulled the trigger, yet with his jacket-back full of cripples retrieved by our first Irisher or her daughter.

Or how Uncle Bill once got home and found such a healthy cripple in his jacket that he added it to his decoy flock, at first tying it to a peg but by spring letting it free to waddle about with the gang. One day the next fall he was working in the yard and heard the high-in-the-sky gabble of migration. His tame mallards, hatched in captivity, never looked up. But the one born wild answered, and Uncle Bill watched it climb to join the flock headed for Mexico.

Or how we never ate ducks. Dad gave them away to city folk who thought duck was a delicacy, partly because they'd never had a chance to develop a taste for the Chinese pheasants Dad shot on upland hunting trips and reserved for the home table.

Had the two hunters been able to hang around long enough I'd have confessed I visited The Flats in the 1930s but never hunted there. Shot a lot of Norway rats and stung a few dogs in the rump, but only once, at the age of ten, turned my gun, a .410, on a bird. The bird was a quail, one of a covey I'd known all spring and summer because I jumped them in the tall grass behind our house so I could enjoy the massed wings exploding underfoot. Dad and Uncle Bill were on hand, and Dad had a bit of fun joshing Uncle Bill about how all Mannings were crack shots, born with it. Mother served up the morsel to me that night as if it were a Chinese pheasant, and I dutifully ate my first kill, my last.

I didn't know if our shack had been in this area. The dike between Big Ditch and Tom Moore Slough felt vaguely familiar, as if it might have been our walking route from Milltown. I pushed on past the second village to a scant half-mile from Milltown, for old times' sake. Recent hunters had been commuting by boat. Hellberries crept up the dike slopes to slash my ankles and knees, snaked down from overhanging willows to rip my cheeks and ears, arched across the dike to wrap my chest and belly and go for my heart and liver. At 3 o'clock, pants and shirt in tatters, umbrella stolen from my rucksack by the grasping arms of the hellberries, fearing for my life, I retreated.

A litter of white feathers said something just had eaten something.

A hawk sailed over.

In the flooded field across Big Ditch a hunter was wading, a dog splashing. A cow chewed cud on a hummock isle.

The Olympics were blue-gray against a wide band of yellow. The islets-peaklets north in Skagit Bay were black profiles in cream. The lights of Stanwood began winking on. Blackbirds said, "Click, click." Peep wheeled overhead. Far out in the bay rose an unholy clamor, the mysterious yelping of a thousand hounds.

The last color faded as I crossed Big Ditch at 4:20 and was splashed by the day's first rain, a brief shower, cool on the cheeks, and nice. The access road took me to railroad tracks at the foot of the bluff. My feet found the ties and followed the steel rails homeward.

Back on Cougar Mountain I picked up the newspaper, which had gone to press about the time I was being taught the meaning of the little blue map lines, and read the headline, "Major Floods." I turned on the TV and watched reporters in hardhats hold microphones to the mouths of mayors and colonels in hardhats. The governor in hardhat declared a Disaster Area. Over helicopter footage of Noah and his ark, an anchorperson solemnly pronounced, "Most of the state west of the Cascades is under water."

I was in the middle of the great big media flood all day and missed it.

37. Milltown to Conway Mile 84¼–86¼

Monday, December 19, 1977

All that remained of whatever had once been Milltown was a solitary house, grandly signed "Milltown Elev. 7 Ft." I parked nearby at the Milltown Access of the Skagit Wildlife Recreation Area. Rotten-looking timbers and rusty iron with a "No Vehicles" sign crossed Tom Moore Slough, so narrow here that it was completely arched over by alder and cottonwood. The bridge got me to Milltown Island. Nearly two miles long and a half-mile wide, the island was entirely ringed, according to the map, by a dike, perhaps *the* dike we walked from Milltown in the 1930s. I'd have no chance to search for the past today; a few steps north and south from the bridge the dike was breached, and the fields of the interior were a sea so deep the cattail brushes barely broke the surface.

The hundredth meridian is the line beyond which midwestern prairies were found by sad experience to be too dry for sustained farming; Milltown Island apparently lay beyond the too-wet line. Just as Grandfather Hawthorn finally gave up on North Dakota, the diker whose fields and buildings are on the map of 1911 must have been happy to sell out to the ducks and the Game Department. It happened well before 1956—the map of that year shows the Christian white reclaimed by Mother Nature's blue tussocks.

The maps show other defeats and victories. Neighboring Ericson Island, diked and inhabited in 1911, has been abandoned so long that the modern map bears no trace of man. Three islands to the west were diked and inhabited in 1911; now the smallest has returned to a state of nature and the two larger have been united, the Old River that divided them reduced to a ditch by a closing dike. Closure of other sloughs here left the river only Tom Moore, Steamboat, and Freshwater sloughs as important channels.

At least since the mapping of 1866, and probably for centuries, the Skagit River, upon debouching from the Cascades at Sedro Woolley, has turned sharply south to flow close under the mountain front, emptying to saltwater on the southernmost reach of its delta. My upstream route on the mainland dike of Tom Moore Slough was parallel to, and only a scant mile from, the frontal scarp's startling leap to the summits of Devils Mountain.

Cirrus clouds lightly streaked the blue sky. Shadows were chilly, splashes of sun cheery. I passed the head of Milltown Island, where the smaller Tom Moore Slough splits off from the larger Steamboat, and then passed the head of the two nameless islands made into one. Here the South Fork Skagit divides into the equal-sized Steamboat and Freshwater. Here begins the dividing and redividing which continues three more river miles (via Freshwater) or four more (via Tom Moore) to the MUD AND SAND of Skagit Bay.

At noon I entered Conway, a quiet town with little plastic and less neon but plenty of white paint. Well-kept old houses evidenced pride in their history, dating back to 1873—not counting the Scatchets, shown by tent symbols on the 1866 map as having a village here: Kikiallus. To a walker-through the major industries appeared to be antique shops and the Conway Tavern, noted by a modest plaque as "Established 1932."

I sat in a grove of cottonwoods and alders to eat my kippers and apple. Across the river rose the steeple of a white church that is featured frequently in Sunday pictorials. The 1911 map shows it and six others nearby, and four more in Milltown—eleven houses of worship to serve two hundred households, assuming none of the local folks did their praying in Stanwood (five churches) or Mount Vernon (too many to count).

> And He walks with me,
> And He talks with me,
> And He tells me I am His own...

The results hereabouts of a century and some decades of His land ethic tended to push my sympathies over the tops of the dikes to Mother Nature; whoever was in charge, though, it remained true now as in the Sunday school song of my childhood that while walking I felt walked *with*, talked *to*, owned. Only when the feet stopped did the darkness crowd in. One wonders about night thoughts in the years before 1911, when farmers pulled on boots and oilskins and went out with lanterns in raging storms to walk new and untested dikes; a powerful lot of Him must have been wanted to combat the seeming omnipotence of Her. Eleven churches may have been scarcely enough.

Near my lunch spot were buildings signed "Diking District No. 7," and without having to think more about it I understood where the dikes came from.

After the TV pathos of cows marooned on pasture islands and rowboats in the streets of Stanwood, the pork barrel is rolled out to buy a few doughnuts, pile a few sandbags. But the compassion is turned off soon after the TV. In the main, the wetfeet must help themselves, particularly through diking districts, units of local government on the pattern of fire districts and sewer districts. This is not to say the dikers won't snap up any dollar they can wheedle from county, state, National Guard, U.S. Army Engineers, or Red Cross.

With a bit more map study I understood Big Ditch, which starts at these buildings and flows from the river in an underground conduit to the above-ground ditch, and thence to the bay. When the rains and snowmelts from a thousand mountains gather together in the Skagit, they "pile up" and slop over the dikes. Big Ditch assists the natural distributaries in carrying away the pile of water. One doubts it was needed before His dikers and Army Engineers closed off so many of Her primeval distributaries.

38. Conway to Brown's Slough   Mile 86¹/₄–92

Monday, December 19, 1977

I fetched the beetle from Milltown and crossed the river on the Conway bridge to Fir Island, the fifteen-odd square miles of delta between the South Fork and the North Fork of the Skagit. I intended to walk downstream along Freshwater Slough but the dike was topped with a row of houses, then rental duck shacks, so I continued driving to the Headquarters Access of the Skagit Wildlife Recreation Area. The trailhead brochure told me I was in the center of 12,761 acres of publicly owned delta treasurehouse. There were marshes of saltgrass, cattail, and sedge-and-bulrushes; willow swamps; cornfields; homes or resting places for brant, whistling swans, sandhill cranes, 200 species of songbird, three species of geese, and 26 species of ducks, not to mention harbor seals, river otters, mink, deer, and beaver. I wished for binoculars, little knowing that before day's end I'd be glad not to have them.

In Dad's time on The Flats most farmers gave free run to any hunter who promised not to shoot the cows. In the more crowded, less amiable America of the 1980s the shooting is jealously guarded from poachers, perhaps shared with friends, but more likely sold to a gun club. Ducks are among the delta's most valuable crops.

This crop is maintained on a sustained-yield basis, the slaughter of Dad's era having been curtailed in the nick of time to save the flocks from extinction. The sport itself was not saved, however, because non-club-members found their old accesses blocked by No Trespassing signs. They therefore taxed themselves, with hunting licenses, to purchase public accesses through private lands to public waters and wetlands, and to buy abandoned too-wet farms. And so, the 12,761 acres.

The sun was cirrus-dulled and cooling as I set out, at 1:40, on the most popular public dike in the state, ringing an island created for recreation, and thus left undrained. In one mile I passed swamp (dark willow hideaways), marsh (reed jungles and nooks of open water), boggy meadow (no open water but water everywhere at the roots of sedge and moss), and field (turf solid enough to walk on and to grow grain for the birds). A bird unable to find pleasure in one or more of these wetlands was not born to be happy.

The dike bent right, around the island foot, from Freshwater Slough to Wiley Slough. I went left on a spur dike, built only to provide a trail, downstream to a dead end in tawny-glowing meadow-marsh. I'd thought to continue over peeping sand but the tide was high and the brown of river and marshes was backed up by the shining blue of Skagit Bay.

My view on the return upstream was over the immensity of Flatland to the 1,700-foot scarp of Devils Mountain. Beyond it were the 4,000-foot scarp of Cultus Mountain, its blue-green forests whitened by fresh snow; Komo Kulshan, whitest of the volcanoes, and its companion, Shuksan, often described as "the most beautiful mountain in America;" Whitehorse, the first mountain other than Rainier whose name I knew; Big Four, where I'd climbed through the snow gullies and ledges without figuring out which of them composed the numeral; and Pilchuck, the incomparable Nanga, the supreme connector, from whose mile-high summit we look west to the Whulj where we live and east to the fossil winters where we adventure.

In 1864 the Fir Island frontier was opened by the first European settler. Since then, says the U.S. Geological Survey, 60 percent of the wetlands of the eleven major delta systems of the Whulj have been civilized. In 1889 all tidelands of the new state of Washington, including the deltas, belonged to the state. They were sold off so vigorously over the years that before the legislature called a halt in 1971, 2,000 miles had been transferred to private hands: 63 percent of the total of 3,174 miles. That's according to the state. (Using different definitions of tidelands, the Army Engineers count 2,337 miles, University of Washington geographers 3,600.) A diker could buy a chunk of public marsh or bay and do it in at his leisure, pleasure, and sole discretion. If he prospered, there rose upon the land a three-story mansion with three brick chimneys, and if his generations thrived, it is sturdy and freshpainted to this day, and if not, faces peer out from upstairs windows.

Unlike such conversions as that of the Duwamish, where the delta has been lidded over by freeways and industry to create a holocaust for the ducks, diking-farming merely requires the ducks to shift their eating habits; in fact, the Skagit delta may now spread before wildfowl a table groaning as never before.

Or maybe not. The bird that prefers eelgrass to peas wouldn't think so. Supermarkets groan, too, and half their glossy foods cause cancer in rats. How hazardous is it to the health of ducks to swim those ditches whose vileness so offended my nose and terrified my skin? At least they have 12,761 acres where the worst they have to fear is getting shot.

Returning along the spur dike I passed hundreds of sawed-off stumps-and-roots, feet-mouths of trees that were logged over the course of a century. They'd been attacked by misery whip or chainsaw; bull-team, donkey, lokie (locomotive), cat, or truck; skidroad or ground-lead or high-lead or skyline; then were ripped out of clearcut slopes by floods and swept down the river to the dump. The lowering sun silhouetted Medusa heads of writhing roots weathered to the color of old bones, skeletons of giants that lived five or a dozen human lifetimes before being assassinated.

At 2:30 I turned north on a trail that crossed Wiley Slough on a wide and sturdy footbridge and climbed over a fence on a stile. It was good to feel welcome.

To my left, beyond Skagit Bay and Whidbey Island, the Olympics were clouding, bad news for tomorrow. Dead ahead and far away, ice giants of the British Columbia Coast Range were shining. To my right, Komo Kulshan grew more brilliant by the minute.

At 3 o'clock the dike trail was blocked by a mean-it fence and signs that made threats surely no one could really mean. Bold and nimble as Jack on the beanstalk, over I went, onto a mown path that led to a cozy cove harboring a fleet of kickerboats and a cabin. Suddenly I was surrounded by a pack of howling hounds, and the cabin door swung open to reveal a specter in long-handled underwear. I pretended an idiocy that in my sudden fear wasn't far from the fact and spun an incoherent tale about my car being at Brown's Slough and I'd got turned around and could I get there from here? The specter closed his eyes and passed a hand over his forehead, as if weary or ill or sick up to here of idiots, called in the hounds, and slammed the door shut.

The dike crossed Dry Slough, which in 1911, before being closed off by a dike, was called Deer Slough and was in effect a middle fork of the Skagit. The map showed other old dikes of the field-by-field conquest of Fir Island. A fence marked the boundary of Long Johns' principality; as at the other fence, signs threatened fine, imprisonment, and disembowelment, and it now seemed to me possible they really meant it.

Beyond the fence the path was overgrown by tall grass and blocked by thickets of hellberry and wild rose that forced me down to short wades in the marsh. Boughs of crooked little trees were hung with wizened crabapples.

The dike curved in around a small bay, the head of a slough. And then another. The mountain front had gone dark, only Komo Kulshan and Shuksan still aglow. I glanced over my shoulder to the enormous pink snowball of Tahoma.

At 3:40 the dike turned sharp right at Brown's Slough which, having been diked off, now contained only what had seeped in. The sun had left Komo Kulshan but—oddly—still lit the tip of Shuksan. Sinking into California, the fireball had found a gap in the ranges to throw a spotlight on the Summit Pyramid.

Brown's Slough turned orange. I walked off the dike onto Fir Island Road, my return route—not twice in one day would Long Johns swallow my poppycock.

In 1911 Fir Island, hitched to the rest of the delta by one bridge and several ferries, had some 125 buildings (including two churches), mostly along rivers and sloughs. Two towns existed: Conway (since moved to the other bank of the river) and Skagit City, formerly the metropolis of the entire delta. A lone fifty-foot hillock crowned by Douglas firs presumably gave the island its name; amid elevations ranging from three feet (the field) to ten feet (the dike top) the grove of trees reaching a hundred and more feet above sea level is a stupendous eminence for the area.

Island roads are narrow. Every square inch of rich brown soil removed from production is begrudged. On both sides the walker is closely hemmed in by fields that emit the aroma one probably learns to love, as with the reek of mud flats in summer sun, if not asphyxiated by it first.

Island roads are quiet at night. No farmer or hunter—no *human* hunter—has reason to be abroad. The fields murmur softly of peace and contentment. Yet the corner of the eye catches the flight of dark wings, silent wings, seeking a quiet supper.

Under the big orange sky, violet clouds, and gibbous moon, in the deepening night of the grandest Flatland west of the Columbia Plateau, veteran of the dikes, at home in the treasurehouse, I walked.

Forest walking, clearcut walking, meadow walking, rock walking, snow walking, desert walking, railroad walking, river walking, beach walking, marsh walking, dike walking, road walking....

At age nine or ten, after many a tumble and crash that engendered a permanent distrust of wheels, I mastered the bicycle and cut by two-thirds the time of the commute to Ronald School. Time saved—for what? One spring morning when thirteen I left the bike home on an impulse and walked through the orchard—the orchard of the quail, the scotchbroom in yellow flame, the salal and Oregon grape and tall fir, the mossy barren of a knoll of glacial gravel, and my Secret Camp—none of which could be seen from wheels. Bicycling is not evil in itself but is the next thing to motorcycling, which leads to jet airplanes and playing golf on the moon. It's the wrong way to point the arrow.

> Walk, walk, walk about
> Freely o'er the plain,
> Merrily, merrily, merrily, merrily,
> Never feeling pain.

Walk (don't run) to cure the imbalance of blood, phlegm, yellow bile, and black bile that can cause a paroxysm of sanguinity or melancholy, apathy or choler. Walk (never jog) to rewire the electrical circuitry whose disarray can trigger a fatal storm.

Walk (and walk by yourself) for the isolation that defines where self leaves off and family and society begin.

> Merrily, merrily, merrrily, merrily,
> Everybody sane.

"Solvitur ambulando [it is solved by walking]—the motto of the philosophic tramp," said the English essayist, Edward Maitland. The Australian aborigine, when too much put upon, says the hell with it and goes off on a walkabout.

Experimenters and interrogators can produce psychosis by waking a sleeper whenever instruments detect the start of the rapid eye movement (REM) that accompanies dreaming. Deprived of REM the victim soon is in the fetal crouch, whimpering, confessing to every crime. Dreaming is the way the subconscious mind links the present with the past and future. The subconscious cannot keep the underside of the head organized without dreaming. Not to dream is to go mad.

Walking lets the conscious mind organize the upperside of the head, gives space to review the past, forecast and plan the future, sort out and evaluate and connect. After nearly two years of daily walking I felt saner than since my years of—of *climbing*. Aha! The truth is out! Wonderland is on *this* side of the looking glass!

In the deep dusk of 4:45 I returned to the headquarters trailhead. A fellow gazing over the marsh watched me unsling my rucksack and asked where I'd been. He laughed at my answer and called to a companion, "Here's a man who's just walked the dikes *all the way to Brown's Slough!*" The companion whistled.

Along the way, I learned, were dikers of the hundredth generation, descended from the reclaimers of the Garden, great-great-grandsons of the Dutch boy who stuck his finger in the dike, magnates of the delta, and what they hated *second*-worst in all the world was bolsheviki hunters who trespassed from the Soviet Recreation Area onto the shooting preserve they maintained for themselves.

What they hated *worst* was peasants who watched birds rather than shooting them. Only the lack of binoculars around my neck saved me from being torn to pieces by the hounds while dikers watched from their cabins, cackling.

I was congratulated on my escape—and warned of dangers ahead.

Capital projects are group efforts by the diking district; routine maintenance is the responsibility of individual reclaimers. On my route ahead lurked notorious ne'er-do-wells perhaps related to the Jukes family of *Tobacco Road*, who went barefoot, chewed tobacco, and made moonshine. The House of Lords didn't mind all *that* but wouldn't tolerate their neglect of their dikes, which three days earlier, during the Conjunction of Three, had been overtopped, flooding their fields and, inevitably, those of their neighbors. When brought up on charges of neglect, they launched into diatribes against the Wildlife Recreation Area—the WRA—and its clientele of trespassers. The foreign birdbusters were bad enough but now they were outnumbered by bloodless, psalm-singing bird*watchers,* so numerous their heavy birdy feet were tramping down the dikes faster than the Jukes relations could pile sand on top. They demanded a campaign to pass a law that nobody be allowed on the WRA without a gun.

My friend in the dusk laughed. The House of Lords knew the ne'er-do-wells of old and had ordered them to bulldoze their hellberries and heap up riprap and sand. Little as the nobles liked foreigners and peasants, they knew the WRA was invulnerable to their assaults, being too

heavily defended by hunters, whose fees originally established the public preserve, and birders, who had contributed to its enlargement
through the federal Land and Water Conservation Fund. Though it was
true that binoculars now outnumbered guns, the two stood together
against the paver-polluter-poisoner, whether oiler, pulper, dammer,
highwayman, subdivider, or diker.

"Listen!" said my friend.
"What?"
"The widgeons."
"Where?"
"All around, everywhere, thousands of them."
The pitch of the whistling was too high for my low-fi ear. I also
failed to distinguish the other night sounds he picked out, voices of
many species, myriad individuals, in from the bay where they'd spent
the day, now resting and feeding in preparation for another great day for
the ducks.
"What does the Game Department do? Sound the 'all clear' at sunset?"
"Doesn't have to. Fifteen minutes after the guns have to quit at
night, in come the birds. Fifteen minutes before it's legal to shoot in the
morning, off they fly to the bay."
No wonder Dad abandoned The Flats in the 1940s. The ducks got
too smart.

39. Brown's Slough to Hall Slough to North Fork Access

Mile 92–96

Tuesday, December 20, 1977

It's well not to know the future. If one did, often one wouldn't go.
Yesterday evening was still vividly with me as I drove by frost-

white fields, complacently anticipating another comfortable day on the delta that was becoming my second home. At 10:40 I climbed from Jensen Access onto the dike and turned south. Immediately I had to ignore a vicious sign and climb a mean-it fence. Then began the hell-berries. Thus far in my apprenticeship I'd learned to cope with dikes, little blue lines, and MUD AND SAND. It was time to come to grips with blue tussocks and beguiling saltmarsh that perhaps could liberate me from barbed wire and thorns.

I headed straight bayward on a grassy peninsula that soon broke into a chain of grassy islets so squishy my socks were quickly soaked. I skirted reed thickets and step-hopped across black-muck basins from one tussock of bunchgrass to the next, and in this manner sortied hundreds of feet out from the dike, to the edge of MUD AND SAND, heaped this morning with sheets of bay ice stranded by the tide.

Delighted with my success, I turned south—and found sideways progress quite another matter. The marshes were drained by a network of sloughlets a few inches to several feet wide, and though some could be stepped over and others leaped, a certain number demanded getting right down in there with both feet. At this stage of the tide the channels were empty, with black ooze floors. I tested—and drew my foot back in haste at the sound of a monstrous stomach grumbling deep underground. Muck seemed a problem not fit for a solitary walker to study; a companion was wanted to retrieve the rucksack so the family would have something, at least, to put in the casket.

A half-mile short of Brown's Slough I gave up and retreated north, past the Jensen Access, to Hall Slough. Pale sun probed thin clouds. Frozen ponds glinted. Far south on the bay there was that mysterious yelping, as of an armada of dogs, but now it also was close ahead in the north, hidden by reeds. As I stepped through the screen a thousand wings beat the air, a massed pulse battered my eardrums, a nova exploded in the sky, and I met the delta superstar, the snow goose.

The Game Department says about 200,000 of these birds annually journey south on the Pacific Flyway to spend October to April in wetlands from British Columbia to Mexico; about 40,000 stop off between the Fraser River and Port Susan. Thousands never fly north again because they get shot in the Wildlife Recreation Area; as with "reclamation," there are paradoxical theological implications in "re-creation."

Legal hunting of the snow goose pains those of us who consider it a crime to slaughter so beautiful a creature in the name of sport, and it also pains the individual birds, but it doesn't endanger the species. Regulations require anyone hunting from a boat in the bay to cut the kicker and drift or row into the flock, giving the prey a chance to evade, the next best thing to a fighting chance. However, an estimated 10 percent of hunters are slack-jawed, drooling thugs who race into the fleet at top speed, guns blasting. Additionally, an estimated 10 percent of airplane pilots are yahoos whose special delight is to razz down from the sky to stir up the great white superstars.

Flocks that are scattered in panic and denied the chance to feed in peace through the winter are not up to full strength when the time comes in spring to fly north to breeding grounds on Wrangel Island, above the Arctic Circle in Siberia, and they don't make it.

I agree with the Jukes clan; nobody should be permitted on the WRA unless armed, such as with a Kawasaki Long Lance, a scale model of the torpedo that in World War II terrorized the American navy, or an L.L. Bean Backpacker's Ack-Ack, imported from the Ho Chi Minh Trail, to sink drooling thugs or shoot down yahoos.

After a short drive from Jensen Access I parked at North Fork Access and set out south to Hall Slough. The dike path tunneled through millions of what seemed to be cherry tomatoes—rose hips—that in early winter give the walker color for his eye, tartness for his mouth, and plenty of vitamin C to stave off the ague and scurvy.

Every slough floated a raft of driftwood logs, some of whose branches were herons. A small hawk zipped past my nose and over the field, eyes sharp for bits of gray amid green cabbages.

Before me rose Tahoma, a blue-gray silhouette in a pale red sky. (Sailor take warning.) The ice-calm air was clouded by clots of wings. The glassy bay was strewn with ice mirrors reflecting the sun. There were gabbling navies, and honking navies, and enormous floating snowfields that yelped.

Here the dike so boldly invaded the bay it had been given the protection of a palisade—now very old, neglected, and rotten. What long-ago disaster had stimulated its construction? Was the Dutch boy, finger stuck, overwhelmed by storm surf? The delta is the banal and the mysterious, all together: the present and the frontier, bustle and rot, white paint and hellberries, smirking prosperity, and faces in upstairs windows.

On the return from Hall Slough I sat for lunch on a boulder. Birds hopped along driftwood, scooted through bushes and reeds, perched in fields. A tiny raptor rested atop a piling stub—what meal had Mother Nature provided for so small a mouth? Through the distant yelping of the Great White Fleet slipped a limpid call as haunting as a solo oboe.

I used to pack so much mineral out of the mountains that moraines crowded my typewriter, tumbled from desk to floor, avalanched down stairs to the kitchen, spilled out on the patio and through the trees of Cougar Mountain, frightening my neighbors. But eventually my curiosity grew a couple feet upward, out of the rocks and into the flowers, and many a spring and summer I spent trying to put names to long-known faces.

On this journey my eyes were being drawn higher still, to the birds, the most satisfying of all trail scenery because there are more of them than beasts and they bloom all winter, but a difficult study because they rarely stand still close to the eye.

The sun was dimming. A blackness to the northwest was sheeting vertical lines I recognized as rain, doubtless very cold. Soaked socks were freezing my feet. Thanks to the snow geese the day was already full. But when I'd returned to the North Fork Access it was barely 2 o'clock, with hours for exploration left.

A path along the marsh-meadow below the dike led a few yards to the North Fork of the Skagit, where I stepped back in fright from the horrid brown churning. A wave burst on the beach and I nearly fled.

Beside the South Fork, eating kippers at the headquarters of Diking District No. 7, I'd felt as secure as within the Vatican walls. This place was outside the walls of Christendom, this was the Skagit of 1911—of 1866—of all the Scatchet eons. However domesticated upstream, here was wild river, swift and terrible, that on a whim could roil up over the narrow beach of gray sand and drown undefended meadows, willows, and me.

> he come up once before he
> drowned toujours gai kid he
> gurgled

Bales of hay floated by—against the current; then I made out the boxy hull of an aged scow and heard an antique *chug-chug-chug*. The captain of the *African Queen* took a swig from a bottle of gin.

His nonchalance caused the first of the day's Momentous Decisions. Warily, watchfully, I walked downstream through an alder grove to a resumption of tidal meadow. Across the North Fork, atop a 200-foot cliff, cows grazed a pasture. A half-mile from where I'd left the dike the path split, the right fork continuing along the bank, the left diverging over meadows toward....

I couldn't believe it. Since Stanwood I'd been gazing longingly over Skagit Bay to the faery archipelago of the San Juan Islands, dreaming of one day borrowing or begging a boatride to the islets-peaklets. This meadow path appeared to lead directly to Craft Island. The second Momentous Decision was forced on me.

Surely there would be sloughlets? Certainly I'd be halted by a too-wide gap of black muck? Or would it by now be brown soup? On dikes as on railroad tracks the water is of purely scenic interest, and I'd not been paying attention to the tide chart. Mud flats had been exposed this morning. So the tide must now be rising. The question was, toward what height?

I hurried. No channels stopped me. In a third of a mile, a half-dozen minutes, at 2:17 I stepped up from grass onto the hard rock of the San Juan Islands.

Flatland extended seven miles east to Devils Mountain. Flatwater extended four miles west to Whidbey Island, eight miles south to Camano. All the flats of land and water were displayed as on a map from this massive eminence.

Massive? Craft Island? With dimensions of 400 by 200 feet, a couple of acres? Where the substance of creation is water, muck, and grass, a couple of acres of hard rock are a Gibraltar. Eminence? At 85 feet above mean high tide? Where the summits of the dikes are 10 feet, 85 feet is Everest.

The archipelago lay before me. Across one and a half miles of glassy bay, Ika Island thrust violently steep to an astounding 450 feet. Beyond rose McGlinn Island, at the mouth of the Swinomish Channel, and Goat, former site of Fort Whitman (which war?). Closest was Bald, mostly a meadow.

I climbed to the summit in elfin forest stunted by sun and contorted by wind; huddled cedar, fir, madrona, and western juniper. I ascended through thickets of cherry tomatoes, snowberries, and head-high mahonia, and beneath walls hung with ferns. I descended the far side on little buttresses and cliffs rounded and plucked by the glacier, down little chimneys and ledges. I walked on carpets of brown grass and green moss and a pale yellow moss that grew airily ankle-deep, and over slabs quilted green, black, and orange by lichen. Near the water the mountain's conglomerate had been sculpted by waves into knobs and pocks, splashed brilliant yellow by algae. A prow of rock was littered with bits of clamshells, shrapnel of bombs dropped by gulls to break into the meat.

It was an island-mountain without a fault—save me, blundering like Gulliver. Shrink me to six inches and the peak would grow to 1,020 feet; to an inch, and it would tower above Nanga Pilchuck. I could see myself, then, hiking through a grass forest, roping up to climb pebbles, watchful for bugs as large as elephants.

Breezes suddenly rippled the bay. Only briefly would the new waves dance in the sun. Doom was rushing on.

A *dozen feet* above the water I noted a *very fresh* litter of driftwood. A *dozen feet…*

> Lord, Lord! methought, what pain it was to drown!
> What dreadful noise of waters in mine ears!
> What ugly sights of death within mine eyes!
> The wills above be done! but I would fain die a dry death.

Heart pounding, knees jittering, hands shaking, hair standing on end, I recalled the Conjunction of Three, four days earlier, when Dad looked out his window to find the dock missing. It was terrible to know the sea could rise *that high.*

I looked suspiciously down to the saltgrass plain, the half-mile between island and dike. The water had been over my ankles much of the way. By now the insidious tide, hidden from my eyes, might be climbing higher and higher on stems of grass, to abruptly overtop them and become a half-mile of sullen sea.

At 2:55 I stepped off the rock. Was the meadow squishier? My foot thought so. The sun was extinguished by a main force of clouds advancing as cruelly as Oliver Cromwell's fearful regiments, the Ironsides. An icy wind gusted over the boggy plain and I was afeared.

The squishing and sloughlets proved to be about the same as an hour earlier. I got away clean.

But humble. There was much to learn about deltas. I could tell a sedge from a grass by the feel of the stems, but didn't know delta sedges apart, nor delta grasses, nor any of them from mountain sedges and grasses. I recognized a cattail and probably a bulrush but used "reeds," "saltmarsh," and "tule" to camouflage my ignorance. I had a smattering of flowers and a flurry of birds and a pocketful of rocks but no mosses, lichens, liverworts, algae, or molds at all. Mosquitos, flies and spiders? Clams, snails, fish, and worms? How many lifetimes to know all the treasures of the delta?

Moreover, the bumpkin was certain, now, there was a lot more around here to worry about than firecrackers.

I'd seen the snow geese and walked onto the San Juan Islands and there was still an hour before night. Sheer greed provoked the Momentous Third Decision. At 3 o'clock I set out *downstream* on the North Fork of the Skagit.

On the far bank I saw a row of shacks shown on the map as derelicts, labeled "Fish Town." They snuggled against the wild, free, undiked river as if it were a friend. Was it so during the Big Media Flood of December 2? On Conjunction Morning? Above the shacks, cliffs rose to the forests and cow pastures of another San Juan islet-peaklet, this one attached to the delta but nevertheless formerly—and still, to me—Fish Town Island.

The single surge of the North Fork began frittering away. A lesser north branch curved off toward Bald and Ika; the pattern of isles and sloughs was precisely as shown by the 1911 map, untouched by diking, dredging, or damming. The branch I was walking along, the south, took most of the flow another half-mile to the bay. At 3:24, on the tip of a marsh peninsula, I stood atop a grass tussock that was washed on my left by wavelets of the bay, on my right by the brown roil of the river. The soles of my feet were three inches above sealevel—not mean high tide, but the level *now*.

The South Fork had denied me this fulfillment: Here, just here, mountain water met saltwater, exactly beside my feet. At long last I stood at the ending of the great stream—the one that makes all other rivers of Western Washington seem dribbles, because it has so many well-remembered beginnings:

Sauk, White Chuck, Suiattle, Baker, and Cascade rivers; Thunder, Granite, Canyon, and a hundred other creeks. The snowfields of Silvertip, Goblin, Sloan, Cadet, Monte Cristo, Portal, White, Kodak, Pugh, Glacier, Fire, Kennedy, Pumice, Cinder Cone, Buck, Plummer,

Mabel, Spire, Grassy, Sulphur, Flower Dome, Liberty Cap, Green, Komo Kulshan, Challenger, Shuksan, Anne, Table, Whatcom, Eldorado, Forbidden, Hidden, Sahale, Timbercone, Spider, Slowdown, Magic, Buckner, Logan, Hardy, Slate, Tamarack, Colonial, Luna, Devils Dome, Crater, Spickard, Red Top, Elbow, Snowfield, Sourdough, and scores of nameless other peaks.

How many times have I kicked steps into steep snow, belayed over crevasses, crept up cliffs on spider trails, walked on air, swum through clouds, fled the fire, and clutched rocks as a wild storm ripped the tarp and stripped me naked?

There was danger where a thousand snowfields sparkled out rills, a hundred glaciers gushed rock milk, up there so near the sky. It didn't feel too safe here, either, three inches above sealevel.

This was the sort of place where a person, given time, might achieve a mystical experience, Wordsworth-and-Shelley style. But there wasn't time. This shortest day of the year had merely eight hours and two minutes between sunrise and sunset—no, not that many, for the sun already had been swallowed by the onrushing storm. I shivered and shook in the freshening wind and fading twilight.

> wind come out of the north
> and pierce to the guts within
> but some day mehitabel s guts
> will string a violin

A climber in a delicate spot must keep fright submerged lest he develop "sewing-machine leg." Once I allowed the realization to surface that the dike was one and a half miles distant, I developed sewing-machine body. I hurried upstream through tussocks, reeds, and meadows. Passing through a grove of naked trees I shuddered to see driftwood stranded in branches high above my head. I felt awful forebodings as I leaped sloughlets of brown water that minutes before had been black muck.

In the dusk of 4 o'clock the trap was sprung. Directly across my path there now rolled a brown river as wide as the North Fork.

Knees sagged, heart raced triple-time, stars sparkled inside my eyes. It was a *spring flood,* the sort of sneaky-swift tide that on other days had chased me up bluffs. Could I climb these scraggly willows or alders? Cling there in wet clothes and cold wind until the ebb?

Should I yell for help? Fish Town was a ghost village and even if it was inhabited no ear could hear a yell above the drowning murmur of the river.

A tidal channel as broad as the North Fork.... I blinked, gasped—it *was* the North Fork! I'd forgotten that on the way downstream I'd made a shàrp left turn to follow the south branch.

Undrowned but unstrung, the bumpkin jumped on his pony and galloped for the Great Wall.

40. Skagit City to Fish Town   Mile 96–104

Wednesday, December 21, 1977

At the split of the North Fork and the South Fork the Boundary Survey map of 1866 shows a village, Skagit. It was so located due to the importance, in a green and tangled land where commerce was by canoe, of the junction of three water roads. One, however, required portaging; upstream on the undivided Skagit the map shows "Rafts," denoting three separate logjams—jackstraws from bank to bank—along a three-mile stretch of river.

The rafts determined the site of the river's first European settlement, Skagit City, which opened for business at the head of Fir Island in 1869. It quickly became more important than the trading post established near Conway in 1863 and the first town in Skagit County, La Conner, founded in 1867. Steamboats paddled to Skagit City via Steamboat Slough, carrying supplies to the hand-loggers who since 1865 had been cutting down the giant cedars, trappers searching for beaver and muskrat, prospectors who hadn't struck it rich elsewhere and were seeking bonanzas in the Cascades and grubstakes in the saloons. In the wake of the first homestead, in 1859, reclaimers turned up, scouting for likely swamps.

There were also townboomers arrived too late to get in on the ground floor. To establish other ground floors, they promoted the area's first great engineering project, the clearing of the Skagit rafts. In 1878, after two years of labor, the task was done, and steamboats paddled as far as Rockport in time to serve the Ruby Creek gold rush of 1878 to 1879. Skagit City was mortally wounded, and Mount Vernon and Sedro were in business.

Skagit City lingers on maps of 1911 and 1973. Walking the dike to the site, seeing a sand bar dividing the brown surge from a mighty one into a mighty two, I felt a cityful of ghosts in the alder groves. Where, though, was the county or state park celebrating the Momentous Spot? The historical society's story board? The sons of the pioneers' memorial plaque? Nothing. Brown water, gray sand, and cowflop.

Walking the river dikes on other days, I hitched the dead Skagit City to the living Mount Vernon and Burlington. A long mile short of Sedro Woolley, a dozen miles upstream from the forks, the dikes stopped and so did I, halted by the swampy sloughs of a river permitted, beyond that point, to meander and overflow as it pleased.

I ate kippers and listened to the barking of trumpeter swans on Barney Lake. Here the river's elevation above mean high tide was 20 feet (on the diketop, 43), sloping to Mount Vernon's 10 feet (diketop, 33), Skagit City's unlisted feet (diketop, 24), and—some seventeen miles downriver—at the North Fork Access, 0 feet (diketop, 10). To a person whose home is at an elevation of 200 meters, the minuscules were ridiculous. Flatland, however, lives and dies by inches; when the sky falls and snows melt and tides rise, dikewatchers rush to their posts to sit all night in pickups and hardhats, talking jargon on the CB; and when the water starts up they give the signal to stand by to sandbag, warn the Red Cross to lay in more doughnuts, and call out the TV.

At dikes' end I connected the saltwater to the mountain front. From the sandbar I looked up to twin massifs rising 4,000 feet on either side of the flood plain. Many years I'd driven between them on the way to high Cascades. Finally I hitched the two of them together and to much else as well. In a winter sunset I once stood atop Cultus and hitched Flatland to the Issaquah Alps. Another day, in soft spring snow I floundered to the summit of Woolley Lyman and hitched Flatland and Flatwater to the Great White Watcher, Komo Kulshan. (The volcano was itself being watched in hopes it might fire the predicted resumption of Cascade violence. The plume rose so close I could feel the heat. The sky was full of geologists vying to be the first blown up.)

I walked the river dike from North Fork Access to Phil's Boathouse, an establishment consisting of a mossy restaurant and store, cabins, campground, and rental boats. There was also moorage for kickerboats and "Skagit arks," the distinctive local craft that had the look of a farmer's invention—chicken coops nailed to wagon beds. I drove off Fir Island on a bridge that arched from delta silt to the rocky heights of Pleasant Ridge, or to my mind, Pleasant Ridge Island. Riverbank homes forced me to concede a mile of walking; I drove to Dodge Valley, a finger of delta enclosed by forested "islands," and Al's Landing, across the North Fork from Phil's. Footpaths and cow trails led up through fir forest to pastures and a view south to Stanwood's damned stack. Tahoma and the Olympics had been enveloped by darkness. Last night's threat had backed off but the clouds were coming on again today. Pale sun shone wanly on tidy fields, the dike-hedgerow boundary line, unruly marshes, and Craft Mountain.

Fish Town began.

First was a workboat floating at the foot of the cliff that edged a pasture. Its paint was flaking, but the vessel appeared tight and snug, stovepipe jutting from the pilot house.

Second was a cluster of shanties on the far side of the pasture and another cluster at the foot of a path dropping to the marsh. Several old cars were parked at the dead end of the farm lane.

Most of Fish Town lay around a nose of conglomerate washed by the river—Gage's Point, I later learned, named for the original homesteader family. An exciting walkway, two planks wide, supported by posts driven in the riverbed, rounded the corner and became Main Street. To one side of the planks, in willow swamps, boathouses moldered and boats rotted. To the other side, a dozen homes lined the river on pilings or floats, the structures ranging from small to tiny, crude to neat, carelessly or lovingly built, old or young, of such materials as could be brought in by boat, carried by hand, or found floating in the front yard. As for utilities, the river had plenty of water, and plank sidestreets led to privies in the swamp, but surely the solitary TV antenna was a jest.

Another good joke was the sole exception to the color scheme of weatherbeaten gray, a clapboard houselet painted bright white, set off by the green of a tidily mown four-by-ten lawn.

Atop a mountain-size boulder at the end of Main Street soared *stupor mundi*, Fish Town Castle, taller than wide, with two stories complete and a third under construction. The architecture suggested: (1) a satire on the Rhine; (2) inflammation of the imagination; (3) community orgies devoted to erecting a counterpart of Chartres Cathedral, the Great Pyramid, or the Tower of Babel. Cockeyed windows, precarious balconies, gables, widow's walks, flying buttresses, turrets, and gargoyles—how much was in fact the inflammation of *my* imagination?

A path climbed over a rocky ridge to delta and dike and the final neighborhood, a row of houseboats in a riverside willow swamp. So ended Fish Town, clearly not a community of duck shacks.

The dike pointed at Bald Island but was blocked by hellberries. A farm lane took me through fields to a splendid yellow farmhouse (shown on the 1911 map) beside Dodge Valley Road. At 1 o'clock I stood wondering what to do next when there came walking down the road a young woman in a patchwork skirt and quilted coat, rings on her fingers and bells on her toes.

As if it were the most natural thing in the world, she offered me a ride into town. Learning that La Conner was not my immediate goal, she described a better return to the Castle. She also told me I absolutely must climb Quarry Mountain, the island-peak that rose 260 feet from where we stood—at an elevation of 5 feet.

I knew something now about the what—or at least the who—of Fish Town. They climb mountains.

I turned off the road on a path across Dodge Valley, a long-ago course of the Skagit, corn stalks to the right, cabbages to the left, fir-green peaklet ahead. From the forest emerged another pedestrian.

Thomas Jefferson wrote, "Walking is the best possible exercise. Habituate yourself to walk very far. The Europeans value themselves on having subdued the horse to the uses of man; but I doubt whether we have not lost more than we have gained, by the use of this animal."

This Fish Towner was walking to La Conner, only two more miles to go. He knew the water road, too; the vessel moored beneath the cow pasture was his home, which—winds and engines cooperating—he could relocate on whim to Coupeville or Port Townsend.

The 1911 map shows a farmhouse on Fish Town Island, near the present one atop Gage's Point. For all the birds and bulrushes, I knew Flatland never could be mine, the stink of the excretions of farm animals and chemical factories never would touch my heart the way a tide flat in the noon sun does. But I could sleep easy enough in a bed in a house in a meadow on a mountain, and perhaps could live among farmers who chose rock and forest, flowers and broad prospects. The muddy-booted, hard-hatted Dutchmen down below, fingers in dikes and noses, undoubtedly sneered at mountaineers scraping a barebones existence from stony soil. But in the highlands the spirit lifts cleanly from the primordial, and that apparently is the story of Fish Town: the sharing tolerance of mountaineer farmers who homesteaded the island and live there yet, and never in all the generations have posted a "No Trespassing" sign.

The 1911 map shows no Fish Town—not, at least, on the present site. Across the river are shown four outside-the-dike buildings, as well as one on Craft Island. An earlier Fish Town?

For years I've watched the to and fro of commercial fishing boats and never understood how they work. Dad tries to explain. He says the purse seiners are the big boats, 60 or 70 feet long, with crews of five or eight. A skiff towing a fine-meshed net circles an area with a circumference of perhaps 1,500 feet. A line strung through the net bottom is drawn tight to close the purse. The big boat draws in the net and empties—or used to—thousands of fish into crushed ice piled in the hold.

Around about World War I boat engines became compact and cheap, and trollers became common, smaller vessels equipped with several mastlike fishing poles, each trailing a line of baited hooks that simulate a school of herring.

The bulk of the catch nowadays, south of the San Juan Islands at least, is by other little boats with small crews, the gillnetters, which use a net of such mesh that salmon can push their heads through but not their bodies, and upon trying to back out are held by their gills.

Despite Dad's efforts, I can't tell, from looking at them, which is which. I certainly can't guess which sort of fishermen built Fish Town, except I know they weren't the owners of the big boats, nor the operators of the fishtraps that used to intercept salmon swimming from Deception Pass to the mouths of the Skagit. The people here had little boats and lived in swamp shacks and were overjoyed to feed a hunter's pothole with corn during the week and collect a jug of corn whiskey on the weekend.

When did they leave? Perhaps they thrived when fishtraps were outlawed and they moved to Ballard and bought purse seiners. Perhaps when World War II broke out they got jobs at Boeing making tin pots for the Army Air Corps. Who moved in? Hunters. Also folks seeking any roof in a Depression.

When did the raggle-taggle gypsies arrive? When the houseboats, garrets, basements, and garages of Seattle's University District—my homes when I was in school—were demolished to make room for apartment houses and student residence halls, and the dense concentration of students and professors ruined the neighborhood. The outmigration began then, led by pioneers with a discriminating eye for Nature's today and Man's yesterday that give a place character. They chose the genteel decay of Seattle's Broadway District, the pastoral mellowness of Duvall, coal-mining Roslyn, settled-in Coupeville, elegant Port Townsend, and diverse La Conner. And whosoever comes to La Conner must inevitably find Fish Town.

I couldn't be comfortable there, not now. The swamp miasma and river fog would seep through the walls into my old bones. On a drizzling morning the aches would wake me to the desperation of being trapped by the treacherous planks of Main Street. In the berserker night I'd try to escape to the bright lights, and in morning they'd find me, only the soles of my boots in sight, sticking straight up from the muck.

But when I was one and twenty?

There'd have been the river flowing by my front porch as interminable as the novels of Thomas Wolfe, traveled only by fish and ducks and otters and arks. I might have lasted out a winter—at least until a Conjunction of Three.

I drove from Al's Landing to the Fish Town parking lot and climbed above the quarry on paths through a forest that had been highgraded (that is, a few of the choicest trees had been cut) by bullteam loggers a century ago and then left alone to regain its virginity. Rising high above squared, diked, drained, fenced, plowed, and fertilized Christendom, Quarry Mountain was a temple of the acute and obtuse and irregular and curving, the savage, the pagan, the useless.

In years of driving the delta's inner edge on Interstate 5 (and before that, Highway 99), I'd supposed Flatland was all one; this lofty view from near the outer edge revealed it was trisected. I looked south to the North Fork and Craft Island, over Fir Island to South Fork sloughs and Stanwood's damned stack now ten air miles distant: all this was the Southern Delta. I looked north to Padilla Bay and Bayview Ridge, marking the end of the Middle Delta, and to Blanchard Hill, twenty air miles distant, the end of the Northern Delta.

I sat on a mossy slab under a dour sky that might hold back its snow and let me go home tonight. Contemplating Flatland, I mentally deleted houses and barns, roads and dikes, and substituted saltgrass meadow and willow swamp and Scatchet canoes sliding along sinuous sloughs. A century and some decades ago...Yet only several days ago the claiming saltwater crept quietly higher on dikes than in recent memory, and here and there poured over the ramparts. The primeval is ever near, a century is not so long; the pale Galilean has won a battle, but Mother Nature may win the war.

At 3:24 I drank an ice-cold Pepsi to honor the solstice. In three months would come the equinox, the dancing and tearing off of clothes, the Dutch boys sticking fingers in their ears against the chorus reverberating from Quarry Mountain to Craft Island to Devils Mountain: "Evoe! Evoe!"

41. McGlinn Island to La Conner to Swinomish Point
Mile 104–111½

Monday, December 26, 1977

When the cold sun ignites the northern winter, the natives have to be put under restraint to keep them from elevating their vocabulary to the Shelleyan ecstatic, such as:

> No merely blue sky, this, that one gazes upon from McGlinn Island, but a frosty cerulean dome, lofty azure rounding o'er a broad sea mirroring fires of the mighty orb arcing the south. Rocky heights seeming close enough for Icarus to attain in one flap of his wax wings, Ika soared 450 feet from the wavelets set sparkling by the Arctic zephyr; if Goat Island lacked beetling crags it delighted with meadows as soft and tawny as a maiden's behind. Fish Town Island and Craft Island bestrode the boundary of the greenly infinite Southern Delta. Cascades marched south to nullity; Pilchuck was an isle of bright snow floating in the brown exhalations of Puget Sound City....

The greatest wonder of McGlinn was exactly here, where the cliffs fell a sheer 100 feet to a saltwater river barely 200 feet wide, walled on the far bank by a mountain only barely lower and less steep than Ika. A Hudson's Bay trader, John Work, first to record the name of the original residents, "Scaadchet," was the first European to see this impressive southern entry to the Swinomish. In 1824, Work canoed the "narrow winding channel" six miles through the delta marsh and swamp to the northern entry. Swinomish Slough, it was then, having at one time in centuries past been a double-exit mouth of the Skagit, exactly as South Pass-West Pass now are of the Stillaguamish. Close on the heels of the dikers and ditchers came the dredgers to make it the Swinomish Channel. Standing on the brink of a McGlinn cliff, I saw the beacons delineating the narrow lane that extended two and a half miles out through MUD to the open blue of Skagit Bay. A riprap jetty connected McGlinn to Goat. Beyond the jetty a bay of logs was organized by pilings, the first active booming grounds I'd seen on this journey; tugs would tow the rafts through Saratoga Passage to Port Gardner.

At every turn in the forest path McGlinn sprang a pretty surprise. I walked over mossy slabs of bedrock polished by ice, around clean granite erratics dropped by ice, along brinks of cliffs plucked by ice. I looked down to a scrap of sand beach tracked by footprints—bare feet. A tiny cove sheltered a houseboat. A rowboat rounded the point, perhaps returning from a Christmas visit to Fish Town, boat and rower stinking of naught but sweat and possibly fish, making no sound but the rattle of oarlocks.

From McGlinn Island I drove north on a mile-long artificial isthmus, built up of dredging spoils, the channel to my left, the delta marsh and a scattering of houseboats to my right. In forests of "Pioneer Park Island," a 145-foot mountain, I found a stone dedicating the park "In memory of Louisa A. Conner, for whom La Conner was named in 1870." The mountain supported the mainland end of the High Orange Bridge that crossed to Fidalgo Island. At the mountain foot I met another wayfaring stranger, the New England Fish Company, which my Nova Scotia ancestors may well have met on the Grand Banks.

Sullivan Slough, east of town, ruined my hypothesizing about Mesopotamians and Dutchmen. Michael Sullivan, in 1863, was one of the first two Skagit dikers, the other being his partner, Samuel Calhoun, an Utsalady mill worker with a knowledge of diking, Scot though he was.

The sign in town identifying the world-famous "Tillinghast Seed Company" reminded visitors that much delta soil is too rich to be wasted merely growing food. The flowers that in springtime splash the delta red and yellow are a byproduct of maximum soil use. More narcissus, iris, and tulip bulbs are produced here than in any other place in the nation.

Though it's of the delta, serving the outer edge as Mount Vernon does the inner, La Conner is not of Flatland. The people who pioneered the town were too sensible to shiver and wheeze in mud and miasma or go bleary-eyed gulping Injun whiskey to keep off the ague; they stayed dry-footed and bright-eyed on the heights of the San Juan Mountains. A cabin in town bears a plaque telling it was built on the the North Fork in 1869 by Magnus Anderson, who had rowed nine miles across Skagit Bay to the Utsalady mill for planed lumber. The cabin was moved here in 1952. (Was it perhaps the building shown by the 1911 map atop Craft Mountain?)

Ever since its 1867 beginnings as Swinomish, a trading post, La Conner has been seafaring. Even before the dredging, a canny skipper of a shallow-drift steamer could slip through the slough at high tide and thus avoid the alternative route, five times longer, via tricky Deception Pass and the ocean-windy Gulf of Vancouver. Here was based the La Conner Trading and Transportation Company, Joshua Green's corporate vehicle for financiering and finagling with the Peabodys, the railroads, and Wall Street, to build the Black Ball shipping monopoly. A few fishing boats still unload at New England Fish and at the San Juan Island Cannery.

The scenery and the history (City Hall, 1886; Gaches Mansion, 1883; and La Conner House, 1878) have generated the Sunday-pictorial tourist town that has antique shops stocked from Charles Addams mansions. La Conner's restaurants sell seafood and steak, hamburgers, deli, yogurt cones, alfalfa tea; shops owned by Fish Towners sell books, pottery, paintings, prints, beads, stained glass, wall hangings, driftwood sculptures, weldings, handknit sweaters, patchwork skirts, and quilted coats.

Another La Conner is devoted to selling real estate, Winnebagos, and Chriscraft, and across the slough lies the 7,172-acre Swinomish Indian Reservation established in 1873 for the "Skagit and South Indians." On the reservation, where the 1911 map shows a marsh a mile long and a half-mile wide, is Shelter Bay, a millionaires' dredge-and-fill community of super-stinkpots and super-splitlevels.

I decided I wouldn't want to live in La Conner, but it was a nice town to walk through. On the outskirts I'd watched a rowboat rounding a point, coming home from the bay. At the foot of a mountain I met a raggle-taggle gypsy. On a path through cornstalks and cabbages I talked to a ship captain.

At the north edge of town lay a final La Conner, the Port of Skagit County, a half-mile long and nearly as wide and crammed to the boathouse rafters with stinkpots.

On a Memorial Day weekend, an old climbing friend, Ted, and I crossed Obstruction Pass, from Orcas Island to Obstruction Island, in his twelve-foot aluminum cockleshell and camped in the woods beside Peavine Pass. Each day we sortied out to fish for kelp greenling and to fetch cold beer from the resort on Blakely Island—and half our time afloat we were frantically oaring the cockleshell to take bow-on the wakes of stinkpotters who otherwise would have swamped us as casually as they swilled their gin-and-tonic. Each evening we sat around the beachfire drinking beer and baking fish, scowling at the noise and refining the concept of a recreational torpedo that would provide rowboaters and beachwalkers a rich source of innocent merriment. In the sunset of the last day the racket abruptly ceased as the fleet headed for port—La Conner—and in the sudden quiet a river otter, the first we'd seen on this trip, swam close by and stared at us intently, as if to ask, "Why don't you *do* something?"

Power corrupts. Stinkpots corrupt absolutely. In 1980 the Army Corps of Engineers counted 161,000 play boats on the Whulj and predicted 253,000 by the year 2000. If boats have oars, paddles, sails, or modest little eggbeater kickers, there can be peace on the Whulj. Some stinkpotters could be taught better: inside many a Chriscrafter is a rowboater crying to get out. As for the rest, they're as hopeless as dirtbikers, and the prescription is a spread of Long Lances. Scratch 'em off the list, they never will be missed.

Across the 600-foot-wide channel, beyond decks of logs waiting to be floated to the booming grounds for shipment to Japan, Fidalgo Island sloped steeply to the uplands of the Swinomish Reservation. The Swinomish Tribes—the "Skagits and Souths"—apparently live by selling taxfree nicotine and booze and cherry bombs, by letting their millionaire tenants on Shelter Bay foul the waters, and by collecting their rental share of Weyerhaeuser's log-export business. One would condemn them more harshly if their reservation lands were not too stony and arid to grow valuable trees, much less cabbages and tulips, and had we Europeans not decimated the primeval fisheries, as we earlier decimated the Skagits and Souths themselves.

The Great Pestilence came from the Orient to the Crimea in 1346, to Italy and England in 1348, and to Germany and Scandinavia in 1349 to 1350. In three years it killed a third of Europe's people and, as further waves of plague rolled over the continent at roughly ten-year intervals, perhaps half by 1400. Philosophy and art dwelt on the Dance of Death. Society at every level wallowed in immorality. In 1358 the Jacquerie swept France and in 1381 in England Wat Tyler led the Peasants' Revolt. The Germans massacred thousands of Jews.

The Conquerors' Pestilence came to the Northwest Coast with Cook, Meares, Eliza, Quadra, and Vancouver. In 1805 Lewis and Clark found the Chinooks at the mouth of the Columbia River riddled with smallpox, measles, and syphilis; even so, the population was an estimated 5,000. James Swan in the 1850s counted fewer than 100. The combination of "children's diseases" (domesticated plagues), venereal diseases, and the unspecified "death fever" was not so instantly devastating to the Northwest as plague to Europe, yet comparing the 1346-to-1400 disaster to that of 1775 to 1850, one feels the Indians got more than twice the worst of it.

Moreover, whereas in Europe all nations were afflicted simultaneously, permitting international hostilities to continue as vigorously as ever, if on a reduced scale (the Hundred Years War is dated 1337-1453), the stricken Indians were overwhelmed by dikers, loggers, fishermen, seamen, platters, and spoilsmen who'd gotten through the plagues in childhood and were rarin' to go, as were the U.S. Cavalry and all the colonels of the Washington Mounted Rifles.

Is it permissible for a person to walk along merrily simply to keep his metronome regular and his thoughts away from the dark? Must not every journey be a crusade? Does one have the right to be ignorant?

I walked miles along the moat and knew nothing of the Swinomish people except what I had learned from their cousin, the Tulalip girl, thirty-odd years ago.

My way across the Southern Delta had so curled and looped that I was interminably haunted by the damned Hamilton Lumber stack. Here the dike ran due north, swift as a railroad. Pleasant Ridge "Island" and Quarry Mountain quickly sank to the rear and Bayview Ridge "Island" rose to the front. The Middle Delta sprawled nine miles east to Little Mountain, on the outskirts of Mount Vernon; I now could see past Little and Cultus and up the Skagit thirty miles to Sauk Mountain. New things were happening northward: the ever-higher peaks of Cypress and Lummi islands, the ever-bigger blocks of ice in Canada. Closer, vapors floated from the forests of Fidalgo Island.

The dike passed a Formerly Momentous Spot where in the not too remote past the Skagit frittered into distributaries that flowed over the Middle Delta to saltwater; Higgins Slough—dike-tamed, now— meandered from the east and split into Blind Slough and Telegraph Slough.

Telegraph Slough was named for its contribution to international communication.

The Western Union Russian Extension Telegraph was to guarantee North America telegraphic contact with Russia, and with Europe as well, via a system, primarily overland, to Siberia and beyond. This system, it was widely agreed, would be of great value for international commerce and peace.

The building party for the telegraph line left Portland, Oregon, on July 6, 1864, aiming for New Westminster in British Columbia, 300 miles distant. North of Seattle, the crew was forced to stay close to the water. According to the *Pacific Northwest Quarterly:*

> The outlook was very discouraging, and the conclusion was reached to follow the shore line of the Sound, taking advantage of the clearings the few settlers had made, and cutting across the bases of points jutting into the Sound. A light draft steamer was employed, which carried the building material and provision, and was the ferry boat and camp for the expedition. The work was generally kept within an average of one-half mile from the shore. The steamer was kept apprised of the locality of the working party, and upon the close of day called them on board with her whistle, and then ran to some inlet or cove for the night....
>
> The builders left Seattle on the first of November, 1864, and arrived at New Westminster April 1, 1865, without serious damage to man or steamer....Telegraphic communication was established with Victoria in the fall of 1865. The route was from a convenient

point on Swinomish Slough, which was crossed by an air line, and thence across Fidalgo Island, thence [by] cable to Lopes Island, to San Juan Island, to Vancouver Island....Victoria was a place of considerable importance, besides being the seat of the Colonial Government and the rendezvous of the British North Pacific Fleet.

The dike passed an assemblage of bridges. Westbound automobiles whizzed through the sky on a new concrete span arching over the channel; eastbound traffic was waiting while an old, low, intricate Rube Goldberg contraption lifted its center section, between a pair of fretted-iron towers, to let a gillnetter chug by on the water.

The railroad swing bridge was open, as it almost always is. The modern map calls the line the Burlington Northern. In 1911 it was the Rockport and Anacortes Branch of the Great Northern, intersecting the Seattle-Vancouver tracks at Burlington. The Northern Pacific paralleled it to the east, running from Arlington, beneath Cultus Mountain, to Sedro Woolley and northward. The 1911 map shows numerous "Tram Lines" climbing the Cascade front to elevations as high as 1,000 feet. These railroads were to continue upward another two decades before locomotive logging gave way to the truck logging that in the World War II era reached the summit of Cultus, twenty-odd years before I did.

I crossed a gravel-sorting yard, climbed over a dike, and walked onto undefended wasteland at the mouth of the Swinomish Channel.

North from the dike sprawled a sea meadow peninsula a half-mile long and a quarter-mile wide. It was not reclaimed marsh—the sand and grass were undiked and only sparsely dotted with cow pies. It resembled a plain of sand dunes that had been mangled by dune buggies, but I saw no buggy tracks, and anyway the winds were wrong for dunes. The map explained: "Channel." The channel continued two more miles through MUD to the solid blue of Padilla Bay; the peninsula was composed not of dunes, but of piles of dredging spoils.

At 3 o'clock in the chill afternoon, sunset barely an hour off, I descended a "dune" to salt grass edging the third great bay of my route north from Everett. A mallard flock, spooked, hustled away, settling down farther out on the rippling waters. A cloud of peep enclosed me in flashing wings.

Skagit Bay had seemed a lake ringed by the Northern Isles; Port Susan had opened south to home seas; Padilla Bay, to the north, opened to far seas. The long jut of Samish Island didn't quite close off the bay mouth, but left between itself and Guemes Island a glimpse of the route once taken by Dad's tanker, the *Standard Service*, to Alaska.

The northern horizon was a confrontation between the peaks of the San Juan Range—the summits of Orcas, Cypress, Guemes, and Lummi islands—and the westernmost peaks of the Cascade Range—Chuckanut Mountain and Blanchard Hill. So distant last week from Quarry Mountain, they were very near today. There no longer was any doubt I'd get there, and that was sad.

At 3:54 the sun fell behind the oil refineries on March Point, whose thin plumes I'd seen floating up from the Fidalgo forest. Devils Mountain and Whitehorse turned pink, and then the water of Swinomish Channel, and finally Tahoma.

By 4:15 the lowlands had all dissolved in darkness. At 4:28 Komo Kulshan went in a blink from garden rose to tomb ice. To the east above Flatland the evening star was rising. The Cascade skyline was backlighted by a brightness that promised more: a full moon.

I walked south, leaving my flashlight in my rucksack, feeling my way through the shades of black that distinguished the dike path from barbed fences and mucky pits, keeping feet and head in proper relationship by the different nights of earth and sky.

Ambulo ergo sum.

42. Swinomish Channel to Bayview

Mile 111½–124

Tuesday, December 27, 1977

For a while, Flatland's favorite Pork in the Sky was a jumbo version of the Big Ditch, the proposed Avon Bypass, which would drain off the waters of the Skagit from a point near Mount Vernon and lessen the stress on the Fir Island dikes by diverting excess water to Padilla Bay. That dream lasted until the Army Engineers confessed that no matter how they jiggered the figures, the computer refused to fabricate a positive benefit-cost ratio, as required by Act of Congress. Had the by-passers got their economics straightened out they'd still have faced the environmentalists. However, the Engineers would not have preached their usual sour sermons against Mother Nature's sloppiness; they'd have claimed they were putting things back the way she used to have them.

The 1911 map shows Indian Slough splitting off from the Skagit at the hamlet of Avon, and meandering from there to the bay; old-timers say some of the Skagit flowed this way until blocked by a diker in the 1870s. On maps old and new can be traced the Skagit's ancient fritter-ing away into Higgins, Telegraph, Blind, Swinomish, and Sullivan sloughs. To walk the southern shores of Padilla Bay today is to see how the South Fork delta country would appear if the Skagit had packed up and moved away.

For intricacy my route here beat the route of Fir Island, the dikes here deviously curving in and out of major sloughs and minor. At 11:12 on a sunny morning (but there was ice on the puddles) I set out where I'd left off the day before, at the gravel factory, two air miles from Bayview. After following the dike over the mouth of Blind Slough (crossed via tidegate) and inland along the wide estuary of Telegraph Slough to the railroad tracks, and having walked two and a half miles, I was still two air miles from Bayview.

My next tour would have been a three-and-a-half-mile circuit of the peninsula enclosed by Telegraph and Indian sloughs. However, in the center of the fields were a large red barn, a derelict three-story mansion, and a mobile home from which, as I watched, a diker baron emerged with a gun and headed for the dikes, probably to hunt birds but perhaps willing to settle for a birder.

I fetched the beetle and put in again, this time from the Bayview-Edison Road, walked one and a half miles down Indian Slough and up a tributary, and now was only one and a half air miles from Bayview.

The walking distance proved to be three miles, and as happy a time on the delta as I'd known. Part of the dike was freshly topped with mud, by dikers evidently motivated by the recent Conjunction. The tide was nearly low, and a narrow strip of sand-gravel beach where straw-yellow grass was growing, gave me easy passage. The dike bent in and out, not quite enclosing all the primeval tidal meadow, leaving many marshy juttings and grass-tussock archipelagos. I passed concrete bun-kers large enough for several hunters to hunker in and, nearby, their fake ducks frozen in shore ice. Offshore was a puzzling island, three-quarters of a mile long and very few feet wide, a willow forest on its centerline ridge. (Later I came upon a map that noted the ownership as "Dike Is. Gun Club," which had taken over the artificial island from a failed subdivision.)

Peep flashed, hawks swooped, ducks paddled, a heron took flight. At the confluence of the tributary with Indian Slough I passed a splendid big farmhouse, uninhabited and boarded up, yet painted freshly white, lovingly preserved. On the 1911 map it is connected by road to the Padilla post office at Whitney and a train station at Fredonia. The map shows the water road, too, and sure enough, beside the farmhouse I saw old docks. The modern map shows the meanders of Indian Slough, onetime course of the Skagit, continuing out into Padilla Bay, a navigable lane of clear blue through a vastness labeled "MUD."

Peep tracks in the mud led to the mouth of Indian Slough. A breeze pushed broken ice against the beach gravel. The ice meant the bay was not excessively salty, that some of the Skagit flowed here still, seeping through the sloughs.

Padilla is described as *estuarine*, a mixture of sea and land, fresh and salt, that nourishes the richest and most diverse of life communities. According to experts, "Phytoplankton, macro-algae, eel grass, and marsh vegetation" draw energy from the sun, brewing "a great vegetable broth that feeds tiny shrimp, worms, or shellfish, which in turn provide the diet for creatures on up the chain." The bay grows North America's largest single bed of eel grass, which feeds the largest single assemblage of black brant. Probably every one of these little geese on the Pacific Flyway spends part of the winter here, mingling with an average of 60,000 wintering ducks. A myriad other living creatures in water, mud, and marsh feed 210 other species of birds.

Said John Work of the clam-diggers he met here in 1824, the "Scaadchet are fine looking Indians....They go quite naked except a blanket about their shoulders; many use in lieu of blankets little cloaks made of feathers or hair. The bay in which they reside is a handsome place."

Edmund Coleman, in 1868, watched other harvesting: "We observed a long pole with a cross-piece to it at the top. It is the native arrangement for catching wild-fowl. A net is spread on the crosspole, fires are lighted at night, the wild-fowl seeking at this time their food, and not seeing the net, fly against it with such force that they drop down."

At 2:30 the dike ended—the Middle Delta ended. Ahead of me stretched cobble beach. From it rose a 20-foot bluff of glacial drift over-hung by alder. I was welcomed home by a "Gark" that flapped out of the alders, and another "Gark," and "Gark, Gark, Gark," and then five more, ten herons, all in a gang. A bald eagle sailed close along the beach.

The Rozemas Boat Works pier forced me off the beach, up the wall, over a lawn to the Bayview-Edison Road. English sparrows, twittering and hopping, testified that Bayview was a longtime urban center. Platted in 1884, in 1911 it had seven blocks and a three-mile dead end logging railroad. Now it had nine moldering blocks centered around a gas sta-tion; the ruins of a public dock were connected by a half-mile of totter-ing pilings marking a channel through the map's "MUD" to the Indian Slough lane.

Bayview may ultimately prosper and sprawl. The uplands of Bay-view Ridge Island have been good for little but starving cows since the logging ended. Today, though, most have been bought by corporate speculators betting against the eel grass and the brant, the gark and the peep.

Port Susan is walled by bluffs. Whatever man can do to its shore he's already done, just about. Wherever man can live, he lives, almost. What is left of Port Susan's wildness may well survive until it thrives again in the next major Conjunction.

Skagit Bay, edged by land that is half water, has been invaded by diking and farming to the practical maximum. The pastoral is likely to prevail, assisted by Great Big Media Floods.

Padilla Bay, on the other hand, makes a walker worry. Long ago the bay floor was sold by the state to oyster-growing entrepeneurs; their enterprise failed, but it opened the door to the oil refiners, whose pay-rolls and taxes enabled Anacortes to win a national award as an All-American City. Other free-enterprisers sought to follow: more refin-eries, a magnesium smelter, a pulp mill, a lime plant, a concrete plant, a food factory, a dogfood factory, a log-export terminal. Scratching and screaming, the militia of friends of the bay managed to fight them off.

But then, in the early 1960s, the Orion Corporation sought to buy *the entire bay* for a New Venice in the MUD, a Codger City of 25,000, where a sizable part of retired Kansas could come to live like bees in glass-and-cedar hives beside plastic stinkpots parked at their front doors next to the porcelain gnomes in their gardens. The scheme could not be halted by Mother: a mile from shore is the map's first blue line denoting a depth of six feet below lower low water. Except in the Indian Slough boat channel, the depth four miles out *still* is only six feet; dredgers-spoilers readily could fill Padilla Bay with codgers, dredging a system of lanes for their pots, and heaping the spoils into sites for their hives. The Washington Shorelines Management Act of 1971 designated Padilla one of the state's five Shorelines of Statewide Significance—nice words, but no teeth.

At 3 o'clock I walked down through Bayview State Park to a narrow sand beach beneath a 50-foot jungle bluff. Herons garked up and down the bay. A goldeneye paddled by. The eagle made another low pass. I proceeded north, trailing clouds of peep.

What was *that*? What was skimming the glassy water with a roar of antique machinery? A Camel? A Fokker? A Spad? Surely I saw a white scarf trailing from the cockpit, between the wings of the biplane? Certainly the pilot was wearing goggles and a Lindy helmet?

Dad, who as a lad in Lowell, Massachusetts followed the exploits of the Lafayette Escadrille in the daily papers, never missed a chance after World War I to bum a ride with a touring barnstormer. In 1923 he hitchhiked in a Curtis float plane, a scout for battlewagons, and the pilot, on Dad's dare, buzzed the piers at Long Beach, California, as women fainted, children cried, police tweeted, and admirals turned purple.

A decade later I wore my Lindy helmet everywhere, drew page upon page of pictures of dogfights between Eddie Rickenbacker and Baron von Richtofen, revered Commander Byrd because he flew over both poles, raised my eyes worshipfully to every noise in the sky, and one thrilling day joined with my schoolmates at Daniel Bagley Grade School and all the schoolchildren of Seattle in filing outdoors in fire-drill formation to gaze up in awe at a silver dirigible of the U.S. Navy.

The evolution of aircraft should have stopped with the likes of this Padilla Bay Camel-Fokker-Spad, before the sky noise became a daily burden, before movie theaters jetted over the Greenland Icecap, gooks were 'palmed in Nam, and hikers stunned in the Cascades, while Lindy was a hero and there was adventure on high.

There remained the low.

The beach was invaded by a half-dozen cottages at the foot of the bluff. Then the fill upon which they were built gave way to tidal marsh that widened until the strand of pebbles and sand was cut off from the bluff by 500 feet of tussocks and sloughlets. Marsh yielded to a soggy meadow that had been a pasture once; inside the skinny lane of beach were dike remnants, and outside, a palisade of rotten, algae-yellow pilings.

At 3:30 a creek flowed through the dike ruins to meet the saltwater, now rising fast; all but two boots' width of beach had been consumed; dike and meadow would soon go under. It occurred to me that this would be a better walk in bright morning. However, this strip of marsh and meadow that wrapped around the corner of Bayview Ridge Island was the start of the Northern Delta. I was on the verge of entering my third Flatland. I stepped off shingle onto sun-dried seaweed.

> toujours gai kid he
> gurgled

Cold water had slyly crept in under the seaweed. Wet to my crotch I fought through slimy tentacles to a genuine dike that came straight out from the bluff and turned north. Oddly, it enclosed no crop except saltwater. Fake ducks floated. Sentry-box blinds were tacked to the inner wall of the palisade. A short distance ahead a second crossdike led to the bluff, promising an easy escape in case of emergency—if I could get to it.

There was a gap in my dike, and a torrent of cold water pouring into the drowned field. Don't think—jump. A second break—*jump*. A third, too wide—wade and be quick, the flood is running strong, safety is close ahead and golly knows what's to the rear by now. A fourth gap—a river—too deep to see or guess the bottom.

I would fain die a dry death.

Turn back, it may already be too late. Wade (it's deeper), jump (it's wider), jump (alas, it's too wide—'tis cold, 'tis bitter cold). The dike leading inland to the bluff was a lane between two seas, the path a trench through rose thorns that ripped pants and shirt and cheek. But at 4:00 I climbed to the Bayview-Edison Road, five miles from the beetle.

I assumed the broken dike meant a failure of reclamation. Later I learned it was a triumph of clamation. Born in 1896, Bayview resident since 1900, Mrs. Edna Breazeale liked Padilla Bay the way Mother made it. She bought sixty-eight acres of marsh and field along a mile of shore and gave it to the State Game Department. Mrs. Breazeale and others of her persuasion were why there still was a Padilla Bay rather than a Codger City.

The map of the bay-floor ownership would be a thing of beauty to a medieval philosopher (how many angels can dance on the head of a pin?) and a Euclidean geometrician (how many drunken sailors can walk a straight line?). Each tract emanates from a single "control point" which is located—for reasons probably arbitrary—two-fifths of a mile southwest of Hat Island in Padilla Bay. The wedge-shaped tracts radiate from that point north to Samish Island and southeast to Bayview, extending over the three or four miles to the edge of the bay, which is to say, the reach of mean low tide. When this scheme was devised the number of possible ownerships approached infinity. A small portion of the pie that belonged to Associated Oyster Lands Inc.—only one of many owners—had 943 tracts, each six feet wide at the shore.

The Orion Corporation simplified the situation; the modern map shows most tracts as "Orion" or "Option to Orion." However, interspersed amid wide Orion slices are little non-Orion slivers, firmly held by folks who confounded Orion by having a motivation other than greed. As any geometrician can plainly see, even a single six-foot—or six-inch—strip can deny passage to a dredge and forbid passage to the Stinkpot Navy. Handsome Orion, which thought itself most beautiful of the hunters, went chasing the wild dollar in Padilla Bay and was shot dead in the water by lethal slivers from the bow of Diana (Edna) Breazeale and friends. (In 1982 she was the star of ceremonies dedicating the Padilla Bay National Estuarine Sanctuary, then one of only eight such preserves in the nation.)

The five miles to the beetle seemed unnecessarily many, but the populace had gone indoors and such few cars as saw my upraised thumb swerved to flee the torn and bloody and seaweedy alien.

> As for me, I walk abroad o' nights,
> And kill sick people groaning under walls.
> Now and then I go about and poison wells...

At 4:14 the fireball burned a hole in the horizon; with the blaze gone I could look directly there to see that it vanished into Olympic peaks familiar to dikers, not to wanderers from Puget Sound.

At 4:20 I sat by the side of the road to drink a winter-cold Pepsi and fill my eyes with the twilight arching from the summit ridge of Lummi Island on the north to the peak of Ika Island on the south. When had I last seen so much sky? White wisps floated across the dark green haystack of Mount Erie, my connector to the Issaquah Alps. Off March Point lay two tankers so huge that the *Standard Service* would have served as a dinghy, so long they seemed to jostle the islands. Yet these were not the state-of-the-art superdragons lurking off the coast; by law those could not be here on the Whulj because they were more than 120,000 tons—which is to say, the size of four U.S.S. *New Mexicos*.

At 4:25 the orange band stretching across the pale blue west exploded. I walked on, around a bend—Tahoma was burning to the ground!

At 4:41, I descended from island to delta, to cows, barns, and murmurings in the fields. A car passed, the first since Bayview. I offered no thumb, only my Quasimodo rucksack. I did not regret this journey.

> by cripes i have danced the shimmy
> in rooms as warm as a dream
> and gone to sleep on a cushion
> with a bellyful of cream

Far south, La Conner twinkled starlike.

> dance mehitabel dance
> till your old bones fly apart
> i ain t got any regrets
> for i gave my life to my art

Nearby, to the south, Highway 20 headlights flowed east and west.

> On every hand the roads begin,
> And people dash with zeal therein;
> But wheresoe'er the highways tend,
> Be sure there's nothing at the end.

On this Third Day of Christmas, yellow flames erupted from electrical trees on March Point, red lights celebrated Swinomish Channel.

Above in eternity shone the evening star.

The western sky shaded from pale blue on high down to yellow, orange, soft rose—and these were also the colors of the bay.

"Gark! Gark!" A black silhouette flapped up from night and dissolved in the prehistoric past.

Walking, chaps, becomes your thing
The night you hear the angels sing.

43. Bayview to Samish Island

Mile 124–129

Saturday, December 31, 1977

On the Seventh Day of Christmas I parked on the Bayview-Edison Road and revisited, from the northern crossdike, the site of Tuesday's sunset. The tide was just starting to ebb so the water gap was even wider, a couple of hundred feet, though not now a river because the abandoned field was a placid arm of the glassy bay. As I recalled my thrilling escape from the water, four days ago, when I found the broken dike, a hunter in rubber pants waded past, fifty feet offshore, towing a line of wooden ducks, the water barely to his hips. Competence is the death of adventure.

Ice-clear air brought southern connections close: refinery plumes and three supertankers; Mount Erie and Quarry Mountain and Ika Island; the Olympics. To the west, against the mountainous backgrounds of Fidalgo and Guemes islands, little Hat Island, its crown towering 292 feet, lorded it over tiny Saddlebag Island and minute Dot Island.

Where Bayview Ridge, a former San Juan Island, sloped down to a former inlet of the bay, a former mouth of the Skagit meandered to the salt. Joe Leary Slough, named for Josiah Larry, who settled here in 1859, was a trespasser's horror. The mile of dike that bent inland upon the estuary and out again to the bay was a series of trials by hellberries and mean-it fences, and I dared not cry aloud in pain lest I catch a baleful eye from the nearby farmhouse and have the dogs set on me.

I almost didn't see the hunter crouched in the reeds beside the dike, and I was barely by when he vented his spleen with a *blam blam* meant for no duck. Silly man. Having fired two shots heard round the world, he began tootling on his patent gabbler, sounding the plaintive call of the wooden duck.

The dike now stretched open and lonesome for three miles, guarded by the rotten and tottering palisade. The blue waters of Padilla Bay were bounded for five miles on the northwest by the long thrust of Samish Island. The stubble-brown and plowed-black fields of the Northern Delta were bounded for five miles on the northeast by Blanchard Hill. Flatland opened east to, and beyond, the gateway masses of Cultus and Woolley Lyman, and extended far up the Skagit Valley.

To my left, pilings and sentry boxes, peep and goldeneyes and bufflehead; Padilla Bay and San Juan Islands. To my right, winter-tawny fields, red barns and white houses, the chiseled ice of Komo Kulshan.

A scant half-mile from Samish Island, a clot of civilization lay in wait for Saturday skulkers. To my rear, though, lay Joe Leary Slough, and between me and the Bayview-Edison Road spread broad fields gridded with evil blue lines. Nearing a dikeside house I lowered my profile and quickened my pace. Hounds came roaring and ramping and slathering. Now the door would fly open to reveal a specter in long-handled underwear. Instead, though, a kindly woman emerged, called off the dogs, and welcomed me to use her driveway to the public road.

Padilla Bay ended. Minutes later, across the island neck, Samish Bay began. The map shows a cunning shore, a masterpiece of miniaturization in the Craft Island style, with a little marsh, peninsulas, and isles, all connected by and enclosing dikes and lakes, embellished with pilings and tidegates, trails, "Footbridges," and "Ruins." However, at every possible entry a mean-it array of signs proclaimed: "Residence—Keep Out." "Duck Club—Keep Out." Fee Fi Fo Fum. For two air miles from Samish Island to Edison the route would have to be the public road.

I started south to fetch the beetle. A car approached and I idly stuck out the thumb that had terrified Bayview.

"Great day for it." The driver smiled as he opened the door. "Soon as I get home I'm walking to La Conner. Charlie needs the exercise."

A nice man, good to his friends, including me and also Charlie, who lived with him on the Swinomish and was perched on the back of the front seat. Charlie wouldn't be getting his exercise by walking because Charlie was a gull.

44. Samish Island

Friday, November 11, 1977

The gospel according to von Humboldt: In the beginning—which is to say when sea and land stabilized near their present relationship, four to five millennia ago—there were *two* Samish Islands. As the lands completed their postglacial rebound, an isthmus rose up to connect the two. The Skagit Delta meanwhile was growing westward, and when the first European settled on Samish in 1867 (or 1853?) the delta had pushed a dozen miles from Sedro Woolley to the inner island. Canoes still could shortcut through sloughs from Samish Bay to Padilla Bay, but dikers put a stop to that, converting island to peninsula. Canoeist complaints were few, the Samish population having declined between 1847 and 1855 from 2,000 to 150.

My hiking partner, Dick, and I drove three miles from the delta to the outer end of the isthmus, all the way barred from the water by continuous beach homes, the Riviera of the Flatlands. We were let through at last by Eddie Adams and Mr. and Mrs. Ben Bourns, who were noted on the sign as having given the state, in 1960, the Samish Island Public Beach and Picnic Site.

Views over Samish Bay were new and dazzling, but they would have to wait because the tide was rising, the future uncertain. From the put-in we hastily walked a half-mile of shingle and sand beneath a 100-foot wall of varved clay and iron-stained gravel. A prow of bedrock schist, green with lichen and yellow with algae, cleaved into deep water, forcing us to scramble up the bluff.

A path wound through island-top wildwoods to an old farm. The 1951 map shows the house standing; shingles now were a mossy heap beside the last wall still erect—and even that was leaning. Thickets of wild rose ringed the pastures, millions of cherry tomatoes shaming the scattered apples on lichen-gray trees. A road that hadn't felt wheels in years curved down to an abandoned quarry in the gray metamorphic rock that lies at the core of Northern Delta dikes. A trail led to North Point.

We hadn't expected to go to sea. We'd thought to take a little stroll close by the delta and found that for all the sedimentation by the Skagit, and all the diking by the Dutch boys, Samish remained a free island, westerly waves breaking against its bow. Straw-yellow grass and green moss sloped to the brink of a cliff that plunged fifty feet to water and (said the map) then plunged sixty feet more.

Pale sun filtered through thin clouds, casting mellow warmth on the isles. We were not looking *to* the archipelago, we were *in* it, as intimately as if aboard a ferry. To the northwest sat little Vendovi Island, near enough for us to see shrubby trees dotting tawny meadows, bald rocks buttressing the 327-foot peak. Larger Sinclair, beyond, rose to 301 feet beneath the looming background of Mount Constitution, 2,049 feet, summit of the San Juans and only fourteen miles distant, not so far as Sedro Woolley to our rear. More northerly Eliza Island, actually several islets become one (so said von Humboldt), sported a jaunty pair of 90-foot peaklets.

The thundering star was Lummi, nine miles long and one and a half miles wide, and we *wow-ee*'d at the profile of the Lummi Wall, four miles long, plunging 1,500 vertical feet—and continuing downward underwater. Von Humboldt pondered what made the wall, which in all the Whulj hasn't a rival. When in doubt, say "glacier." But sometimes say "strike of the strata" or even "fault line." We also were now viewing the 2,000-foot plunge of Chuckanut Mountain to Samish Bay, less steep than the Lummi scarp yet nearly as impressive and exactly parallel, and the deep canyon of Oyster Creek that divides Chuckanut from Blanchard Hill in an identical alignment.

We'd unexpectedly escaped the delta, and man as well. The sea chanced at the moment to be empty of ships, and whatever civilization there was on the lands was dissolved in distance. The sky, too, chanced to be momentarily empty, so that amid the wash of waves and the splash of tippy-ass ducks the loudest sounds were our *wow-ee*s.

The spot cried out (to a developer) for a row of millionaires' ticky-tacks, but their absence did not set us to praising the sensitivity and wisdom of government. Along about 1970 the Snohomish County Public Utility District bought 100 acres here, at the same time it bought, in partnership with Seattle City Light, Kiket Island in Skagit Bay, in both cases to put the salt sea to work cooling nuclear reactors. The technology happened never to be perfected, but after holding a fair trial Dick and I ruled that the utility managers could not be let off on that account. The plotting of a crime was held by us to be a crime. Those who conspire to kindle hellfires in Paradise must burn in Hell. If the atheists prove there is none, we'll build one.

(In 1980 the PUD put its Samish property on the block for $1 million; afterward when Skagit County zoned the land to preserve the scene by forbidding the proposed building of half-a-thousand boxes, the PUD sued the county! Two Hells will be required, the second to continue the punishment after the first is burnt out.)

We returned to the farm, descended to a cove for lunch, and climbed to the meadows and cliffs of Point William, westernmost jut of Samish. At our back the Douglas firs on the forest edge massed thick-barked trunks and heavy limbs to protect the inner forest from the west winds, the north winds, and the south winds, which have blown winter and summer through the centuries from the crossroads of Padilla, Samish, Fidalgo, and Bellingham bays, Guemes and Bellingham channels, and the straits of Georgia and Rosario. The crossroads itself, the momentous gulf, was left nameless by the navigators, and remains that way, despite all the other names they passed out.

In July of 1791 Narvaez, on behalf of the Eliza (Island) expedition, double-honored Juan Vicenta de Guemes (Island) Pacheco de Padilla (Bay) Horcasitas y Aguayo, second Conde de Revilla Gigedo, Viceroy of Mexico.

In 1792 a British naval officer, William (Point) Bellingham (Bay) was double-honored by Vancouver, who mis-honored Cypress (Island), which ought to have been Western Juniper, that being the correct name of the tree. Puget and Whidbey, who named Hat Island and guessed Padilla Bay had a "communication by rivulets" with Skagit Bay, camped one June day at Point William, during which time a marine stepped on "an animal called a skunk…and the intolerable stench it created absolutely awakened us in the tent."

Charles Wilkes, who in 1841 took soundings all around Guemes Island ("Lawrence" to him) through "Hornet Harbor," "Levant Passage," "Penguin Harbor," and into Padilla Bay nearly to March Point, established that Fidalgo ("Perry's") was an island and mapped Swinomish Channel. He honored a crewman, Jack (Island), named Sinclair Island for an American naval officer and Vendovi Island for a native abducted from the Fiji Islands and brought along as a mascot—a cannibal chief who was reputed to have eaten eight sailors from the Boston whaler *Charles Daggett.*

But these busy mariners didn't name the crossroads gulf where mingled the ships of three nations and the canoes of Lummi, Samish,

Skagit, and Haida. Neither did they distinguish the 600-square-mile expanse of water within which they named most of the interruptions, the San Juan Islands (or "Archipelago of Arro"). Had the earliest European explorers been landsmen, and had they come afoot to William Point, the first thing they'd have named would have been the "Sea of San Juan."

On seacliff balds beside gnarled firs and contorted Oregon white oaks whose bark reminded me of the corks in bottles of madeira, we rounded the shore from lee to windward. Meadow grass danced, forest sighed, an eagle sailed. Ahead now were Guemes, one of the broad islands, mostly low and rolling but with a 720-foot peak on the southeast tip; and beyond one of the bulky islands, Cypress, with double peaks of 1,484 and 1,514 feet—the higher one known to the Lummis as She-ungtlh, home of the great thunderbird. Small islands sprinkled the foreground waters: Jack, Huckleberry, Saddlebag, Dot, and Hat. Plumes from March Point drifted across the forests of Mount Erie.

We scrambled down to a little beach and over a rock ridge to Kirby Spit and walked away from hard-rock Samish Island, traipsing a half-mile out between driftwood and surf to Dean Point. We wondered: why did it point southwest? In our home waters that couldn't happen because that's the direction of the storm winds, the heavy engines driving the spit-building longshore currents. Here, one supposed, currents from the southeast have a major advantage over competitors because of the abundance of alluvial mud-sand they can pick up in Padilla Bay; further, winds in the Sea of San Juan are bounced about as crazily as billiard balls; moreover, gales from the water horizon to the northeast between Vendovi and Lummi—the Gulf of Georgia that connects to Alaska—may come in storm or sun or whenever they please.

We didn't linger on Dean Point amid the cross-chopping waves colliding and exploding, the sands shuddering underfoot, wild water everywhere. Our attachment to the continent was insecure, the wild west wind deafening ears and slitting eyes and threatening—promising—to carry us away like dead leaves.

Returning along the spit to the bluff, and so to the isthmus and the car, we passed cabins of the Campfire Girls camp, not unlike those of Camp Sealth on Vashon Island or Camp Parsons on Hood Canal.

45. Samish Island to Blanchard   Mile 129–136$^{1}/_{2}$

Saturday, December 31, 1977

The green wall of Blanchard Hill rose so near that trees could be singled out in the forest. I drove past diketop houses and commercial fishing boats at the estuary of the Samish "River"—a creek that dribbles from mountains north of the delta, wanders forlornly over Flatland, and would be lost altogether did it not slip into a onetime channel of the Skagit.

Another such channel, Edison Slough, had a white-paint-tidy village, settled in 1869 (Blanket Bill Jarman camped nearby a while in 1852), and is hardly larger now than then. Beyond the last houses I turned off on a dirt lane to the dike. At 1:20 the last lap began.

The ebbing tide had exposed the sliver of beach characteristic of dikes—"artificial-natural"—built by the natural action of waves attacking artificial fill. I tried it for walking, but masses of seaweed were hard-frozen and slick. My way was the high road, ten feet above high tide, in the iced air of December, in a spotlight of bright sun, through a world all aglow and aglitter, holiday happy and kindly.

Except for several boat basins and frequent gaps where pilings had toppled, the palisade was continuous; von Humboldt hypothesized a single burst of delta-wide engineering a half-century or more ago—after a Conjunction of Four? Perhaps the Great Flood of 1909? Or was this a relic of the original diking? In a newspaper I once saw a 1910 photograph of farmers with shovels and wheelbarrows building a dike "near Edison," apparently on the bay shore.

Plankwalks led out to ladders that climbed pilings to platforms where gunners could man the ramparts in case those tens of thousands of ducks and geese and swans floating on the brilliant bay turned surly and came to eat up all the spinach and peas.

I sat alone on a piece of stone for a Christmas feast of kippers and apple and Pepsi, and reviewed my inventory of islands from long Samish to little Vendovi to massive Lummi. Close ahead rose Chuckanut Mountain, its brown band of sandstone layered across slopes of dun brush grown up since the forest fire of the mid-1960s.

I passed a hunter crouched in the riprap, another hunter crouched in the reeds sounding the quack of the wooden duck, and a farmer by a tidegate fiddling with a pump that spewed ditchwater onto the glistening plain of mud. Out to sea the yelping of the fleets of snow geese mingled with the muttering-croaking-gabbling of other fleets unknown.

At 2:42 the dike ended (fanfare) beside Chuckanut Drive and I walked (drum and colors) along a gravel lane to the estuary of Colony Creek, at the northernmost edge of the northernmost delta, at the foot of the westernmost thrust of the Cascades. I stood on a heap of oyster shells and 1977 was done, and so (trumpets and cornets) were the deltas.

And so (recorders and hautboys) exeunt all, to another room in the castle.

PART FIVE

Blanchard to Bellingham

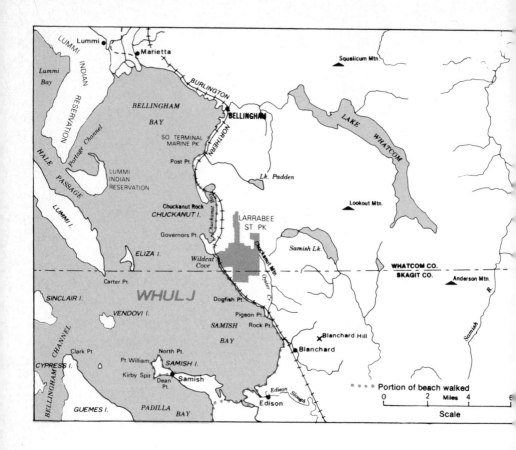

Portion of beach walked

Scale
0   2   Miles   4

46. Blanchard to Chuckanut Bay

Friday, November 4, 1977

Beyond the 7-11 frontier I always keep an eye out for old country stores and think up something to buy. At Blanchard I was too late. The two-story box of a building, white paint flaking, was signed "Blanchard Grocery" and the window advertised "Lipton's Tea," but the only living thing to be seen was a TV antenna on the roof. However, a modest placard, "1885," showed somebody remembered.

Blanchard must have had its day, sited where bay and mountain meet. The map shows a navigable blue line starting at Colony Creek, northernmost ancient mouth of the Skagit, named for a socialist colony, Equality, that was located upstream for a decade or so after 1897. Out through "MUD SAND & GRAVEL," the line proceeds to the open blue of Samish Bay. Mosquitos docked here and fishing boats harbored. Ruins of an oyster-packing plant at the estuary mouth are so freshly charred as to suggest it operated until quite recently. The Seattle-Vancouver telegraph of 1865 had a station here. In 1896 a wagon road was completed along the mountain scarp north from this point to Bellingham Bay, and was later improved into the first highway connection between Bellingham and the delta, Chuckanut Drive. The 1911 map doesn't reach this far north but has the Seattle and Vancouver line of the Great Northern running off the edge as if intent on going the whole way. The map doesn't show the Mount Vernon-Bellingham Interurban Railway, presumably built a bit later. Telegraph, wagon road, railroad, interurban—at Blanchard all transferred from delta to mountains.

At 10:15 so did I, shouldering my rucksack and walking away from the grocery, from dikes to tracks. There'd be no difficulties with the route these final few miles, following, once again, the well-beaten trail of the iron horse—no tides to watch or barbed-wire fences to clamber.

There'd also be no memories—our family never lived in these parts nor came here Sunday-driving or vacationing. There'd not be much new to see—and nothing (for me) old. Of course, that's when a tramp gets some of his best thinking done, settling into the autonomic pace of tie-walking, spending the hours inward looking and backward because there's so little to look forward to.

A concrete bridge lifted Chuckanut Drive up from Flatland onto the mountainside, high above the railroad, to be seen or heard little more the rest of my walking way. Rotten pilings marched across the mouth of the estuary, recalling vanished rails of the interurban. Poles footed in water carried the telephone line north, as others, long since toppled, once did the telegraph. Jim Hill's bridge took me over Colony Creek onto the base of the mountain, to end as I'd begun, on Jim Hill's tracks.

Hill's tracks brought Mother from North Dakota to meet the *New Mexico*. The tracks of other empire-builders led me from Seattle to Portland and San Francisco; from New York to Boston, Philadelphia, Connecticut, and up the Hudson River; from Vancouver to Saskatoon; from Golden to Glacier to climb Mount Sir Donald; and from Newhalem to Reflector Bar to climb Colonial Peak and Snowfield Mountain. I expected more. The Orient Express. The Trans-Siberian. Grand Central Station and fame, fortune, pretty girls.

There were other tracks, more homely, in Seattle. As freshmen at Lincoln High in 1938 we rode streetcars to football games at Civic Field. As seniors we went by trackless trolley or diesel bus. The loss of the streetcars was like a death in the family, because aside from a few photographs and anecdotes, my only connections to Grandfather Hawthorn were the great ships of the streets he had commanded as conductor on the Ballard line.

From ships of the seas I expected more than rides to football games, more than Grand Central Station. I was planning to go to California on the *Alexanders* and to England on the Cunard White Star liners. They quit too soon for me, though. I did take a *Princess* to Victoria, saw retired British majors with white mustaches riding bicycles through the rose gardens, and smoked Players and Black Cats. I slept a night aboard the *Standard Service.* I've often driven Suibhna the Sailor Man to his ship, berthed on the Duwamish Waterway, and drunk very old Scotch in the radio room.

With littler vessels I've done better. I've ferried a dozen routes on

the Whulj between Anderson Island on the south and Vancouver Island
on the north; over Lake Washington from Seattle to Kirkland; across the
Columbia River at Megler, Biggs, and Vantage; and across some other
big river between there and Massachusetts—the Mississippi? I knew the
old mosquito fleet when it was a going business, and now I honor the
last survivor, the *Virginia V*, a steaming museum. I ride the modern mosquitos—the *Goodtimes*, to the beaches of Blake Island, and the
Speedway and *Lady of the Lake* to the mountains of Lake Chelan and
Stehekin.

Incredibly, I was only just a little late for the sailing ships which
from the seventeenth to the nineteenth centuries carried my family over
the Atlantic (or in the case of Great-great-great-grandfather Horton, to
the bottom of the Atlantic). My best friend at Winslow lived on a sailing
ship moored in Eagle Harbor, awaiting its next cargo, and I went to his
birthday party aboard. There never was another cargo. Among the
funeral pyres I attended at Richmond Beach may have been that of my
birthday-party ship.

I managed to travel a little by wind. On a blustery winter day four of
us college boys and girls borrowed, or maybe temporarily stole, a sailboat on Portage Bay and ran north before the wind on Lake Washington
until we ran out of lake. As we were about to smash into the shore, one
of us remembered enough high school physics to come about and tack
south. An October afternoon I enlisted with Suibhna to crew on his
cabin sailer for what he predicted to be an hour's run from Portage Bay
to Leschi Marina to have the dead auxiliary fixed. We ran out of wind,
then out of daylight, finally out of whiskey sour, and late at night were
arrested by the Harbor Police as a menace to navigation.

Steamships and motor vessels, naphtha launches and kickerboats
and stinkpots, sailboats and float boats and paddle boats and rowboats,
I've voyaged some in all of these, and in 1931 or 1932 lifted my eyes to
a mighty airship, precursor—so thought we children and the U.S.
Navy—of a new Pacific Fleet of battlewagons of the sky.

I mourn the passing of the Navy dirigibles still, and of the *Graf Zep-
pelin* and *Hindenburg* as well, and thus am rather sentimental about the
Goodyear blimps. For the rest, though, I'd as soon the sky had been
left to the stars. A dozen years after Bleriot made the first human flight
over the English Channel, Dad skimmed the Long Beach piers, a dozen
years after that I watched Wiley Post and Will Rogers fly over Vashon
Island, and less than a decade later I was a laborer in the boneyard at

Sand Point Naval Air Station, stacking pieces of aircraft crashed by World War II pilots-in-training. A decade more and I began flying to New York and San Francisco in DC-3s, DC-6s, 707s, and DC-10s, and after several years of never getting where I wanted to go, planted both feet on the planet to stay. Too much. Too fast.

> Entropy, entropy, entropy—
> Thinketh it dwelleth i' the dark o' the moon.

In 1841 the hustle-bustle England of the Industrial Revolution hailed the improvements in road surfaces and ingenuities of undercarriage construction which permitted the "rapid coach" to fly from London to Exeter in a breathtaking eighteen hours. In 1845 the rail express shrank the route to six and a half hours.

> Revolution, revolution, revolution—
> Thinketh the wheel never stoppeth, but
> Goeth ever faster, round and round and round.

Starting with the Liverpool-Manchester line, between 1830 and 1850 more than 6,000 miles of railway were built in Britain. By 1850 there were already more than that in the hurly-burly United States.

At Sidmouth, in the 1840s, was founded the first society for the preservation of footpaths.

On the Whulj, in the 1970s, was founded the first society for the preservation of wooden rowboats.

Even the wind may be too swift, as Captain Horton will testify from the bottom of the Atlantic. The pace of the railroad seems decently in Earth scale only by comparison with the airplane, which renounces the planet altogether.

> Row, row, row your boat.
> Walk, walk, walk about.

From California through Oregon and most of Washington the Cascades lie far east of the tides. North of the Skagit the range bellies abruptly west to saltwater. The shore from Blanchard is a mountain wall of hard rock, sandstone interbedded with seams of coal and fossilliferous shale, and the only beaches are those of glacial drift deposited by longshore currents. Lacking the railroad, a waterside walker would spend a great deal of time in three-point suspension, climbing with the eyes, testing holds.

Von Humboldt, my scientific alter ego, observing San Juan peaks (Burlington Hill and Sterling Hill) located amid peaks of the Cascade front, and now viewing the startling plunge of Blanchard Hill and Chuckanut Mountain to the Whulj; gazing to Lummi, Constitution, Guemes, and Cypress, and having rather recently heard about plate theory, wondered where the San Juans left off and the Cascades began. He hypothesized a titanic tectonic clash in progress, plates rising and diving and colliding and fracturing. But tectonics were invented after he left school and make him nervous.

So does isostasy. The melting of the Canadian ice—here so thick it overtopped the 4,000-foot summits of Woolley-Lyman and Cultus—exposed a lowland trough that was drowned by saltwater that crept, as sea level continued to rise, far east past the Cascade gateway peaks. The Skagit, counterattacking with the sediments of a thousand headwaters, filled the estuary and pushed a delta far out from the mountain front, enveloping such San Juan Islands as Quarry, Fish Town, and Bayview Ridge, and bumping against Craft, Fidalgo, and Samish. However, the post-melting rebound must have been (must continue to be?) tremendous hereabouts. Are the San Juan Islands still rising? Was it that these islets were *not* enveloped by delta silt but rather erupted through it like so many adolescent pimples?

The sun was paled by clouds that appeared insufficiently pregnant for an umbrella. Tiny waves lapped the skinny beach below the tracks. From the tip of Windy Point I looked over four miles of Samish Bay to Samish Island, and beyond to Mount Erie and the Olympics, well remembered by old feet.

To fly over the Greenland Icecap may be to "see" it, in the sense of experiencing an electro-chemical excitation of a neural mechanism. To *know* it, though, one would have to ski or sledge, at the pace that gives time to be *with* a place, not merely *at* it, that allows the lineaments of the land to be indelibly etched in the memory. Once a mountain has been walked—has been read, Braillelike, by the feet—it can be recognized at a very great distance from subtle details that mean nothing to the person who hasn't been there.

An outlander, looking from Samish Bay to the Olympics, would see a jumble of anonymous rocks patched and streaked with interchangeable snows, foreign and meaningless. I saw rocks my fingers had clutched, rocks I'd sat upon for lunch, snows I'd slowly ascended, kicking steps, and snows I'd slid down upon my bottom faster than a speeding bullet. I knew the Olympics, they were home.

Seen from the Issaquah Alps, this northernmost scarp of the Cascades had stirred about as much emotion in me as snapshots of a neighbor's cousin's vacation in Hawaii. Approaching closer, I'd wondered at subtle colorings quite different from the general green uniformity. Walking the base of the scarp, I saw gray-brown cliffs of naked sandstone, winter-tawny slopes of meadow grass, dun thickets of leafless shrubs, and black snags charred by the fire which so recently had burnt the mountain so bare. Henceforth, viewing the scarp from the Issaquah Alps, I would feel (if not quite see) the subtleties. Not to be ungracious to my host, Jim Hill, but in two-thirds of a century his wheels never had gotten to know the mountain as well as my feet in a few hours.

To make a place your home, walk it. Or row it.

A railroad sign said "Samish" at a small peninsula that jutted to "Rock Point Oyster Co. Retail Hours 8–5 weekdays, 1–6 Sat–Sun." I looked in a window to workers at the sorting table, which was fed from a roof-top hopper outside the building. While I watched, a scow-dredge chugged in from the bay and hooked into a conveyor belt that carried oysters up to the hopper. I stepped in the retail shop to browse.

The very first oyster of my life I swallowed on the beach of Camp Parsons for my initiation into the Royal Order of the Raw Oyster. Some Scouts couldn't keep theirs down and had to try a second time—or a third. Years passed before my stomach could hear about an oyster without convulsions. Eventually introduced to them in fried, baked, or chowdered condition, my taste developed, grew to an appetite, and became a passion. I now considered a dozen merely a snack; a whole beach was needed for a proper meal. Luckily, Dad now lived on such a beach and I was able to indulge in the occasional orgy, eating enough at a sitting to satisfy me for months. So far had I progressed in overcoming my aversion to raw oysters that while Dad and I were shucking on the Hood Canal beach I popped one in every-so-many into my mouth instead of the jar and chewed the slimy bugger to death. Alacazam.

At Rock Point I considered buying a dozen in the shell for a beachfire luncheon of oysters Rockefeller, or a dozen in a jar to swallow raw as I walked. Inspection of the price list reminded me why I never bought oysters, only stole them.

The tracks burrowed through the jutting cliffs of Pigeon Point. Rather than enter the black hole where a diesel Cyclops might lurk, I turned up Oyster Creek, the incongruously small dribble that issues from the disproportionately grand cleft that separates Blanchard Hill from Chuckanut Mountain. Its little delta was a pig farm. The swine rushed out snuffling and oinking, restrained by the electric wire from offering me a warmer welcome. I wondered how it would be to eat our dogs (such a delicacy to the Indians they saved them for holidays and guests) and take our pigs walking.

From Chuckanut Drive I descended a woods road to regain the tracks. A duck squadron took to the air to join the main fleet in the bay. Pigeons strutted and crows hustled. A hawk cried "spee-oo!" A gull whined. An ivy-covered ridge ten feet high and a hundred feet long paralleled the tracks. Probing the ivy, I found the ridge was entirely composed of shells, and in my mind's eye saw mountains of oysters being gobbled by Diamond Jim Brady and John D. Rockefeller and James J. Hill and a whole history book of scoundrel nabobs, through the whole of the Gilded Age.

The meadow peninsula of Dogfish Point ran out to pilings of a one-time dock. A lone madrona stood on the brink of the sandstone wall, its bark silky tan and its leaves green-leathery, its fruit clustered in balls of red berries. A tiny beach, overhung by the madrona branches and enclosed by the sandstone wall, was a jewel-like miniature with bleached driftwood heaped against the base of the rock and then, in concentric arcs progressing outward, white shells, green-red seaweed, gray gravel, and, finally, waves rippling lucid water.

I was under clouds. The San Juans shone in the sun, and the Olympics shone too, fifty miles away, the same distance they are from Cougar Mountain. At Parsons, to achieve the Silver Marmot award, we had to memorize the Olympic rivers. The Hood Canal rosary—Skokomish, Hamma Hamma, Duckabush, Dosewallips, Quilcene—were invisible from here. The northern valleys were in view, however, as they are not from further south: the Dungeness, in whose headwaters lay Marmot Pass and Home Lake (which I first encountered in 1938), Lost Ridge (1940), Royal Basin and Graywolf Pass (1946), and the Elwha, headwaters in the Elwha Basin, through which I walked in 1949 on a traverse from the Hoh River over glaciers of Mount Olympus and meadows of the Low Divide to the Quinault River.

A broad terrace (identified by von Humboldt as a fossil beach raised up by the Great Rebound) sprawled out from the cliff. I left the tracks to walk a quarter-mile of pure sand beach beneath a sand slope rising 20 feet above the driftwood. The beach ended in a gallery of sandstone filigree and fretwork—walls, buttresses, and caves eaten at by waves as if by a plague of moths.

Against one wall lay a talus of broken glass, pieces of the thousands of bottles that had been hurled against the rock during the nights of many years, by the lights of many beachfires and stars.

> i wake the world from sleep
> as i caper sing and leap
> when i sing my wild free tune

To the south, trestle remnants marched in from the bay to meet a road-trail angling inland north. The map shows the abandoned interurban grade crossing Chuckanut Drive and proceeding to Bellingham. As loonily lovestruck as Toad of Toad Hall, people of the Whulj were all too eager to desert watercraft for motorcars, and mourned the mosquito fleet only after they killed it. So, too, when the people of America had the beginnings of a rapid-transit system that might have kept pace with growth and made suburbs rational appendages of healthy cities, they fell in with the General Motors plot to remove every competitor to the motorcar. Our family collaborated. Though the Seattle-Everett Interurban ran so near our house that the clanging bell was as familiar as roosters crowing, we rode the GM bus on Highway 99 instead, and in 1939 the bell didn't clang anymore; the Toonerville Trolley ran only in the funny papers.

The railroad swerved from the shore to tunnel through forest, to pass cozy coves, to cross deep ravines. This was Larrabee State Park, 2,000 acres of wildland sloping steeply up from Samish Bay to the summit of 1,940-foot Chuckanut Mountain.

At 1:20 I sat on a log by the wavelets of Wildcat Cove eating my kippers and apple and listening to a recorder duet by two girls on a neighbor log. Vendovi, the Cannibal Isle, was falling away south. The north shores of broad Guemes and tall Cypress Islands were rounding into view. Eliza was taking a turn in the spotlight, perky little snip of an island at the foot of Lummi, no longer seen bow-on as a thin slab but enormously broadside, a ship-of-the-line that could speak with not seventy-four but seventy-four hundred guns, and demast and hull

Chuckanut Mountain before its marines could scramble into the rigging with their muskets.

Larrabee State Park to Chuckanut Bay

Had I turned around at the park I could easily have walked back to the beetle by dusk and been home for dinner. But a man's reach must exceed his grasp, or what's a thumb for?

> the things i had not ought to
> i do because i got to

The railroad, having climbed to 66 feet for the purpose, crossed a sandstone ridge. Whiskey Rock, Governors Point, Pleasant Bay, and Chuckanut Point, all tantalizing on the map, were all denied me by stern signs at every lane: NO BEACH ACCESS.

A freight train passed from the north. I looked ahead and behind on the tracks to ensure no other was approaching and scooted through Tunnel No. 19, so numbered, and also identified, by numerals indented in the concrete, as dating from 1912. As I entered Tunnel No. 20 I saw a devil dog silhouetted at the far end. But I too was in black silhouette and my devil noises sent the devil dog yipping.

A pair of tangled ravines reminded me of childhood shores. A slow-croaking frog, remembering or anticipating spring, reminded me of long-ago days and nights.

> i once was an innocent kit
> with a ribbon my neck to fit
> and bells tied onto it

Suburbs continued on a strip of fossil beach, and when that pinched out, they leaped up atop the sandstone wall and perched high above the tracks. I descended a path for the sake of being with the water—a new water, Chuckanut Bay. The very little Chuckanut Island, its meadow summit 50 feet high, and the even littler Chuckanut Rock, were foreground grace notes to the enormous background of Lummi, six miles out and 1,600 feet high, blotting out a huge amount of sky.

A fellow came running down the path and asked for a hand in lauching his cockleshell, cradled in a tree, offering in return to fill my rucksack with crabs. As he rowed out to the buoy that marked his crab pot, visions of bacchanal danced in my head.

A heap of cracked crab, loaves of hot garlic bread, jugs of white wine, jolly friends around the table, and under it the Alley Kats, the mehitabels, the Krazy Kats. Crab is particularly excellent for sociable feasting because extricating the flesh is a slow business, the dining goes on and on, morsel by morsel, and so too the drinking and the laughing, the capering, singing, and leaping.

To be sure, too much seafood grows tiresome, and a person can understand the delight of the Skagits when Hudson's Bay introduced them to the Irish potato, and why the Clallams were willing to kill for a share. (What would they have done for garlic bread?) Shrimp, clams, oysters, and crab are best gone at not too often—but when they are gone at, it ought to be done all-out.

During Depression years, Dad would often be driving along Railroad Avenue and spot a fishing boat unloading. He'd stop the car and give a holler and a high sign, and a Norwegian would laugh and toss him a chicken halibut. Supper at our house that night would include potatoes and cole slaw, but purely for table decoration. The serious business was halibut, one steak after another, hot from the frying pan. We had no refrigerator, the entire halibut had to go in our stomachs immediately, and when ours were stuffed full, into those of the household mehitabels.

In our family, salmon has never been something to buy in a market, much less a restaurant. Mainly, nowadays, we get ours from Dad when he returns from an ocean voyage out of Westport, where the son of one of my Consani cousins is a sea captain. When our kids were little, we often car-camped at Mukkaw Bay on the Olympic Peninsula, and I'd drive to the Co-op Dock at Neah Bay to buy a silver, blackmouth, humpie, or whatever was running, right out of the bin, fresh off the boat, an eight- or ten-pounder, costing four or five bucks. Betty, meanwhile, would have built a big fire on the beach, and when I returned would scrape it away and dig a pit in the hot sand. Wrapped in seaweed, enclosed in foil, the salmon would go into the pit, covered by hot sand. We might then go mushrooming in the sea pastures and find fairy rings to saute and wash down with sips of madeira. The foil package would at length be exhumed and opened to loose upon the ocean air a cloud of steam redolent of fish and seaweed, and we'd eat salmon until the moon went down. Next day there'd be salmon for breakfast and salmon for lunch and salmon for dinner again, and about then we'd have had enough to last us a while.

The cockleshell returned to shore with awful news—a recent storm had tipped over the pot. However, the fellow gave me his entire catch, a single crab, luckily a big one, and even cleaned it, ready to pop in boiling water as soon as I got home. It would be a modest bacchanal.

I realized then that I was going to have to find a spot to anchor my own crab pot. And a shrimp pot, too. I wanted also to discover where scallops and abalone grow, and how to get them. Nor could I indefinitely ignore the mussels. What about the barnacles, said by the experts to be tastier than oysters? Would I, in the end, be seen shuffling along the waterfront wearing a blanket, digging in waste bins for the makings of fish-head chowder?

Houses retreated up the cliff and vanished in the forest. Railroad-track wilderness resumed. Thickening clouds hurried on the dusk. Too late now to turn back. A kingfisher flew by—the last bird, there were no more—I was alone.

I stopped at a tiny rock point topped with a lone madrona, a shell beach below. From here the railroad crossed the bay on a boulder causeway. I found a trail up the bluff and climbed 200 steep feet through old-growth Douglas fir to Chuckanut Drive, to a sign that said "Entering Bellingham." It was 4:05 and night was falling and all tramps and Siwashes were going to be afoot till morning, and many a mile stretched south to the beetle, and it was cloudy in the west, looking like rain, and my damn old umbrella was in the wagon again.

Such a great lot of people I wasn't meeting. I knew their frontyard gardens and their backyard wildlands, but not the people because they all had run away or died of the plague. Oyster-sorters, swine, girls playing recorders, devil dog, and crab man—where were they now? Where was I? If the gimp in my left hind leg didn't tighten up, and if the rain didn't soak through to my cockles, and if there was enough footpower in an apple and a Snickers, I'd make the beetle by 8 o'clock, but I scarcely think we'll get a drink till we get to Buffalo-o-o.

Headlights approached, the Last Car from Bellingham. Who would stop to pick up the likes of what those lights saw? *I* wouldn't. But this couple did, their tiny English car stuffed full of camping gear, and never mind that it was November, they were on gypsy tour, raggle-taggle-o, unafraid of Quasimodos in the night, disciples as they were of Thoreau, who said "Distrust any enterprise that requires new clothes."

47. Chuckanut Bay to Bellingham

Mile 145³/₄–148¹/₂

Saturday, November 5, 1977

I recognized the granite blocks of the railroad causeway crossing the bay as having come from the Index quarry, beneath the North Peak of Mount Index. In a half-mile the granite terminated at buttresses of sandstone-conglomerate pocked with incipient caves. The tracks entered Tunnel No. 21, dated 1913, a quarter-mile of dreadful night; I didn't enter, preferring to climb a path to the ridge crest and descend to a cove in Bellingham Bay.

Bellingham Bay. A new water. My last. Little more than a mile of it to look forward to. So look back.

To Chuckanut Bay, to Samish Bay, to Padilla Bay, to Skagit Bay, to Port Susan, to Port Gardner, to Possession Sound, to Puget Sound, to Elliott Bay, the first water of the journey—of my life.

From the last I see the first clearly. From the first I could pretty well have guessed the last, had I bothered. First and last are points on the same circle. Round and round she goes, and where she stops nobody knows. The trip's the thing, wotthehell.

For each creature there's a fitting trip. To Mount Everest or the Pole. To Paris or the Grecian Isles. To Disneyland or the Space Needle. These are common trips, for the common imaginations. The routes are crowded because the generality of the world's creatures are more common than not.

Spiders earn their livings on the common routes, the best for capturing and eating common travelers. When time comes for vacation, though, they take uncommonly imaginative—imaginatively uncommon—trips.

Resting beside a mountain trail, gazing in the sky, I'll spot a silvery glint and offhandedly remark, it being nothing out of the ordinary to me, "There goes a flying spider."

My companions see nothing because the glint is already gone. They give me a look and return to their cheese and crackers. It takes a knowing eye to see the nearly invisible strands. First one must be aware they exist. Then one must care. In my childhood *Want to Know Book* I read that at certain times, why I've forgotten, certain spiders, which I don't remember, build airships and sail away in the wind. Knowing they are there, I've seen them frequently, linear webs many feet long, momentarily caught by the sun. So alerted, the eye often can follow the flight great distances and sometimes make out the black dot of the aviator. But few eyes do, nowhere near as many as stare enraptured at rocketships blasting off. Spider-flying hasn't caught on as a spectator sport. My best friends, my own children, walk away on the trail and leave me gazing. Rarely indeed do I come upon a stranger with face lifted, eyes fixed on—nothing.

Another creature introduced to me by my *Want to Know Book* was the ant. Family anecdotes are told of the hours I spent sitting in the dirt by the back door, watching the ceaseless to and fro. It's interesting to try to figure out where they're going, and why. It's also depressing, especially for a person who has spent too much of his life in commuter-hour traffic, our ceaseless to and fro from job to home, home to job. I feel happier with spiders.

In 1943 a spider built a web in the corner of the windshield of my Model A and we went everywhere together—to the University campus, downtown to take my sweetie to see the bright lights, and to the mountains. The A's top speed didn't threaten the web or bother the spider, and I was careful not to use the windshield wiper. This spider didn't have to fly. The A was good enough ship for the both of us.

The finest day I ever knew on Tahoma (the midnight at Steamboat Prow was so mild my boots hadn't frozen, the air was so still I could light a cigarette without cupping the match, and the morning was so balmy we climbed with parkas in packs and shirtsleeves rolled up) butterflies I'd never seen higher than 11,000 feet fluttered over the summit, and bumblebees buzzed my red stocking cap, the grandest flower in all the dazzling-white world of the crater. That day in 1951, at 13,000 feet on the Emmons Glacier, a spidership floated by so slow and so close I could look the traveler in the eye and silently ask, "Why are you here? Where are you going?" and hear the silent answer, "What about *you*?"

In 1957 a bank loan let us enlarge our 200-meter hut on Cougar Mountain. The new cathedral-ceiling living room, crossbeams tied by vertical braces to the ridge beam, became a spider city with scores of webs, hundreds of feet of silken lines, which when finally vacated became feathery ropes of gray dust that, in a draft, undulated as if to whatever music it is that pleases a spider. Then one night a friend, a climber, had to traverse the crossbeams (because they were there) and Betty handed him a broom. I came up from the basement with more bottles of homebrew and howled in such rage and pain as if subdividers had bulldozed the cathedral at Chartres.

I've witnessed only scattered episodes of airship construction, which for all I know extends over many days or is completed in a morning. I've come upon an airship with one end attached to a limb, the other already cut free and trailing in the breeze, and have waited around to wish bon voyage. But before the spider cuts the last tie and sets out on the wind, an endless scurrying seems needed, checking the lines, repacking the suitcases, and always I've lost patience and walked on.

Every spider construction is a mystery. Often webs are strung across forest trails between anchors so distant, demanding such complexities of engineering, one marvels that the spider can see, in the start, the finish. Surely, in building an airship, it can have no notion of a destination. Why does it want to leave home at all? Perhaps it doesn't, just wants a quick change of scene for perspective and expects to be back by dinner. Why did I, in the spring of 1976, cast loose from Cougar Mountain? Where did I think I was going?

The spider I met at 13,000 feet in 1951 never got to the summit of Tahoma, as did I and my companions. A spider never would make it up Everest. An ant would, shuttling to and fro, up and down the glaciers. An ant also would reach the Pole, Grand Central Station and fame, fortune, pretty girls. A spider would be more likely to end up in—well, say Bellingham, for example.

Crossing the Skagit delta in the beetle this morning, I'd seen an immense swirling blackness where Komo Kulshan should have been, but the bay was glassy, the air still and mild, the sky a thin stew of pale blues and soft whites.

Sandstone slabs shelved into the bay. A till bluff kept houses respectfully distant. This springlike Saturday the tracks were busy with photographers, birdwatchers, strollers, and it was polite to avoid the sheltered sandstone nooks just big enough for two. Sails white-dotted the bay, barely making lazy way. The bell buoy off Post Point, where I rested in the grass beneath a pair of picturesque firs, gonged now and then.

I'd not be spending enough time on Bellingham Bay to learn it as well as my earlier waters. Mainly I'd remember the islands. Lummi was the dominant fact of life, the huge bulk looming close to the west. Orcas lay farther away, though near enough to make out the donjon keep on the summit of its highest point, Mount Constitution. South beyond the tall peaks of Cypress and Guemes, the vapors of Anacortes floated across forests of Mount Erie. North rose vapors of the refineries that had been chased away from Picnic and Kayak Points.

The bay was enclosed on the west by a long, low peninsula, on either side of which the double-exit Nooksack River emptied into the Whulj. I knew the Nooksack from headwater glaciers on Komo Kulshan and Shuksan, but this journey wouldn't take me to the outlet, as it had to those of the Snohomish, Stillaguamish, and Skagit Rivers.

The peninsula, said the map, was the Lummi Indian Reservation, authorized for the Lummi, Nooksack, and Samish peoples by the Point Elliott Treaty of January 22, 1855, and established by presidential decree on November 22, 1873. This journey wouldn't take me there, as it had to the Tulalip and Swinomish reservations. No matter, really. I'd learned little enough about *those* people walking "their" lands (the choice beach property had been removed from their ownership generations ago). The same published sources that had informed me about them would serve as well for the Lummi, Nooksack, and Samish.

It was the same old story. Everybody who reads the papers knows that for barefaced thievery and callous massacre the American frontier ranked with the most heinous crimes ever committed by one people against another. Generally, having confessed a share of family guilt, the Europeans whose great-grandparents had done the deed wanted to get on with fishing at their usual and accustomed places and picking the clams and oysters off the beach in front of the family cabins. The hell with the "Native Americans," formerly "Siwash." To insist we Europeans had not yet rendered sufficient justice was to earn for oneself another epithet far from dead and buried in the past.

I'd not set out on this journey as more than a perfunctory "Indian lover." Yet here at the end, having walked along so many miles of the Whulj where so many peoples had lived so long, and now gazing across Bellingham Bay to another of the "reservations" (of this one, 38 percent of the lands—no doubt 98 percent of the *valuable* lands—were now owned by Europeans), I felt a culminating sense of outrage.

The public schools of Seattle and vicinity taught me that in the Battle of Seattle a band of gallant pioneers and fourteen stalwart U.S. Marines fought off 3,000 screaming savages. The textbooks failed to note the testimony of more careful observers that in 1856 there were at most 300 hostiles west of the Cascades, of whom 20 or fewer "attacked" Seattle, mainly by standing behind trees safe from the ship's cannon and yelling dirty words in Chinook jargon.

While the teachers were instilling in my memory the Pledge of Allegiance to the flag that waved on high above the Washington Mounted Rifles, they didn't inform me that in March of 1856 this doughty company of real estate speculators, most of them colonels, had ridden into a Nisqually village on the Mashel River, discovered the men were all away, and vented their frustrated patriotism by murdering seventeen women and children.

The girl I knew at the University of Washington in 1944 described life on the Tulalip Reservation. She didn't put the blame on me, which is to say, on mine. Another young woman, in the 1970s, did. Wearing the uniform of a ranger-naturalist at Lava Beds National Monument, she told how "Shagnasty" was written up as a treacherous murderer in the books about the Indian Wars published by descendants of the settlers who gave him that insulting nickname, stole his land, and hanged him. She, his great-grandaughter, told us that every Modoc and white in northern California and southern Oregon knew him as an amiable incompetent who couldn't shoot straight enough to kill a cow in its stall. Nevertheless, on the chance her equally blameless grandparents might protest the theft of family land, they were hustled off to Indian Territory, where her parents brought her up on tales of treacherous, murdering whites, and of "Captain Jack" and his company of heroic white-fighters in the White Wars.

How much of the fault *was* mine? My Grandfather Hawthorn was a beloved figure in Ballard, conducting his streetcar over the rails to down-town Seattle and back. Aunt Grace, older than Mother, vividly re-membered a few incidents of life with him on the prairies. She told me of prairie fires, of dust storms—and of a ragged band drifting silently into the farmyard, eyes reflecting no memory that they had ridden with Red Cloud and Sitting Bull. Grandmother Hawthorn met them on the back porch and handed out loaves of bread hot from the oven. Aunt Grace had been sniffing the good smells all morning and threw a tan-trum. Grandfather Hawthorn reproved her, "You are hungry, child. The Sioux are starving."

Before the children, before his wife, he'd lived ten years alone on the prairie. The Sioux had ridden taller on their ponies, then, memories fresh of the Little Big Horn. The buffalo were not yet eliminated to hum-ble the people whose professional opponents in the U.S. Army assessed their military forces as "the greatest light cavalry in the history of war-fare." As much as Buffalo Bill, Grandfather Hawthorn eliminated the buffalo. Whenever I go by a bakery and smell hot bread, I think about that. In 1492 an estimated 4,500,000 people lived north of Mexico. When the Sioux rode through my family's North Dakota homestead, the number had fallen to about 350,000.

Mile 93 (from Everett), says the railroad sign. Lunchtime, says my stomach. Sit on a bench in South Terminal Marine Park, provided by the Port of Bellingham, for an apple, kippers, and a Pepsi Cola. Look out over Bellingham Bay. Look back.

There was no Bellingham (save the bay) until 1903, when the vil-lages of Sehome and Whatcom merged under that name, the better to solicit Jim Hill's Tunnel No. 21 (1913). Look back farther.

In 1868 Edmund Coleman, who on August 17 of that year made the first ascent of Komo Kulshan, declared: "Bellingham Bay is the finest natural harbor of the Puget Sound (*sic*) district, and there the fleets of the world might ride in safety and manoeuvre with ease. If the Northern Pacific Railway should be constructed through any of the passes of the Cascade range, this bay would be the best terminus." The mines of Sehome, a mile north of my park bench, then were shipping San Francisco 12,000 tons of coal a month. Coleman called the hamlet "the outpost of American civilization, being the most northerly town in Washington Territory." (Actually, Whatcom was a mile farther north.)

The North West Boundary Survey map of 1866 shows "Mil Rd to

Whatcom." From Seattle (first named settlement north of Steilacoom) the road parallels the shore, passing close by my childhood home. (Highway 99, where I pedaled my bicycle to deliver the *Seattle Shopping News*, was the approximate if not the exact route of Army wagon trains rolling north to put down the natives, three-quarters of a century before we schoolboy patrolmen watched Indian junks chugging south to Seattle.) The first named settlement north of Seattle is Snohomish City, at the river crossing. Next is Sehome ("Coal Mines"), then "Whatcom." In a final mile the road ends at "Fort."

The prospects of Whatcom had been bright. Coleman wrote: "During the excitement in 1858, when gold was discovered on Fraser River, it was expected that it would become the great depot and forwarding place for supplies to the mines. For about three months there were 10,000 people camped around, and it was quite a common occurence for half a dozen ocean steamers, and over a dozen square-rigged vessels, to arrive from San Francisco." The governor of British Columbia then ordered there should be no mining without a license, to be issued only in Victoria, and that was it for Whatcom.

The same year the Europeans were whooping it up at Whatcom, older settlers, nearby, were running for cover. Raiders from the north (Haida or Tsimshian from British Columbia, or Tlingit from Alaska?) destroyed a Lummi village on Orcas Island.

The northerners were even-handed: three years earlier the Europeans on Bellingham Bay (come in 1854 to dig the coal and in 1852 to saw logs in a mill powered by Whatcom Creek) had been besieged, and two killed, by raiders from Alaska's Stikine River. This incident proved reason enough to extend the Military Road.

Look back farther. In 1828 four Hudson's Bay men camped on Lummi Island were murdered. The Company heard the assassins may have been Clallams from the Olympic Peninsula. No other suspects coming readily to ear, the Company bombarded Clallam villages, killing twenty-nine, some of them not women and children.

Local legend, not confirmed by Spanish records (why *would* they?) says intercontinental hostilities commenced on Bellingham Bay in the eighteenth century when 400 Spanish pirates landed and an army of 1,000 local folk wiped them out.

Bellingham. A decent enough city, in all probability, with a waterfront as interesting as those of Everett and Seattle. However, the trip struck me as being over. I didn't feel the need of another waterfront, another river, another Indian reservation, any more bays.

Was *this* my goal when I cast loose from Cougar Mountain in 1976? A Port of Bellingham freight dock and the adjoining Worthy Cause, a pool of sewage being churned up to release upon the air the city's alimentary odors? No. What *did* I have in mind, then?

The meaning of the journey certainly wasn't here. It must have been somewhere along the way. So, look back.

To Seattle. To Jim Hill's one-eyed locomotive steaming south along the shore from Everett. To the prow of the *New Mexico* cleaving the waves south from Admiralty Inlet. Look farther.

Mother's father went to North Dakota from Pennsylvania. There may have been a dab of Pennsylvania Dutch (German) in the family, but mainly his people were of that fictitious nationality invented by and for the convenience of nineteenth-century immigration officials, Yankees who lazily lumped together as "Scotch-Irish" all non-Catholics from the north of England, south of Scotland, and north of Ireland. Mother's mother was from New York, her people English and Hudson River Dutch (Hollanders), settlers from early colonial times.

Dad's mother went to Massachusetts from Nova Scotia. Her grandmother, Elizabeth Ann Simpson, was born near Hyde Park, England, daughter of Captain Horton, who went down with his ship at sea, her widowed mother emigrating to Canada, dying, and leaving her to the care of Captain Narroway, who kept his ship afloat. Her (Dad's mother) Great-grandfather William Simpson was born in Caithness, Scotland, wore the King's red coat as drummer boy in the War of 1812, took up a soldier's grant of land, and married Lydia Hart, whose family had founded Hartford, Connecticut, then fled the rebel rabble of Boston and Virginia.

Dad's father was from New Brunswick. His (Dad's father) Grandmother Manning was fresh off the ship from England when she married Grandfather Manning, who was born in 1817 and still going strong when Dad was born. His (Grandfather Manning) people had left northern Ireland while the Pretenders were galloping about the bogs, remained truculent Orangemen in the Ohio wilderness, presumably scuffling with papist Frenchies, and were such firm Loyalists they moved north to stick with the King.

On his father's mother's side, Dad is (as I've heard on every festive occasion since childhood) the great-great grandson of an Irish lord

(Orange). In childhood I inflated my personal magnificence by adding not one but half a dozen "greats." Later I toyed with the notion of voyaging to the old country to claim my inheritance. Examination of the genealogy showed the chances were slim or none, we being sprung from the loins of Lord Musgrave's daughter, who ran off to Canada with the stable groom, Bill Chittick. It was a good time for the disinherited to be leaving Ireland, what with the famine raging, even as the pestilence was depopulating the Whulj.

None of *this* explains my journey. So, look back farther, to Britain.

To be British is to be a bit Norman—a blend of Norse and Frankish (German) and Gallic (Celto-Roman). In the English midlands and north, a good lot of Danish (ask King Alfred about that) or on the northern coasts and isles, Norwegian with a touch of Swedish (ask King Canute and Ethelred the Unready). Few localities of England lack an abundance of Anglo-Saxon-Jute (German, another name for Dutch), as King Arthur will confirm. In his domains (Wales and vicinity) and in Scotland and Ireland, there's so much Celt (Welch, Cornish, Manx, Scotch, Pictish, Irish) the people can't understand the English and hardly each other. Nearly every corner of Britain has sufficient Celtishness for fairy tales and poetry to break out with no warning.

The Great Armada stranded some Spanish (Celto-Germanic-Romano-Saracenic-Basque-Jewish) in Scotland and Ireland. The Restoration brought over a courtful of Frenchmen; William of Orange was accompanied by a mob of his hungry Dutchmen; and George I was attended by his favorite German cronies.

The Romans scattered seed from provinces of a vast empire; many common wildflowers of Britain have been traced to origins as distant as Illyria and beyond. The British Empire imported seed from the West Indies, the East Indies, and darkest Africa (see the two giggling heiresses in *Vanity Fair*). In Roman times and from the Norman period onward, all important towns required the sophisticated skills of civilized Mediterraneans, notably the Jews (see *Ivanhoe*'s Rebecca, so much more interesting than Rowena, the Saxon twit). Cornwall surely retained a trace of Phoenician from the ancient tin trade, the basis of the Bronze Age. Who was Piltdown Man? A fraud. Not so the builders of Stonehenge, the enigmatic Iberians, small and dark, who, after the arrival of the Celts, withdrew into forest shadows and at last went underground to become the Little People, a score of whom would fit comfortably in a Model A.

Look back over the three millennia from American imperium to British Empire, Angevin Empire to Norse Empire, Saxon Heptarchy to Round Table to Roman Empire, Celtic anarchy to Iberian mystery. My family was there for all of it.

So what?

Look back farther, beyond those three short millennia to the eons when we were roaming the grasslands of Europe, Asia, and Africa, wherever the sun wasn't too hot or the glaciers too thick. When some of us went west to become British, others went east to become Siberian, 15,000-odd years ago crossed to Alaska in pursuit of the woolly mammoth, and as soon as an alley opened at the edge of the ice sheet, headed south. They arrived in the savannahs of the Puget Trough perhaps 12,000 years ago, before the ice had completely melted, before the Whulj had advanced to fill the trough and shift the menu of the ordinary feast from barbecued mastodon to baked salmon with a side of clams.

A person needn't apologize for making a fuss about his Britishness, anymore than a Pole should be ashamed of dancing the polka or Italians of singing opera. Nobody in America is a "native American." We're all English-French-Spanish-Swede-Russian—in sum, European—or we're Asian or we're African. We all ought to remember where we came from. And then remember we all started out together. And see that if America does, indeed, hold any promise for the future, it is as the place where the family of man at last comes together as one again.

Some of the family have been here on the Whulj as many as 12,000 years. That makes me late for the party, but here I am finally, mouth set for a delicious fish-head chowder and a beach of hot and cold oysters.

The latitude of Seattle's King Street Station is 47° 36'; of Bellingham's South Terminal Marine Park, 48° 43'. At this pace, Peary would be sledging yet.

Why not, so long as the dogs held out? The Pole was the excuse, not the reason. The trip was the thing. Nobody ever knows when or if they reach the Pole. You zig and zag back and forth across the white plain shooting the sun, and when you run low on pemmican, turn for home, shrugging, "It must have been around there someplace."

> Every walk is a sort of crusade, preached by some Peter the Hermit in us,
> To go forth and reconquer this Holy Land from the hands of the infidels.
> —Thoreau

Of course, that's not how Peary saw it. He wanted newspaper headlines, which is why he was so nasty to Dr. Cook for getting the headlines first by lying. Dr. Cook's friends (he had more than Peary, being much the nicer man) think Peary lied too, more expertly and with the massive connivance of the Establishment. Personally, I don't care. Wherever Peary and Cook actually went, they had good trips, both of them. So did Amundsen—and Scott, too, up to a point.

So did I. No newspaper headlines, though a couple-three times I was afeared. Plenty of infidels—squatting on the spits, dredging the lagoons. Nothing much to do about them except preach up a Conjunction, and then stand back, because preachings don't always turn out as expected. The Eastern Empire stirred up the Frankish barons against the Moslems who held the Holy Land. The Franks were glad for the excuse of a jaunt but found the Holy Land too far and the Moslems too tough and therefore conquered the Eastern Empire instead. Many a person has gotten excited by college-campus evangelists, enlisted in a cause, and found himself on a Children's Crusade, sold into slavery or frozen to death in the Alps. But that's no excuse for not going on crusade. It just means we should enjoy the trip while we can.

Bellingham was pleasant enough, free enough, warm enough, sitting on a park bench with apple, kippers, and Pepsi Cola. Was the end of the trip the sum of it?

Looking back, I think there was considerably more at Meadow Point, Crown Hill, in the Edmonds sunset, on the log at Picnic Point, at the Everett Massacre, in the twilight of Tulalip Bay, on the White Cliffs of Whidbey, the tawny cliffs of Ebey, beside the maelstrom of Point Wilson, the mouth of the North Fork of the Skagit River, out on the shining sky-sand amid the peep. Of course, I could be wrong.

Still, were I again to meet the girl from Tulalip I knew at the University of Washington, we'd have much, much more to talk about, and I would do some of the talking, not merely all of the listening. If Alexander von Humboldt came on a foray this far north, he and I would have jolly times hypothesizing our way up and down the Whulj. I know my Mother and Dad much the better for having found the beach at Fletcher's Bay where they met one summer evening around a fire of driftwood logs. I know myself the better, having walked the beaches where once, as an infant, I crawled.

Is there meaning in such a journey? Perhaps. mehitabel would say it doesn't matter a lot, one way or the other. In her salad days she had a particular gentleman friend, the fellow who

> went aboard a canal boat
> one day and he got his head into
> a pitcher of cream and couldn t get
> it out and fell overboard

Fondly she recalls how he used to say

> toujours gai kid toujours gai he
> was an elegant cat

If not available at your
local bookstore, this book may
be ordered by sending the cover price
plus one dollar for postage and handling to

Madrona Publishers
Department X, P.O. Box 22667
Seattle, WA 98122

Visa or Mastercard holders can call
(206) 325-3973